Introducing .NET MAUI

Build and Deploy Cross-platform Applications Using C# and .NET Multi-platform App UI

Shaun Lawrence

Apress®

Introducing .NET MAUI: Build and Deploy Cross-platform Applications Using C# and .NET Multi-platform App UI

Shaun Lawrence
St Ives, UK

ISBN-13 (pbk): 978-1-4842-9233-4   ISBN-13 (electronic): 978-1-4842-9234-1
https://doi.org/10.1007/978-1-4842-9234-1

Managing Director, Apress Media LLC: Welmoed Spahr
Acquisitions Editor: Joan Murray
Development Editor: Laura Berendson
Editorial Assistant: Gryffin Winkler
Copy Editor: Mary Behr

Cover image designed by mrsiraphol through Freepik (www.freepik.com)

Distributed to the book trade worldwide by Springer Science+Business Media LLC, 1 New York Plaza, Suite 4600, New York, NY 10004. Phone 1-800-SPRINGER, fax (201) 348-4505, e-mail orders-ny@springer-sbm.com, or visit www.springeronline.com. Apress Media, LLC is a California LLC and the sole member (owner) is Springer Science + Business Media Finance Inc (SSBM Finance Inc). SSBM Finance Inc is a **Delaware** corporation.

For information on translations, please e-mail booktranslations@springernature.com; for reprint, paperback, or audio rights, please e-mail bookpermissions@springernature.com.

Apress titles may be purchased in bulk for academic, corporate, or promotional use. eBook versions and licenses are also available for most titles. For more information, reference our Print and eBook Bulk Sales web page at www.apress.com/bulk-sales.

Any source code or other supplementary material referenced by the author in this book is available to readers on GitHub using this link: https://github.com/Apress/Introducing-MAUI.

Printed on acid-free paper

Table of Contents

About the Author

Shaun Lawrence is an experienced software engineer who has been specializing in building mobile and desktop applications for the past 15 years. He is a recognized Microsoft MVP in Development Technologies; his work helps the community learn and build with Xamarin Forms, the predecessor to .NET MAUI. His recent discovery of the value he can add by sharing his experience with others has thrust him on to the path of wanting to find any way possible to continue to do so.

Shaun actively maintains several open-source projects within the .NET community. A key project for the scope of this book is the .NET MAUI Community Toolkit where he predominantly focuses on building good quality documentation for developers to consume. Shaun lives in the United Kingdom with his wife, two children, and their dog.

Shaun can be found on Twitter @Bijington, on his blog at https://blog.bijington.com, or on LinkedIn at www.linkedin.com/in/shaun-lawrence-53a0099/.

About the Technical Reviewer

Gerald Versluis is a Senior Software Engineer at Microsoft working on .NET MAUI. Since 2009 Gerald has been working on a variety of projects, ranging from front end to back end and anything in between that involves Azure, ASP.NET, and all kinds of other .NET technologies. At some point he fell in love with cross-platform and mobile development with Xamarin. Since then he has become an active community member, writing, tweeting, and presenting about all things tech. Gerald can be found on Twitter @jfversluis, blogging at https://blog.verslu.is, or on his YouTube channel at https://youtube.com/@jfversluis.

Acknowledgments

I have a number of people that I would like to thank for their assistance.

Firstly, Dan: Your assistance in both reviewing my content and also talking through each of my worries and ideas definitely encouraged me to write.

Secondly, Gerald: You have been fundamental from start to finish. You encouraged me to accept this project, helped me with decisions, reviewed the content, and provided fantastic guidance throughout!

Thirdly, the team at Apress: From Joan for initially reaching out to me in order to present this opportunity, to the rest of the team of Jill, Gryffin, and Laura for answering all of my questions and guiding me through this process.

Finally, my family—my wife, Levinia, daughters Zoey and Hollie, and dog, Soco: Without your encouragement I would not have taken the leap to embark upon this writing journey. I am so grateful for all your help and the sacrifices made to help get me over the line.

Introduction

Welcome to *Introducing .NET MAUI.*

This book is for developers who are new to .NET MAUI and cross-platform development. You should have basic knowledge of C# but require no prior knowledge of using .NET MAUI. The content ranges from beginner through to more advanced topics and is therefore tailored to meet a wide range of experiences.

This book provides an in-depth explanation of each key concept in .NET MAUI, and you will use these concepts in practical examples while building a cross-platform application. The content has been designed to primarily flow with the building of this application; however, there is a secondary theme that involves grouping as many related concepts as possible. The idea behind this is to both learn as you go and also to have content that closely resembles reference information, which makes returning to this book as easy as possible.

All code examples in this book, unless otherwise stated, are applied directly to the application you are building. Once key concepts have been established, the book will offer improvements or alternatives to simplify your life as you build production-worthy applications. The book does not rely upon these simplifications as part of the practical examples and the reason for this is simple: I strongly believe that you need to understand the concepts before you start to use them.

Finally, all chapters that involve adding code into the application project contain a link to the resulting source code. This is to show the final product and for you to use as a comparison if anything goes wrong during your building of the application.

PART I

Getting to Know
.NET MAUI

CHAPTER 1

Introduction to .NET MAUI

In this chapter, you will gain an understanding of what exactly .NET MAUI is, how it differs from other frameworks, and what it offers you as a developer wishing to build a cross-platform application that can run on both mobile and desktop environments. I will also cover the reasons why you should consider it for your next project by weighing the possibilities and limitations of the framework as well as the rich array of tooling options.

What is .NET MAUI?

.NET Multi-platform App UI, or .NET MAUI for short, is a cross-platform framework that allows developers to build mobile and desktop applications written in C# and XAML. It allows developers to target both mobile (Android and iOS) and desktop (macOS and Windows) platforms from a single codebase. Figure 1-1 shows the platforms officially supported by .NET MAUI and Microsoft.

© Shaun Lawrence 2023
S. Lawrence, *Introducing .NET MAUI,* https://doi.org/10.1007/978-1-4842-9234-1_1

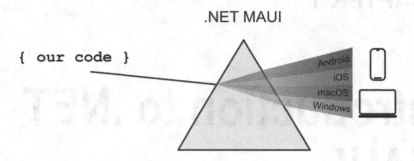

Figure 1-1. *.NET MAUI platform support*

.NET MAUI provides a single API that allows developers to write once and run anywhere. When building a .NET MAUI application, you write code that interacts with this single cross-platform API and .NET MAUI provides the bridge between your code and the platform-specific layer.

If you take a look inside the prism in Figure 1-1, you can start to understand the components that .NET MAUI both uses and offers. Figure 1-2 shows how an Android application is compiled.

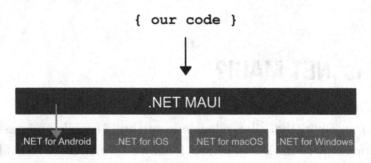

Figure 1-2. *Interacting with .NET MAUI APIs*

Of course, there will be times when you need to directly access a platform feature. .NET MAUI also provides enough flexibility that you can achieve this by interacting directly with the platform-specific APIs:

- .NET for Android

- .NET for iOS

- .NET for macOS

- Windows UI Library (WinUI) 3

Figure 1-3 shows how the code bypasses the .NET MAUI APIs and interacts directly with the .NET for Android APIs.

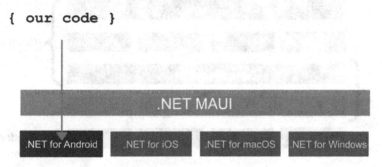

Figure 1-3. *Interacting with platform-specific APIs*

Digging a Bit Deeper

There are some extra steps that the tooling will perform under the hood to get your application built and ultimately ready for use on each of the possible platforms.

When building a .NET application, even if it is not using .NET MAUI, you will very likely hear the term BCL, which is short for the *base class library*. This is the foundation of all .NET applications, and in the same way that .NET MAUI abstracts away the platforms you wish to build for, the BCL abstracts away what that platform implements when your application runs.

To run your application on your desired platform, you need a .NET runtime. For Android, iOS, and macOS, this is the Mono runtime. The Mono runtime provides the ability to run .NET code on many different platforms. For Windows, this is Win32. Each of these runtimes provide the functionality required for the BCL and therefore a consistent working environment across all supported platforms.

I like to think of the BCL as the contract between what we are compiling against and what we are running that compiled code with.

Figure 1-4 shows all of the layers involved in compiling and running a .NET MAUI application.

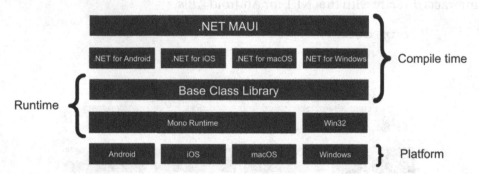

Figure 1-4. *The full breakdown*

To continue with the example of building for Android in the previous diagrams and taking note of the diagram in Figure 1-4, the following can be said:

Your code is compiled against **.NET MAUI**, **.NET for Android** and the **base class library**. It then runs on the **Mono runtime**, which provides a full implementation of the **base class library** on the **Android** platform.

Looking at the above statement, you can replace the parts that are platform specific with another platform (e.g., swapping Android for iOS) and the statement will still be true.

Where Did It Come From?

.NET MAUI is the evolution of Xamarin.Forms, which itself has a rich history of providing developers with a great way to build cross-platform applications. Of course, no framework is perfect, and Xamarin.Forms certainly had its limitations. Thankfully the team at Microsoft decided to take the pragmatic approach of taking a step back and evaluating all the pain points that existed for themselves as maintainers and (more importantly) for us as developers using the framework.

Not only do we therefore gain improvements from the Xamarin framework as part of this evolution, but we also get all the goodies that come with .NET such as powerful built-in dependency injection, better performance, and other topics that I will touch on throughout this book. This makes me believe that this mature cross-platform framework has finally become a first-class citizen of the .NET and Microsoft ecosystems. I guess the clue is in the first part of its new name.

On the topic of its name, .NET MAUI implies that it is a UI framework, and while this is true, this is not all that the framework has to offer. Through the .NET and the .NET MAUI platform APIs, we are provided with ways of achieving common application tasks such as file access, accessing media from the device gallery, using the accelerometer, and more. The .NET MAUI platform APIs were previously known as Xamarin Essentials, so if you are coming in with some Xamarin Forms experience, they should feel familiar. I will touch on much more of this functionality as you progress through this book.

How It Differs From the Competition

.NET MAUI provides its own controls (for example, a `Button`) and then maps them to the relevant implementation on each platform. To continue with the example of a button, this is a `UIButton` from `UIKit` on iOS and macOS, an `AppCompatButton` from `AndroidX.AppCompat.Widget` on Android, and a `Button` from `Microsoft.UI.Xaml.Controls` on Windows. This gives a great level of coverage in terms of providing a common implementation that works across all platforms. With the introduction of the .NET MAUI handler architecture (which will we be looking at in more detail in Chapter 11) we truly gain the power to tweak the smallest of implementation details on a per-platform basis. This is especially useful when the common API provided by .NET MAUI may be limited down to the least amount of crossover between each platform and doesn't provide everything we need. It is worth noting that your application will render differently on each platform as it utilizes the platform specific controls and therefore their look and feel.

Other frameworks such as Flutter opt to render their own types directly rather than mapping across to the implementations provided by each platform. These frameworks provide a common look and feel across each platform. This is a hotly contested topic but I personally believe that making applications fit in with the platform they are running on is a big benefit.

Why Use .NET MAUI?

There are several reasons why you should consider using .NET MAUI for your next application: a large number of supported platforms, increased code sharing capabilities, an emphasis on allowing developers to build applications that fit their style, great performance, and many more. Let's take a look at them.

Supported Platforms

.NET MAUI provides official support for all of the following platforms:

- Android 5.0 (API level 21) and above

- iOS 11.0 and above

- macOS 10.15 and above (using Mac Catalyst) **

- Windows desktop

*** MacCatalyst allows native Mac apps to be built and share code with iPad apps. This is an Apple technology that allows developers to shared code between Mac and iPad. For further reference, go to the Apple documentation at* https://developer.apple.com/mac-catalyst/.

.NET MAUI provides community-driven support for

- Tizen: The implementation is provided by Samsung.

I thoroughly recommend checking out the documented list of supported platforms in case it has changed since the time of writing. The list can be found at `https://learn.microsoft.com/dotnet/maui/supported-platforms`.

Code Sharing

A fundamental goal of all cross-platform frameworks is to enable developers to focus on achieving their main goals by reducing the effort required to support multiple platforms. This is achieved by sharing common code across all platforms. Where I believe .NET MAUI excels over alternative frameworks is in the first four characters of its name; Microsoft has pushed hard to produce a single .NET that can run anywhere.

Being a full stack developer myself, I typically need to work on web-based back ends as well as mobile applications, .NET allows me to write code that can be compiled into a single library. This library can then be shared between the web and client applications, further increasing the code sharing possibilities and ultimately reducing the maintenance effort.

I have given talks based on a mobile game (`www.superwordsearch.com`) I built using Xamarin.Forms, where I boasted that we were able to write 96% of our code in our shared project. I have not yet converted this across to .NET MAUI; however, initial investigations show that this number will only increase.

There are further possibilities for sharing code between web and client, such as the use of .NET MAUI Blazor, which provides the use of web-based technologies inside a .NET MAUI application. While I won't be covering .NET MAUI Blazor in detail in this book, Microsoft does provide some really great documentation and guides on what it is and how to build your first application with the technology at `https://learn.microsoft.com/aspnet/core/blazor/hybrid/tutorials/maui`.

Developer Freedom

.NET MAUI offers many ways to build the same thing. Where Xamarin. Forms was largely designed to support a specific application architecture (such as MVVM, which I will talk all about in Chapter 4), .NET MAUI is different. One key benefit of the rewrite by the team at Microsoft is it now allows the use of other architectures such as MVU (Chapter 4). This allows us as developers to build applications that suit our preferences, from different architectural styles to different ways of building UIs and even different ways of styling an application.

Community

Xamarin has always had a wonderful community. From bloggers to open-source maintainers, there is a vast amount of information and useful packages available to help any developer build a great mobile application. One thing that has really struck me is the number of Microsoft employees who are part of this community; they are clearly passionate about the technology and dedicate their own free time to contributing to this community. The evolution to .NET MAUI brings this community with it.

Fast Development Cycle

.NET MAUI offers two great ways to boost a developer's productivity.

.NET Hot Reload

.NET Hot Reload allows you to modify your managed source code while the application is running, without the need to manually pause or hit a breakpoint. Then, your code edits can be applied to your running app without the need to recompile. It is worth noting that this feature is not specific to .NET MAUI but is yet another great example of all the goodness that comes with the framework being part of the .NET ecosystem.

XAML Hot Reload

XAML Hot Reload allows you to edit the UI in your XAML files, save the changes, and observe those changes in your running application without the need to recompile. This is a fantastic feature that really shines when you need to tweak some controls.

Performance

.NET MAUI applications are compiled into native packages for each of the supported platforms, which means that they can be built to perform well.

Android has always been the slowest platform when dealing with Xamarin.Forms and the team at Microsoft has been working hard and showing off the improvements. The team has provided some really great resources in the form of blog posts covering the progress that has been made to bring the start-up times of Android applications to well below one second. These posts cover metrics plus tips on how to make your applications really fly.

- https://devblogs.microsoft.com/dotnet/
  performance-improvements-in-dotnet-maui/

- https://devblogs.microsoft.com/dotnet/dotnet-7-
  performance-improvements-in-dotnet-maui/

Android apps built using .NET MAUI compile from C# into intermediate language (IL), which is then just-in-time (JIT) compiled to a native assembly when the app launches.

iOS and macOS apps built using .NET MAUI are fully ahead-of-time (AOT) compiled from C# into native ARM assembly code.

Windows apps built using .NET MAUI use Windows UI Library (WinUI) 3 to create native apps that target the Windows desktop.

Strong Commercial Offerings

There are several commercial options that provide additional UI elements and other integrations such as Office document editing or PDF viewing in your .NET MAUI applications. Some options (at the time of writing) are

- SyncFusion

  "The feature-rich/flexible/fast .NET MAUI controls for building cross-platform mobile and desktop apps with C# and XAML"

  www.syncfusion.com/maui-controls

- Telerik UI for .NET MAUI

  "Kickstart your multiplatform application development with a Preview version of Telerik UI for .NET MAUI controls!"

  www.telerik.com/maui-ui

- DevExpress

  "Our .NET Multi-platform App UI Component Library ships with high-performance UI components for Android and iOS mobile development (WinUI desktop support is coming in 2022). The library includes a Data Grid, Chart, Scheduler, Data Editors, CollectionView, Tabs, and Drawer components."

  www.devexpress.com/maui/

Note that while these are commercial products, several of them provide free licenses for smaller companies or independent developers so I recommend checking out their products.

Limitations of .NET MAUI

I hope this doesn't get me in too much trouble with the wonderful team over at Microsoft ☺. This section is not aimed at slating the technology (I wouldn't be writing a book about something I didn't believe in); it is purely aimed at making clear what cannot be achieved or at least what is not provided out of the box, to help you as a reader best decide whether this is the right technology for your next project. Of course, I hope it is, but let's look at what I feel are its main limitations.

No Web Assembly (WASM) Support

.NET MAUI does not provide support for targeting Web Assembly. This means that you cannot target the web directly from a .NET MAUI project, but you can still run Blazor inside your .NET MAUI application. This opens the door for further code sharing; as discussed earlier, it is entirely possible to build Blazor components that can be shared between .NET MAUI Blazor and .NET Blazor applications.

If you do require direct WASM support, then a good alternative to .NET MAUI is the Uno Platform.

No Camera API

This has been a pain point for a lot of developers throughout the life of Xamarin.Forms and continues to be an initial pain point for .NET MAUI. There are some good arguments as to why it hasn't happened. Building a camera API against the Android Camera offering has not been an easy task, as I am sure most developers who have embarked on that journey can attest to. The sheer fact that Google is rewriting the entire API for a third time shows the inherent challenges.

Apps Won't Look Identical on Each Platform

Controls in .NET MAUI make use of the platform implementations, therefore an entry control on iOS will render differently to one on Android. There are investigations into providing a way to avoid this and have controls render exactly the same on all platforms, but this is still at an early stage.

Lack of Media Playback Out of the Box

Playing media has become a very common task. So many apps these days offer the ability to play video or audio. I suspect this is also due to the vast differences between platforms in how they provide playback support.

While this functionality is not officially provided by .NET MAUI, this does not mean the functionality is not possible.

The Glass Is Half Full, Though

I believe that limitations are not a bad thing. Doing some things well is a far better achievement than doing everything badly! I expect the list of limitations will reduce as .NET MAUI matures. Thanks to the fact that .NET MAUI is open source, we as consumers have the ability to suggest improvements and even provide them directly to further enhance this framework. I must also add that the .NET MAUI Community Toolkit is great (of course, I am biased because I currently help to maintain it). It provides value for the .NET MAUI community, and it is also maintained by that community. Another huge advantage is that concepts in this toolkit can and have been promoted to .NET MAUI itself. This gives me hope that one day there will be a solid choice for both camera and media playback APIs in .NET MAUI.

How to Build .NET MAUI Applications

There are several different ways to build an application with .NET MAUI. I will look at each in turn, covering some details that will hopefully help you decide which is the best fit for you.

Visual Studio

Visual Studio is available for both Windows and macOS, but while these operating systems are both officially supported, it is worth noting that the Visual Studio products are separate and themselves not cross-platform. This means that functionality and levels of support differ between the two.

Note that the Windows and macOS versions come with three different pricing options, but I would like to draw your attention to the Community edition, which is free for use by small teams and for educational purposes. In fact, everything in this book can be achieved using the free Community edition.

Visual Studio (Windows)

Visual Studio is a comprehensive integrated development environment or IDE that provides a great development experience. I have been using this tool for years and I can happily say that it continues to improve with each new version.

To build .NET MAUI apps, you must use at least Visual Studio 2022.

In Visual Studio (Windows), it is possible to build applications that target

- Android
- iOS *
- Windows

15

A networked Mac with Xcode 13.0 or above is required for iOS development and deployment. This is due to limitations in place by Apple.

Visual Studio for Mac

Visual Studio for Mac has only been released recently and as of 2022 it has undergone a significant rework to provide a better experience for developers.

To build .NET MAUI apps, you must use at least Visual Studio 2022 for Mac.

In Visual Studio for Mac, it is possible to build applications that target

- Android

- iOS

- macOS

Rider

JetBrains Rider is an impressive cross-platform IDE that can run on Windows, macOS, and Linux. JetBrains has a history of producing great tools to help developers achieve their goals. One highlight is ReSharper, which assists with inspecting and analyzing code. With Rider the functionality provided by ReSharper is built in.

JetBrains offers Rider for free but only for educational use and open-source projects.

Visual Studio Code

Visual Studio Code is a very popular lightweight code editor also provided by Microsoft. Using extensions and the dotnet CLI, it is entirely possible to build .NET MAUI applications using no other tools. It is worth noting, however, that the debugging experience is vastly inferior to the other products we have discussed.

Summary

Throughout the course of this book, you will primarily be using Visual Studio (Windows) as the tool to build your application. I will refer to Visual Studio for Mac in the later parts when I cover how to deploy and test macOS applications.

In this chapter, you have learned the following:

- What .NET MAUI is

- What it offers and what it does not offer

- Reasons why you should consider using it

- The tooling options available to build a .NET MAUI application

In the next chapter, you will

- Get to know the application we will be building together

- Learn how to set up the environment to build the application

CHAPTER 2

Building Our First application

In this chapter, you will learn how to set up your development environment across all of the required platforms. You will then use that environment to create, build, and run your very first .NET MAUI application. Finally, you will take a look at the application you will build as you progress through this book.

Setting Up Your Environment

Before you get into creating and building the application, you must make sure you have an environment set up.

macOS

There are several tools that you must install on macOS to allow support for building Mac Catalyst applications and to provide the ability to build iOS applications from a Windows environment.

This is required if you wish to develop on macOS or deploy to a Mac or iOS device (even from a Windows machine). If you are happy with only deploying to Windows or Android from a Windows machine, then you can skip this part or just read it for reference.

Visual Studio for Mac

As mentioned in the previous chapter, you will be primarily focusing on using Visual Studio on Windows. You will have a requirement to use Visual Studio for Mac much later, but you will set it up now. Also note that while the book does focus on using Visual Studio on Windows, quite a lot of the concepts should still translate well enough to Visual Studio for Mac if that is your preferred environment.

Download and install Visual Studio 2022 for Mac. This can be accessed from `https://visualstudio.microsoft.com/vs/mac/`.

1. Open the downloaded `VisualStudioForMacInstaller.dmg` file.

2. Double-click the **Install Visual Studio for Mac** option. Figure 2-1 shows the Visual Studio for Mac installer.

Figure 2-1. *Visual Studio for Mac installer*

3. You will likely be shown a security dialog making
    sure that you wish to run this installer. Double check
    the details and then proceed if all looks fine.

4. Accept the terms and conditions by clicking
    Continue.

5. In the next window, select **.NET, Android, iOS**, and
    macOS (Cocoa) and then click **Install**. Figure 2-2
    shows the installer with the required options for
    .NET MAUI checked.

21

Figure 2-2. *Visual Studio for Mac installation options*

Please refer to the Microsoft documentation page at `https://learn.microsoft.com/dotnet/maui/get-started/installation?tabs=vsmac` if any of the installation options have changed.

Xcode

Xcode is Apple's IDE for building applications for iOS and macOS. You don't need to use Xcode directly, but Visual Studio needs it in order to compile your iOS and macOS applications.

Thankfully this install is straightforward despite it being a rather large download.

1. Open the **App Store** application.

2. Enter *Xcode* into the **Search** box and press return.

3. Click **Get**. Figure 2-3 shows Xcode available on the
    Apple App Store.

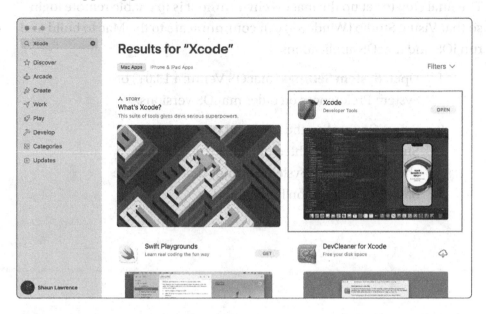

Figure 2-3. *Xcode on the App Store*

4. Once downloaded, open Xcode and wait for it to
    install the command line tools. Note that this is
    usually required to be performed after each major
    update to Xcode, too.

I suggest using caution when applying updates to the whole suite
of applications that you are installing today. Typically, when a new,
big release of .NET MAUI comes out, it likely requires an update of
Xcode. I personally like to keep these expected versions in sync so I
recommend checking for the updates within Visual Studio first and
verifying that it expects a new version of Xcode before proceeding to
update that.

Remote Access

The final step to set up the macOS environment is to enable remote login so that Visual Studio (Windows) can communicate to the Mac to build and run iOS and macOS applications.

1. Open **System Settings** (macOS Ventura 13.0+) or System Preferences on older macOS versions.

2. Select **General** on the left-hand panel and then **Sharing**, as highlighted in Figure 2-4. This image shows the macOS System Settings dialog with the Sharing menu option highlighted.

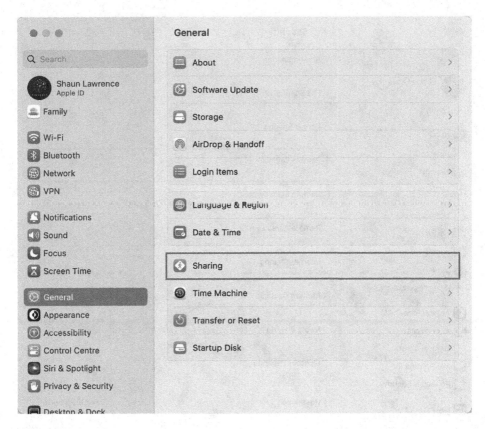

Figure 2-4. *macOS system settings*

3. Enable **Remote Login**. Figure 2-5 shows the Remote
    Login option enabled.

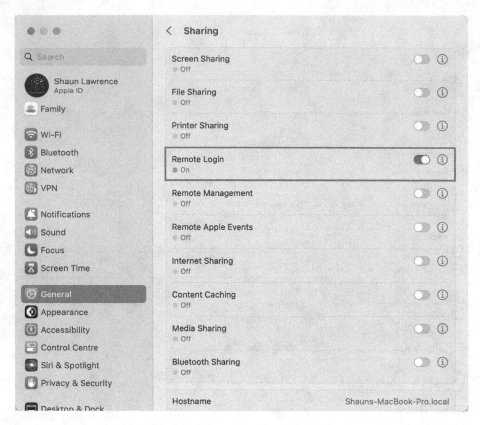

Figure 2-5. *macOS sharing options*

4.   Add your user to the list of allowed users for
     Remote Login. My user is an Administrator so the
     Administrators user group enables remote login
     access for this user. Figure 2-6 shows the Remote
     Login editor to enable access for users on macOS.

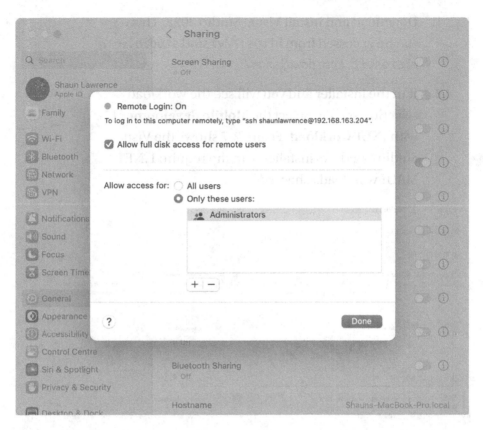

Figure 2-6. *macOS remote login options*

5. That's it! Your mac should now be ready to use.

Windows

Visual Studio

First, you must install Visual Studio 2022. These steps will guide you through getting it ready to build .NET MAUI applications:

1. Download and install Visual Studio 2022. This can be accessed from `https://visualstudio.microsoft.com/downloads/`.

2. Run the installer and you will see the workload selection screen. Select the **Mobile development with .NET workload**. Figure 2-7 shows the Visual Studio Windows installer with the required .NET MAUI workloads checked.

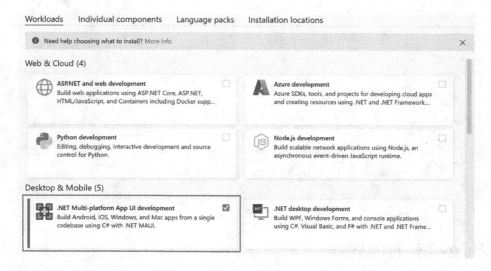

Figure 2-7. *Visual Studio Windows installation options*

Please refer to the Microsoft documentation page at `https://learn.microsoft.com/dotnet/maui/get-started/installation?tabs=vswin` if any of the installation options have changed.

Visual Studio to macOS

The final item to configure in your Windows environment is to set up the connection between Visual Studio and your macOS so that iOS and macOS builds can be compiled.

1. Inside Visual Studio select the Tools menu item.

2. Select iOS ➤ Pair to Mac.

3. Check and confirm the firewall access. Figure 2-8 shows the firewall request dialog that is presented when first running Visual Studio on Windows.

Figure 2-8. *Windows firewall request*

4. Note that you may also see a second firewall popup for the Xamarin Broker.

5. Select your Mac from the list.

6. Click **Connect**. Figure 2-9 shows the Pair to Mac dialog that allows you to connect your Visual Studio running on Windows to connect to your macOS machine.

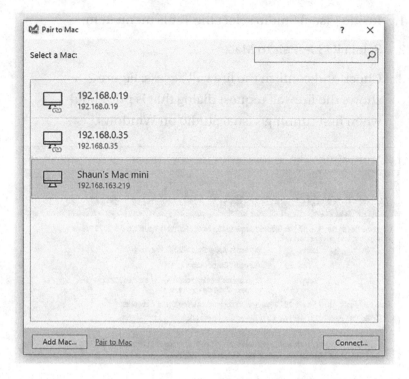

Figure 2-9. *Pair to Mac screen*

7. Enter the username and password that you use to log into your Mac.

8. Wait for the tooling to connect and make sure that everything is configured on the Mac.

9. When you see the symbol shown in Figure 2-10, your setup is complete. Figure 2-10 shows the Pair to Mac dialog with the connected symbol against your macOS machine.

Figure 2-10. *Pair to Mac screen with confirmation*

10. Visual Studio should now connect automatically
    when you open a .NET MAUI solution. Figure 2-11
    shows the Pair to Mac button in Visual Studio on
    Windows.

Figure 2-11. *Visual Studio toolbar with Pair to Mac buttons*

Troubleshooting Installation Issues

Given that there are several moving parts in the development ecosystem when building .NET MAUI applications, there is room for things to go wrong. In this section, I will go over a few common issues and how to check that things are correctly set up.

.NET MAUI Workload Is Missing

In order to check whether the .NET MAUI workload has been installed, you can check either in Visual Studio Installer or through the command line.

Visual Studio Installer

This currently only works on Windows, but you can follow these steps.

1. Open the **Start** menu.

2. Type in *Visual Studio Installer*.

3. Open the installer.

4. Select **Modify** on the Visual Studio 2022 installation.

5. View the workloads and check that the **Mobile development with .NET** workload is ticked.

Command Line

This has the benefit of working on both Windows and macOS.

1. Open a Terminal session.

2. Run the following command:

```
dotnet workload list
```

3. Verify that the results include **maui.**

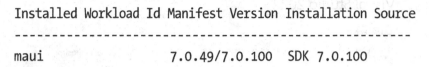

```
Installed Workload Id Manifest Version Installation Source
--------------------------------------------------------
maui                    7.0.49/7.0.100  SDK 7.0.100
```

Creating Your First Application

You will be using the user interface in order to create your application, build, and run it. I will also be including the dotnet command line commands because I find they can be quite helpful when building and debugging.

Creating in Visual Studio

1. Launch Visual Studio 2022. In the window that opens, select the **Create a new project** option. Figure 2-12 shows the initial starting screen in Visual Studio running on Windows with the **Create a new project** option highlighted.

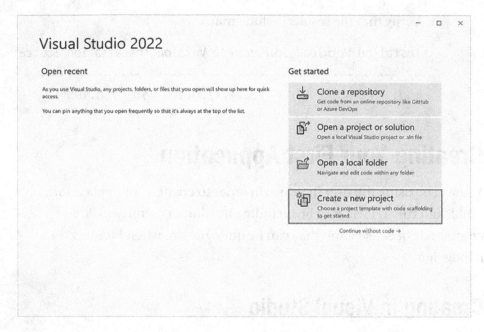

Figure 2-12. *Creating a project in Visual Studio*

2. In the window that follows, type *.NET MAUI* in the Search for templates box. Then select the **.NET MAUI App** option and click **Next**. Figure 2-13 shows the project creation screen with the .NET MAUI App project selected.

Figure 2-13. *Selecting a .NET MAUI App project type*

3. In the next window, enter a name for your project. I
    chose WidgetBoard. Choose a location if you would
    like to store it somewhere different from the default
    location, and click **Create**. Figure 2-14 shows the
    Configure your new project screen in Visual Studio.

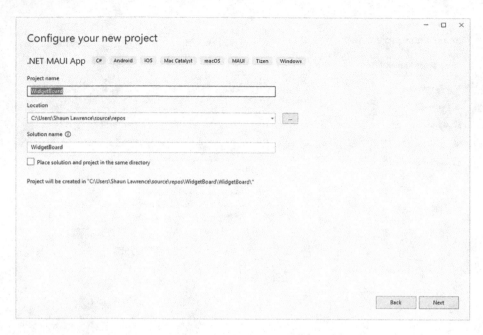

Figure 2-14. *The Configure your new project dialog*

Please bear in mind that Windows has a limitation on the length of the location path. If the path is longer than 255 characters, then strange behavior will follow. Visual Studio will fail to build perfectly valid code and so on. This can be rectified by disabling the path limit (`https://learn.microsoft.com/windows/win32/fileio/ maximum-file-path-limitation?tabs=cmd#enable-long- paths-in-windows-10-version-1607-and-later`).

---

4. Select the version of .NET you wish to use. At the time of writing this book .NET 7.0 is the current version so I am using this version. Figure 2-15 shows the Additional information dialog where you can choose the .NET Framework version for your application.

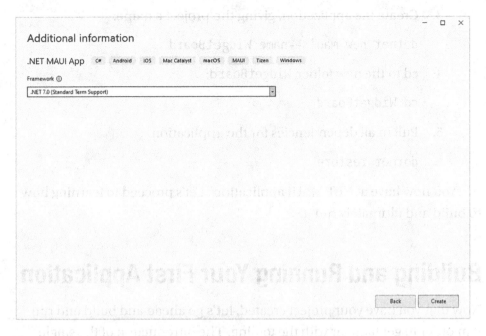

Figure 2-15. *The .NET Framework selection dialog*

5.   Wait for the project to be created and any background restore and build tasks to be completed.

Now admire the very first .NET MAUI application that we have created together.

Creating in the Command Line

While the command line might feel more complicated, at times there are actually fewer steps required than when using Visual Studio.

1.   Open a Terminal/command line session.

2.   cd to the location you want to create your application:

```
cd c:\work\
```

3. Create the application, giving the project a name:

```
dotnet new maui --name WidgetBoard
```

4. cd to the new folder, WidgetBoard:

```
cd WidgetBoard
```

5. Pull in all dependencies for the application:

```
dotnet restore
```

You now have a .NET MAUI application. Let's proceed to learning how to build and ultimately run it.

Building and Running Your First Application

Now that you have your project created, let's go ahead and build and run it in order to get familiar with the tooling. The introduction of the single project approach for .NET MAUI applications may bend your way of thinking when it comes to building applications. In the past, a solution containing .NET projects would typically have a single start-up project, but these projects would have a single output. Now that a single project actually has multiple outputs, you need to learn how to configure that for your builds. In fact, this is done by clicking the down arrow, which can be seen in Figure 2-16.

File   Edit   View   Git   Project   Build   Debug   Test   Analyze   Tools   Extensions   Window   Help   Search

Debug   ▾   Any CPU   ▾   ▶ Android Emulator ▾   ▷   ...

▶ Android Emulator
✓ Android Emulator
Windows Machine

Download New Emulators...

Framework (net7.0-android)   ▶
Android Emulators   ▶
iOS Local Devices   ▶
iOS Remote Devices   ▶
iOS Simulators   ▶
🔧 WidgetBoard Debug Properties

MainPage.xaml   MainPage.xaml.cs ⇄ ✕

WidgetBoard (net7.0-android)

```
 1    namespace WidgetBoard;
 2
      4 references
 3    public partial class MainPage : ContentPa
 4    {
 5        int count = 0;
 6
      0 references
 7    public MainPage()
 8    {
 9        InitializeComponent();
10    }
11
      0 references
12    private void OnCounterClicked(object sender, EventArgs e)
13    {
14        count++;
15
16        if (count == 1)
17            CounterBtn.Text = $"Clicked {count} time";
18        else
19            CounterBtn.Text = $"Clicked {count} times";
20
21        SemanticScreenReader.Announce(CounterBtn.Text);
22    }
23    }
24
25
```

Figure 2-16. *Build target selection dropdown in Visual Studio*

You may also notice the dropdown in the above image that currently says **WidgetBoard (net7.0-android)**. This allows you to show in the visible file what applies to that specific target, but it does not affect what you are currently compiling. Figure 2-17 shows this a little clearer.

1. This is where you set the current target to compile for and run.

2. This is highlighting in the code file what will compile for the target chosen in the dropdown. Notice here that you are compiling for Windows but showing what would compile for Android.

Figure 2-17 highlights items 1 and 2 from the above list to highlight what is compiled vs. what is targeted in Visual Studio.

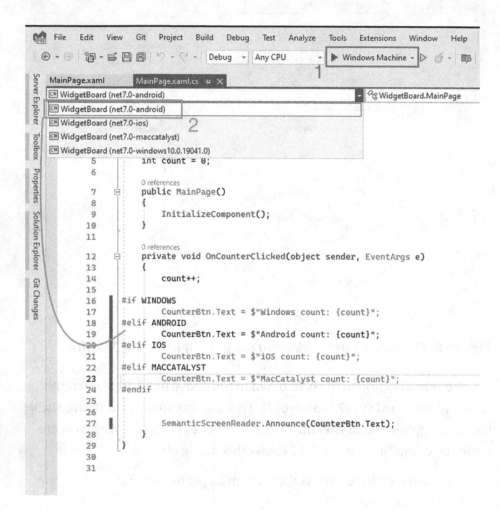

Figure 2-17. *Showing the differences between what target is being compiled and what target is being shown in the current editor*

Getting to Know Your Application

Together we will be building an application from the very initial stages
through to deploying it to stores for public consumption. Given that the
application will play such a pivotal role in this book, I want to introduce
you to the concept first.

I want to try something a little bit different from the normal types of
apps that are built as part of a book or course. Something that requires a
fair amount of functionality that a lot of real-world applications also need.
Something that can help to make use of potentially older hardware so we
can give them a new lease on life.

WidgetBoard

The application that we will be building together will allow users to turn
old tablets or computers into their own unique digital board. Figure 2-18
shows a sketch of how it could look once a user has configured it.

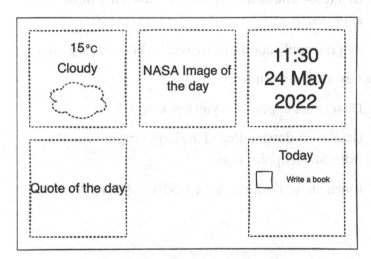

Figure 2-18. Sketch prototype of the application we will be building

We will build "widgets" that can be positioned on the screen. These widgets will range from showing the current time to pulling weather information from a web API to displaying images from your library. The user will also be able to customize the color, among other options, and ultimately save these changes so that they will be remembered when the user next opens the application.

I am planning for this to provide a digital calendar/photo frame for our home. I would love to hear or see what you are able to build.

Summary

In this chapter, you have

- Set up your development environment so that you are capable of creating, building, and ultimately running/deploying the application.

- Created, built, and run your very first .NET MAUI application

- Met the application that we will be building together

In the next chapter, you will

- Dissect the application you just created.

- Gain an understanding of the key components of a .NET MAUI application.

- Learn about the lifecycle of a .NET MAUI application.

Source Code

The resulting source code for this chapter can be found on the GitHub repository at `https://github.com/Apress/Introducing-MAUI/tree/main/ch02`.

CHAPTER 3

The Fundamentals of .NET MAUI

In this chapter, you will dissect the project you created in Chapter 2 and dive into the details of each key area. The focus is to provide a good overview of what a .NET MAUI single project looks like, where each of the key components are located, and some common ways of enhancing them.

Project Structure

.NET MAUI provides support for multiple platforms from within a single project. The focus is to allow us as developers to share as much code and as many resources as possible.

You will likely hear the term *single project* a lot during your time working with .NET MAUI. It is a concept that is new to the .NET world as part of .NET MAUI. Its key feature is that you can build applications for multiple different targets from, you guessed it, a single project. If you have ever built .NET applications that aim to share code, you will have noticed that each application you wanted to build and deploy required its own project. The same was true with Xamarin.Forms in that you would have at least one project with your common code and then one project per platform. The single project now houses both the shared code and the platform-specific bits of code.

S. Lawrence, *Introducing .NET MAUI*, https://doi.org/10.1007/978-1-4842-9234-1_3

Figure 3-1 shows a comparison between the old separate project approach in Xamarin.Forms and the new .NET MAUI project format.

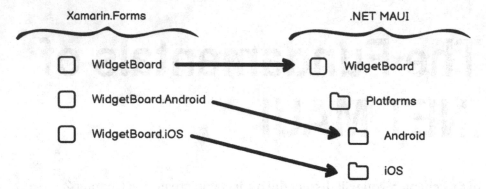

Figure 3-1. *Comparison of Xamarin.Forms projects to a .NET MAUI project*

Let's inspect the project you created in Chapter 2 so that you can start to get an understanding of how .NET MAUI supports the multiple platforms and how they relate to shared code.

The new project has the following structure:

- `Platforms/`: This folder contains all the platform-specific code. Inside this folder is a set of folders, each with a name that relates to the platform that it supports. Thus `Platforms/Android` supports the Android platform.

- `Resources/`: This folder is where you store all your resources for the application. A resource is typically anything you wish to embed in the application that isn't strictly code, such as an image, a font file, or even an audio or video file.

In the past, resource management was always a pain point when building cross-platform applications. For example, building an application for both Android and iOS with Xamarin.Forms could result in needing four or five different sizes of each image rendered in the application.

- `MauiProgram.cs`: This class is where you initialize your .NET MAUI application. It makes use of the Generic Host Builder, which is the Microsoft approach to encapsulating the requirements of an application. These requirements include but are not limited to dependency injection, logging, and configuration.

- `App.xaml.cs`: This is the main entry point to the cross-platform application. Note this line of code from the `MauiProgram.cs` file includes our App class:

  `builder.UseMauiApp<App>();`

- `App.xaml`: This file includes common UI resources that can be used throughout the application. I will cover these types of resources in much more detail in Chapters 5 and 8.

- `MainPage.xaml` and `MainPage.xaml.cs`: These two files combine to make up your application's first page.

- `AppShell.xaml` and `AppShell.xaml.cs`: These two files enable you to define how your application will be laid out through the use of the .NET MAUI concept called *Shell*. I will cover Shell extensively in Chapter 5.

Note that wherever you see a `.xaml` file, there will typically be an associated `.xaml.cs` file. This is due to limitations in what XAML can provide; it requires an associated C# file to cover the parts that XAML does not support. I will cover XAML much more extensively in Chapter 5.

It is also worth noting that you do not have to write any XAML. Sure, .NET MAUI and its predecessor, Xamarin.Forms, have a deep connection to XAML but because the XAML is ultimately compiled down to C#, anything that is possible to create in XAML is also possible in C#. You will look through the different possibilities for architecting your applications in the next chapter (Chapter 4).

/Platforms/ Folder

I mentioned that the platform-specific code lives in the Platforms folder. While cross-platform applications provide a nice abstraction from the platforms we wish to support, I still believe it is extremely valuable to know how these platforms behave. Let's dive in and look at each of the platform folders to understand what is happening.

Android

Inside the Android platform folder you will see the following files:

- MainApplication.cs: This is the main entry point for the Android platform. Initially you should note that it does very little. The bit it does is rather important, though; it is responsible for creating the MauiApp using the MauiProgram class. This is the bridge between the Android application and your cross-platform .NET MAUI code.

- MainActivity.cs: An activity in Android development is a type of app component that provides a user interface. The MainActivity starts when your app is loaded. This is typically done by tapping the app icon; however, it can also be triggered by a notification or other source.

- AndroidManifest.xml: This file is extremely important. It is how you define the components that make up your application, any permissions it requires, the application version information, the minimum and target SDK versions, and any hardware or software features that it requires.

iOS

Inside the iOS platform folder, you will see the following files:

- `AppDelegate.cs`: This class allows you to respond to all platform-specific parts of the application lifecycle.

- `Info.plist`: This file contains configuration about the application. It is like the `AndroidManifest.xml` file discussed in the Android section. You can change the application's version and include reasons why your application requires permission to use certain features.

- `Program.cs`: This is the main entry point.

MacCatalyst

Inside the MacCatalyst platform folder, you will see the following files. It is worth noting that this section is nearly identical to the previous iOS section. It's been kept separate to provide an easy reference to what the platform folder consists of for MacCatalyst.

- `AppDelegate.cs`: This class allows you to respond to all platform-specific parts of the application lifecycle.

- `Info.plist`: This file contains configuration about the application. It is like the `AndroidManifest.xml` file discussed in the Android section: you can change the application version and include reasons why your application requires permission to use certain features.

- `Program.cs`: This is the main entry point.

Tizen

Inside the Tizen platform folder, you will see the following files:

- `Main.cs`: This is the main entry point for your Tizen application.

- `tizen-manifest.xml`: This file is very similar to the `AndroidManifest.xml` file. It is how you define the components that make up your application, any permissions it requires, the application version information, the Tizen API version, and any hardware or software features it requires.

Windows

Inside the Windows platform folder, you will see the following files:

- `app.manifest`: The package manifest is an XML document that contains the info the system needs to deploy, display, or update a Windows app. This info includes package identity, package dependencies, required capabilities, visual elements, and extensibility points. Every app package must include one package manifest.

- `App.xaml` and `App.xaml.cs`: The main entry points for your Windows application

- `Package.appxmanifest`: An application manifest is an XML file that describes and identifies the shared and private side-by-side assemblies that an application should bind to at run time. They should be the same assembly versions that were used to test the application. Application manifests may also describe metadata for files that are private to the application.

Summary

Phew! That felt like a lot to take in! I think I need to take a tea break! Don't worry, though; while this gives an overview of what each of the files are responsible for, you will be modifying most of them throughout this book with some practical examples so if there are any points that aren't clear, or you feel you will need to revisit them, you certainly will be.

/Resources/ Folder

The Resources folder is where you store anything you want to include in your application that is not strictly code. Let's look through each of the sub-folders and key types of resource.

Fonts

.NET MAUI allows you to embed your own custom fonts. This is especially handy if you are building an app for a specific brand, or you want to make sure that you render the same font on each platform. You can embed either True Type Fonts (.ttf files) or Open Type Fonts (.otf files).

A word of warning around fonts. I strongly recommend that you check the licensing rules around fonts before including them in your application. While there are sites that make it possible to download fonts freely, a very large percentage of those fonts usually require paying to use them.

There are two parts to embedding a font so that it can be used within your application.

1.   The font file should be place in this folder (Resources/Fonts).

By default, the font will be automatically included as a font file based on the following line that can be found inside the project file (`WidgetBoard.csproj`):

```
<MauiFont Include="Resources\Fonts\*" />
```

What the above line does is set the **build action** of the file you just included to be of type `MauiFont`.

If you want to perform this manually, you can right-click the file inside Visual Studio, click **Properties**, and inside the Properties panel set the **Build Action** to **MauiFont**.

2. Configure the font.

When bootstrapping your application, you need to specify which fonts you wish to load. This is performed with the following lines inside your `MauiProgram.cs` file:

```
.ConfigureFonts(fonts =>
{
    fonts.AddFont("Lobster-Regular.ttf", "Lobster");
});
```

In the above example, you add the font file `Lobster-Regular.ttf` to the collection of fonts and give it an alias of **Lobster**. This means you can just use the name of Lobster when referring to the file in your application.

Images

Practically every application you build will include some images. Each platform that you wish to support has its own rules on the image sizes that you need to supply to make the image render as sharp and clear on the many devices they run. Take iOS, for example. In order to supply a 24x24 pixel image in your app, you must provide three different image sizes: 24x24, 48x48, and 72x72. This is due to the different DPIs for the devices Apple builds. Android devices follow a similar pattern but the DPIs are not the same. This is similar for Windows.

Figure 3-2 shows an example image that would be rendered at 24x24 pixels. Note that while Windows shows the three sizes, this is just based off recommendations for trying to cover the most common settings. In truth, Windows devices can have their DPIs vary much more. Figure 3-2 shows the required image sizes needed for all supported platforms in order to render a 24x24 pixel image.

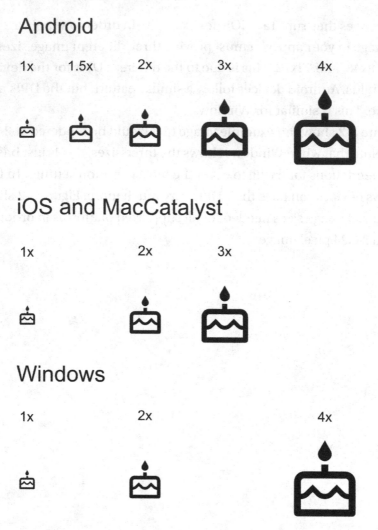

Figure 3-2. *Required image sizes across the various platforms*

You can see from the figure above that it can become painful very quickly if you have lots of images in your application each requiring at least five different sizes to be maintained. Thankfully .NET MAUI gives us the ability to provide a single Scalable Vector Graphic (SVG) image and it will generate the required images for all the platforms when the application is compiled. I cannot tell you how happy all of us Xamarin.Forms old timers are at this new piece of functionality!

As it currently stands, if the SVG image is of the correct original size, you can simply drop the image into the /Resources/Images/ folder and it will just begin to work in your application. In a similar way to how the fonts are automatically picked up, you can see how the images are also handled by looking inside your project file and observing the line <MauiImage Include="Resources\Images*" />

.NET MAUI doesn't render SVGs directly but generates PNG images from the SVGs at compile time. This means that when you are referring to the image you wish, it needs to have the .png extension. For example, when embedding an image called image.svg, in code you refer to it as image.png.

If the contents of the SVG are not of the desired size, then you can add some configuration to tell the tooling what size the image should be. For this the image **should not** be added to the /Resources/Images/ folder as the tooling will end up generating duplicates and there is no telling which one will win. Instead, you can simply add the image to the /Resources/ folder and then add the following line to your project file:

```
<MauiImage Include="Resources\image.svg" BaseSize="24,24" />
```

The above code will treat the contents of the image.svg file as being 24x24 pixels and then scale for each platform based on that size.

Raw

Your final type of resource to embed is raw files. This essentially means that what is embedded can be loaded at runtime. A typical example of this is to provide some data to preload into the application when first starting.

Where To Begin?

.NET MAUI applications have a single main entry point that is common across all platforms. This provides us with a way to centralize much of the initialization process for our applications and therefore only write it once.

You will have noticed that in each of the platform-specific main entry points covered in the previous section they all called `MauiProgram.CreateMauiApp();`. This is the main entry point into your .NET MAUI and shared application.

The `CreateMauiApp` method allows you to bootstrap your application. Bootstrapping refers to a self-starting process that is supposed to continue or grow without external input (Wikipedia quote). This means that your implementation in this method is responsible for configuring the application from setting up logging, general application configuration, and registering implementations to be handled with dependency injection. This is one of the big improvements in .NET MAUI over Xamarin.Forms. This is done through the Generic Host Builder.

Generic Host Builder

I mentioned back in Chapter 1 that one of the benefits that comes with the evolution to .NET MAUI is powerful dependency injection. The Generic Host Builder is tried and tested through other .NET frameworks such as ASP .NET Core and it has thankfully become available to all application types now.

Before we jump in to how the Generic Host Builder works, let's look at what exactly dependency injection is and why you should use it.

What Is Dependency Injection?

Dependency injection (DI) is a software design pattern aimed at reducing hard-coded dependencies in a software application. A dependency is an object that another object depends on. This hard-coded dependency approach is referred to as being tightly coupled. Let's work through an example to show how and why it's named so and how you can remove the need for the hard-coded dependencies thus making your design loosely coupled.

So, my wife is a fantastic baker. She bakes these beautiful, delicious cakes and this is the main reason I have gained so much weight recently. I am going to use the process of her baking a cake to show this concept of dependencies.

```
public class Baker
{
    public Cake Bake()
    {
    }
}
```

The above code looks relatively straightforward, right? She bakes a cake. Now let's consider how she might go about making the cake. She needs a way of sourcing the ingredients, weighing them, mixing them, and finally baking them. We end up with something like

```
public class Baker
{
    private readonly WeighingScale weighingScale = new
    WeighingScale();
    private readonly Oven oven = new Oven();
    private readonly MixingMachine mixingMachine = new
    MixingMachine();
```

```
private readonly IngredientsProvider ingredientsProvider =
new IngredientsProvider();

public Cake Bake()
{
    Ingredient ingredient = ingredientsProvider.Provide();

    weighingScale.Weigh(ingredient);
}
}
```

We can see that for the Baker to do their job, they need to know about all these different pieces of equipment. Now imagine that the WeighingScale breaks, and a replacement is provided. Baker will still need to weigh the ingredients but won't care how that weighing is performed. Imagine that the new WeighingScale is digital and now requires batteries. There are a few reasons why we want to move away from having hard-coded dependencies as in our Baker example.

- If we did replace the WeighingScale with a different implementation, we would have to modify the Baker class.

- If the WeighingScale has dependencies (e.g., batteries in our new digital scale), they must also be configured in the Baker class.

- This becomes more difficult to unit test because the Baker is creating dependencies and therefore a unit test would result in having to test far more than a unit test is designed to.

Dependency injection can help us to address the above issues by allowing us to achieve *Inversion of Control* (IoC). Inversion of Control essentially means that we are inverting the knowledge of the dependency from the Baker knowing about a WeighingScale to them knowing about something that can weigh ingredients but not an actual implementation. This is done through the introduction of an interface which we will call IWeighingScale.

```
public class Baker
{
    private readonly IWeighingScale weighingScale;
    private readonly Oven oven = new Oven();
    private readonly MixingMachine mixingMachine = new
    MixingMachine();
    private readonly IngredientsProvider ingredientsProvider =
    new IngredientsProvider();

    public Baker(
        IWeighingScale weighingScale)
    {
        this.weighingScale = weighingScale;
    }

    public Cake Bake()
    {
        Ingredient ingredient = ingredientsProvider.Provide();

        this.weighingScale.Weigh(ingredient);
    }
}
```

Now our Baker knows about an interface for something that can weigh their ingredients but not the actual thing that does the weighing. This means that in the scenario where the weighing scale breaks and a new one is supplied, there is no change to the Baker class in order to handle this new scale. Instead, it is registered as part of the application start-up or bootstrapping process. Of course, we could and should follow the same approach for our other dependencies.

One additional concept I have introduced here is the use of *constructor injection*. Constructor injection is the process of providing the registered dependencies when creating an instance of our `Baker`. So, when our `Baker` is created, it is passed an instance of `WeighingScale`.

If you have a background with Xamarin.Forms, you will have come across the `DependencyService`. This provided a mechanism for managing dependency injection within an application; however, it received criticism in the past for not supporting constructor injection. This doesn't mean it wasn't possible to achieve constructor injection in Xamarin.Forms applications but it required the use of a third-party package and there are a lot of great packages out there! Now it is all baked into .NET MAUI.

Registering Dependencies

In the previous section, I discussed how to minimize concrete dependencies in your code base. Now let's look through how to configure those dependencies so that the dependents are given the correct implementations.

Implementations that you register in the generic host builder are referred to as services and the work of providing the implementations out to dependents is referred to as the `ServiceProvider`. You can register your services using the following.

AddSingleton

A singleton registration means that there will only ever be one instance of the object. So, based on the example of our `Baker` needing to use an `IWeighingScale`, we register it as follows:

```
builder.Services.AddSingleton<IWeighingScale, WeighingScale>();
```

Then every time that an IWeighingScale is resolved, we will be provided with the same instance. This suits the weighing scale example because we use the same one throughout our baking process.

It is extremely unlikely that you will ever need to register a view model as a singleton. Doing so can introduce bits of behavior that you are most likely not expecting on top of the fact that you can run the risk of leaking memory.

AddTransient

A transient registration is the opposite of a singleton. Every time an implementation is resolved, a new instance is created and provided. So based on the example of our Baker needing to use an IWeighingScale, we register it as follows:

```
builder.Services.AddTransient<IWeighingScale, WeighingScale>();
```

As mentioned, every time an IWeighingScale is resolved, we will be provided with a new instance. A better example here might be the greaseproof paper that lines the cake tins. They are used once and thrown away.

AddScoped

A scoped registration is somewhere in the middle of a singleton and transient. A single instance will be provided for a "scope," and then when a new scope is created, a new instance will be provided for the life of that scope.

```
builder.Services.AddScoped<IWeighingScale, WeighingScale>();
```

This type of registration feels much better suited to a web application where requests come in and a scope will represent a single request. In the mobile and desktop world, your application typically has a single state and therefore is less likely to need scoped registrations. Currently .NET MAUI does not provide any automatic creations of scopes, but you have the power to create your own using the `IServiceScopeFactory` interface and ultimately its implementation.

Application Lifecycle

Sadly, no two platforms provide the same set of behaviors or lifecycle events such as when an application is started, backgrounded, or closed. This is where cross-platform frameworks provide us with a solid set of encapsulated events to cover most scenarios. There are four main application states in a .NET MAUI application.

Application States

These are the application states:

- **Not running**: This means that the application has not been started and is not loaded into memory. This is typically when the application has been installed, the device has been powered on, the application was closed by the user, or the operating system has terminated the application to free up some resources.

- **Running**: This means that the application is visible and is focused.

- **Deactivated**: This means that the application is no longer focused but may still be visible. On mobile, this could mean that the operating system is showing a permission request alert (e.g., an application asking for permission to use the camera) or similar.

- **Stopped**: This means that the application is no longer visible.

You can now see how a .NET MAUI application moves between the above four states and the events that are triggered to an application. Figure 3-3 shows the possible states that a .NET MAUI application can take during its lifetime and how it transitions between those states.

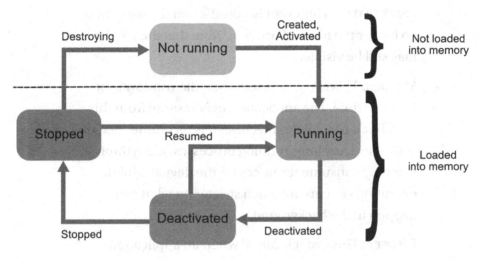

Figure 3-3. *Application state lifecycle chart*

Before we dive into the details of each of the events that are fired between the state transitions, I need to give you some background on how they can be accessed and why. In order to access these events, you must access the Window class. It certainly isn't a common concept to have a window in a mobile application, but you must appreciate that you are dealing with a cross-platform framework and therefore an approach that fits desktop as well as mobile. I see it as follows: a mobile application is a single window application, and a desktop is likely to be multi-window.

Lifecycle Events

Now on to the events that move an application between states.

- **Created**: This event is raised after the platform window has been created. Note that the window may not be visible yet.

- **Activated**: This event is raised when the window is the focused window.

- **Deactivated**: This event is raised when the window is no longer the focused window. Note that the window may still be visible.

- **Stopped**: This event is raised when the window is no longer visible. The application may resume from this state but it is not guaranteed, so it is recommended that you cancel any long-running processes or anything that may consume resources on the device. Mobile operating systems are much stricter on what can happen in the background.

- **Resumed**: This event is raised when an application resumes from the **Stopped** state. It is recommended to prepare your application for full use again (e.g., subscribe to events or messages, refresh any visible content).

- **Destroying**: This event is raised when the platform window is being destroyed and removed from memory. It is recommended that you unsubscribe from events or messages.

Handling Lifecycle Events

By default, a .NET MAUI application won't give you access to the lifecycle events; this is something you must opt in for. In order to opt in, you must modify your App class.

Open Visual Studio. You need to add a new class to your project and call it StateAwareWindow. Your new class will need to be modified so it looks as follows:

```
public class StateAwareWindow: Window
{
    public StateAwareWindow() : base()
    {
    }

    public StateAwareWindow(Page page) : base(page)
    {
    }

    protected override void OnCreated()
    {
        // Initialise our application
    }
}
```

Inside of your application, you can override all methods that will be executed when the specific event occurs. Each override method follows the naming of the events, as described previously, with a prefix of On. Therefore, to handle the Activated event, you override the OnActivated method.

The final step is to make use of the new class, so inside your App.xaml. cs file, add the following:

```
protected override Window CreateWindow(IActivationState
activationState)
{
    return new StateAwareWindow(MainPage);
}
```

This will create a new instance of StateAwareWindow and pass it a reference to the application's MainPage. If you do not pass in a reference to a Page to the Window implementation, you will experience exceptions being thrown.

Cross-Platform Mappings to Platform Lifecycle Events

I strongly believe that despite the fact that .NET MAUI provides us with these events, you should understand how they map to the underlying platforms. If you understand what is being called on the platform-specific side, it can really help to diagnose things when they go wrong or perhaps point you in the direction of a better approach for your scenarios.

Let's break down how the .NET MAUI lifecycle events map to the platform-specific events and then show off the bits that are not mapped if you ever need to use them. See Table 3-1.

Table 3-1. *Cross-Platform Lifecycle Events Mapped to the Platform-Specific Events*

Event	Android	iOS/MacCatalyst	Windows
Created	OnPostCreate	FinishedLaunching	Created
Activated	OnResume	OnActivated	Activated(Code Activated and Pointer Activated)
Deactivated	OnPause	OnResignActivation	Activated (Deactivated)
Stopped	OnStop	DidEnterBackground	Visibility Changed
Resumed	OnRestart	WillEnterForeground	Resumed
Destroying	OnDestroy	WillTerminate	Closed

This list may not provide too much meaning right now and I wouldn't worry yourself with needing to know this. The aim here is to provide you with a quick look-up to be able to then research if any lifecycle events are going wrong or possibly not the right fit for your solution.

Platform-Specific Lifecycle Events

There are actually many platform-specific lifecycle events that .NET MAUI does not map to. What .NET MAUI does provide is a set of lifecycle events that map consistently across all platforms. The rest in this section are really specific to each individual platform. I won't be covering all of the details of each individual event; however, I will cover how to make use of one so that you will know how to make use of an event that better suits your use case.

When searching for information around a platform-specific event, don't feel constrained to searching for .NET MAUI-specific documentation. You have the power to leverage the platform APIs. You should be able to search for information in the context of Android or iOS and the code should be relatively easy to translate into C#.

In order to register for a platform-specific event, you need to make use of the `ConfigureLifecycleEvents` method on the `MauiAppBuilder` class. Let's look at a concrete example for each platform. The code in each of the following examples is largely the same but the duplication has been kept to show the bigger picture. I have highlighted the differences in **bold** to show the key differences.

Android

To receive a notification for an Android lifecycle event, you call the `ConfigureLifecycleEvents` method on the `MauiAppBuilder` object. You can then make use of the `AddAndroid` method and specify the events you wish to handle and how you wish to handle them.

```
using Microsoft.Maui.LifecycleEvents;

namespace WidgetBoard;

public static class MauiProgram
{
    public static MauiApp CreateMauiApp()
    {
        var builder = MauiApp.CreateBuilder();
        builder
            .UseMauiApp<App>()
            .ConfigureLifecycleEvents(events =>
```

```
            {
#if ANDROID
                events.AddAndroid(lifecycle=>
                    lifecycle.OnStart((activity) =>
                    OnStart(activity)));

                static void OnStart(Activity activity)
                {
                    // Perform your OnStart logic
                }
#endif
            });

        return builder.Build();
    }
}
```

For more information on the available lifecycle events, I recommend checking out the following documentation pages:

Microsoft: https://learn.microsoft.com/dotnet/maui/fundamentals/app-lifecycle#android

Android: https://developer.android.com/guide/components/activities/activity-lifecycle

iOS and MacCatalyst

To receive a notification for an iOS lifecycle event, you call the ConfigureLifecycleEvents method on the MauiAppBuilder object. You can then make use of the AddiOS method and specify the events you wish to handle and how you wish to handle them.

```
using Microsoft.Maui.LifecycleEvents;

namespace WidgetBoard;

public static class MauiProgram
```

```
{
    public static MauiApp CreateMauiApp()
    {
        var builder = MauiApp.CreateBuilder();
        builder
            .UseMauiApp<App>()
            .ConfigureLifecycleEvents(events =>
            {
#if IOS || MACCATALYST
                events.AddiOS(lifecycle =>
                    lifecycle.OnActivated((app) =>
                    OnActivated(app)));

                static void OnActivated(UIKit.UIApplication
                application)
                {
                    // Perform your OnActivated logic
                }
#endif
            });

        return builder.Build();
    }
}
```

For more information on the available lifecycle events, I recommend checking out the following documentation pages:

Microsoft: https://learn.microsoft.com/dotnet/maui/ fundamentals/app-lifecycle#ios

iOS: https://developer.apple.com/documentation/uikit/app_and_ environment/managing_your_app_s_life_cycle?language=objc

Windows

To receive a notification for a Windows lifecycle event, you call the ConfigureLifecycleEvents method on the MauiAppBuilder object. You can then make use of the AddWindows method and specify the events you wish to handle and how you wish to handle them.

```
using Microsoft.Maui.LifecycleEvents;

namespace WidgetBoard;

public static class MauiProgram
{
    public static MauiApp CreateMauiApp()
    {
        var builder = MauiApp.CreateBuilder();
        builder
            .UseMauiApp<App>()
            .ConfigureLifecycleEvents(events =>
            {
#if WINDOWS
                events.AddWindows(lifecycle =>
                    lifecycle.OnActivated((window, args) =>
                    OnActivated(window, args)));

                static void OnActivated(Microsoft.
                UI.Xaml.Window window, Microsoft.UI.Xaml.
                WindowActivatedEventArgs args)
                {
                    // Perform your OnActivated logic
                }
#endif
            });
```

```
        return builder.Build();
    }
}
```

For more information on the available lifecycle events, I recommend checking out the following documentation page:

Microsoft: `https://learn.microsoft.com/dotnet/maui/ fundamentals/app-lifecycle#windows`

You may have noticed the usage of #if statements. Due to the nature of compiling for multiple platforms in a single project, you will need to write platform-specific code. If, like me, you do not like the #if statement or at would like to keep its usage to a minimum, then fear not: we will be taking a closer look at minimizing it in Chapter 13.

Summary

In this chapter, you have

- Walked through the main components of a .NET MAUI application

- Earned a tea break

- Learned about the start-up process

- Learned about the life of a .NET MAUI application

In the next chapter, you will

- Learn about the different possibilities you have to architect your applications

- Decide on what architecture to use

- Walk through a concrete example by creating your `ClockWidget`

- Learn how to further optimize your implementation using NuGet packages

CHAPTER 4

An Architecture to Suit You

In this chapter, you will look through some possible architectural patterns that can be used to build .NET MAUI applications. The objective is to provide you with enough detail to help you find the architecture that best fits you. I want to point out that there are no right answers concerning which architecture to choose. The best option is to go with one that you feel will benefit you and your team.

I aim to quash the following myths throughout the course of this chapter:

"You are forced to use XAML."

"You are forced to use MVVM."

There seems to be a common misconception that Xamarin.Forms and .NET MAUI are built largely around using only XAML and MVVM. While this is the most common approach taken by developers, it is not forced upon us.

A Measuring Stick

You will build the same control with each of the options to provide a way to compare the differences. The control you will be building is a `ClockWidget`. The purpose of this control is to do the following:

© Shaun Lawrence 2023
S. Lawrence, *Introducing .NET MAUI*, https://doi.org/10.1007/978-1-4842-9234-1_4

- Display the current time in your app.

- Update the time every minute.

Figure 4-1 shows a very rough layout of the control with the current date and time. You will tidy this up later with the ability to format the date and time information in Chapter 5, but for now let's just focus on a limited example to highlight the differences in options. Figure 4-1 shows how the ClockWidget will render in your application when you have finished with this chapter.

24/05/2022 11:30

Figure 4-1. *Sketch of how the ClockWidget control will render*

Prerequisites

Before you get started with each of the architectures you will be reviewing in this chapter, you need to do a little bit of background setup to prepare.

You need to add a single new class. This implementation will allow your widgets to schedule an action of work to be performed after a specific period of time. In your scenario of the ClockWidget, you can schedule an update of the UI. Let's add this Scheduler class into your project.

- Right-click the *WidgetBoard* project.

- Select **Add ➤ Class.**

- Give it the name of *Scheduler.*

- Click **Add.**

You want to modify the contents of the file to look as follows:

```
using System.Threading.Tasks;

public class Scheduler
{
    public void ScheduleAction(TimeSpan timeSpan,
    Action action)
    {
        Task.Run(async () =>
        {
            await Task.Delay(timeSpan);
            action.Invoke();
        });
    }
}
```

In the following sections you will be looking at code examples rather than implementing them directly. This is aimed at providing some comparisons to allow you to find out what will be a good fit for you as you build your applications and grow as a cross-platform developer. At the end of the chapter, you will take your chosen approach and add it into your application so you can see the final result of your `ClockWidget`.

Model View ViewModel (MVVM)

Model View ViewModel is a software design pattern that focuses on separating the user interface (View) from the business logic (Model). It achieves this with the use of a layer in between (ViewModel). MVVM allows a clean separation of presentation and business logic. Figure 4-2 shows the clean separation between the components of the MVVM architecture.

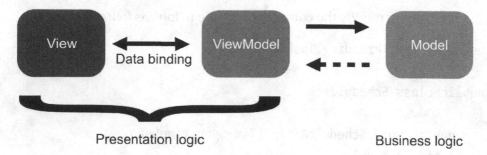

Figure 4-2. An overview of the MVVM pattern

The result of creating this separation between UI and business logic brings several benefits:

- Makes unit testing easier

- Allows for Views to be swapped out or even rewritten without impacting the other parts

- Encourages code reuse

- Provides the ability to separate UI development from the business logic development

A key part to any design pattern is knowing where to locate parts of your code to make it fit and abide by the rules. Let's take a deeper look at each of the three key parts of this pattern.

Model

The Model is where you keep your business logic. It is typically loaded from a database/webservice among many other things.

For your business logic, you are going to rely on the Scheduler class that you created earlier in the "Prerequisites" section of this chapter.

View

The View defines the layout and appearance of the application. It is what the user will see and interact with. In .NET MAUI, a View is typically written in XAML where possible, but there will be occasions when logic in the code-behind will need to be written. You will learn this later in this chapter; you don't have to use XAML at all so if you don't feel XAML is right for you, fear not.

A View in .NET MAUI is typically a `ContentPage` or an implementation that will inherit from `ContentPage` or `ContentView`. You use a `ContentPage` if you want to render a full page in your application (basically a view that will fill the application). You use a `ContentView` for something smaller (like a widget!). For your implementation you will be inheriting from a `ContentView`.

I discussed in Chapter 2 that the majority of XAML files come with an associated C# file. A XAML-based view is no exception to this rule. With this in mind, let's take a look at the contents you need to place in each of the files.

XAML

```
<?xml version="1.0" encoding="utf-8" ?>
<ContentView xmlns="http://schemas.microsoft.com/
dotnet/2021/maui"
             xmlns:x="http://schemas.microsoft.com/
             winfx/2009/xaml"
             xmlns:viewmodels="clr-namespace:WidgetBoard.
             ViewModels"
             x:Class="WidgetBoard.ClockWidget">

    <ContentView.BindingContext>
        <viewmodels:ClockWidgetViewModel />
    </ContentView.BindingContext>

    <Label Text="{Binding Time}"
```

```
            FontSize="80"
            VerticalOptions="Center"
            HorizontalOptions="Center" />

</ContentView>
```

C# (Code-Behind)

The following code will have already been created for you by the .NET MAUI template. It is included for reference.

```
namespace WidgetBoard;

public partial class ClockWidget : ContentView
{
    public ClockWidget()
    {
        InitializeComponent();
    }
}
```

The InitializeComponent method call above is essential when building XAML-based views. It results in the XAML being loaded and parsed into an instance of the controls that have been defined in the XAML file.

ViewModel

The ViewModel acts as the bridge between the View and the Model. You expose properties and commands on the ViewModel that the View will bind to. To make a comparison to building applications with just code-behind, we could state that properties basically map to references of controls and commands are events. A binding provides a mechanism for both the View and ViewModel to send and receive updates.

For your ViewModel to notify the View that a property has changed and therefore the View will refresh the value displayed on screen, you need to make use of the INotifyPropertyChanged interface. This offers a single PropertyChanged event that you must implement and ultimately raise when your data-bound value has changed. This is all handled by the XAML binding engine, which you will look at in much more detail in the next chapter. Let's create your ViewModel class and then break down what is going on.

```
public class ClockWidgetViewModel : INotifyPropertyChanged
{
    public event PropertyChangedEventHandler PropertyChanged;

    private readonly Scheduler scheduler = new();
    private DateTime time;

    public DateTime Time
    {
        get
        {
            return time;
        }
        set
        {
            if (time != value)
            {
                time = value;

                PropertyChanged?.Invoke(this, new PropertyChang
                edEventArgs(nameof(Time)));
            }
        }
```

```
    }

    public ClockWigetViewModel()
    {
        SetTime(DateTime.Now);
    }

    public void SetTime(DateTime dateTime)
    {
        Time = dateTime;

        scheduler.ScheduleAction(
            TimeSpan.FromSeconds(1),
            () => SetTime(DateTime.Now));
    }
}
```

You have

- Created a class called ClockWidgetViewModel

- Implemented the INotifyPropertyChanged interface

- Added a property that when set will check whether it's value really has changed, and if it has, raise the PropertyChanged event with the name of the property that has changed

- Added a method to set the Time property and repeat every second so that the widget looks like a clock counting.

Model View Update (MVU)

Model View Update is a software design pattern for building interactive applications. The concept originates from the Elm programming language. As the name suggests, there are three key parts to MVU:

- **Model**: This is the state of your application.

- **View**: This is a visual representation of your state.

- **Update**: This is a mechanism to update your state.

Figure 4-3 shows how each of these components relate and interact with each other.

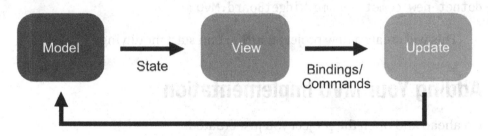

Figure 4-3. *An overview of the MVU pattern*

This pattern offers several benefits:

- Clearly defined rules around where state is allowed to be updated

- Ease of testing

A key part to any design pattern is knowing where to locate parts of your code to make it fit and abide by the rules. Let's take a deeper look at each of the three key parts of this pattern.

Getting Started with Comet

First, you must install the Comet project templates. To do this, open a terminal window and run the following command:

```
dotnet new -install Clancey.Comet.Templates.Multiplatform
```

This will install the template so that you can create a new project. Sadly, this is different enough to the WidgetBoard project that you have been working with so far.

Next, you need to create the project. This is again done via the terminal for now:

```
dotnet new comet --name WidgetBoard.Mvu
```

This will create a new project that you can start modifying.

Adding Your MVU Implementation

Go ahead and open the project you just created.

The first thing you need to do is make use of the same `Scheduler` class that you created in the MVVM Model example for your MVU implementation. Here it is again to make life easier:

```
public class Scheduler
{
    public void ScheduleAction(TimeSpan timeSpan,
    Action action)
    {
        Task.Run(async () =>
        {
            await Task.Delay(timeSpan);
            action.Invoke();
        }
```

```
    }
}
```

Finally, go ahead and create your `ClockWidget` class:

```
public class ClockWidget : View
{
    [State]
    readonly Clock clock = new();

    [Body]
    View body()
        => new Text(() => $"{clock.Time}")
            .FontSize(80)
            .HorizontalLayoutAlignment(LayoutAlignment.Center)
            .VerticalLayoutAlignment(LayoutAlignment.Center);

    public class Clock : BindingObject
    {
        readonly Scheduler scheduler = new();

        public DateTime Time
        {
            get => GetProperty<DateTime>();
            set => SetProperty(value);
        }

        public Clock()
        {
            SetTime(DateTime.Now);
        }

        void SetTime(DateTime dateTime)
        {
            Time = dateTime;
```

```
scheduler.ScheduleAction(
    TimeSpan.FromSeconds(1),
    () =>
    {
        SetTime(DateTime.Now);
    });
    }
  }
}
```

Now that you have added a load of code, let's summarize what you have done.

- You have created a new class named ClockWidget.

- You have defined your state type as Clock.

- You have initialized (known as init in the MVU pattern) your **model** field clock.

- You have defined your **view** with the body() function.

- You have defined your **update** function in the form of the SetTime method.

Note that there are two common scenarios when an update is called: when there is user interaction (e.g., a click/tap of a button) and around asynchronous background work. Your example here applies to the second scenario.

XAML vs. C# Markup

XAML has proven to be a big part of building application UIs in Xamarin. Forms and it will likely continue in .NET MAUI, but I want to make it clear that you do not have to use it. So, if like some friends and colleagues, the verbosity of XAML makes you feel queasy, there is a solution!

Anything that you can create in XAML can ultimately be created in C#. Furthermore, there are ways to improve on the readability of the C# required to build UIs.

Some benefits of building user interfaces solely with C# are

- A single file for a view. No pairing of .xaml.cs and .xaml files.

- Better refactoring options so renaming properties or commands in XAML won't update the C#.

Let's work through how you can build your ClockWidget in C# in all its verbosity and then I will show how you can simplify it using C# Markup. (I must add this is an open-source package that you need to bring in). Also, these examples are still built using MVVM.

Plain C#

As mentioned, anything you can build in XAML can also be built in C#. The following code shows how the exact same XAML definition of your ClockWidget can be built using just C#:

```
using WidgetBoard.ViewModels;

namespace WidgetBoard.Views;

public class ClockWidget : ContentView
{
    public ClockWidget()
    {
        BindingContext = new ClockWidgetViewModel();

        var label = new Label
        {
            FontSize = 80,
```

```
        HorizontalOptions = LayoutOptions.Center,
        VerticalOptions = LayoutOptions.Center
    };

    label.SetBinding(
        Label.TextProperty,
        nameof(ClockWidgetViewModel.Time));

    Content = label;
  }
}
```

The code above does the following things:

- Creates a single file representing your `ClockWidget`

- Points your widget's `BindingContext` to the
  `ClockWidgetViewModel`

- Creates a label and set its `Text` property to be bound to
  the view models `Time` property

- Assigns the label to the content of the view

C# Markup

I have recently come to appreciate the value of being able to fluently
build UIs. I don't tend to do it often because I personally feel comfortable
building with XAML or perhaps it is Stockholm Syndrome kicking in ☺
(I've been working with XAML for well over 10 years now). When I do, it
needs to be as easy to read and build as possible given it is not something I
do often.

As a maintainer on the .NET MAUI Community Toolkit, one of the packages we provide is CommunityToolkit.Maui.Markup. It provides a set of extension methods and helpers to build UIs fluently.

```
using CommunityToolkit.Maui.Markup;
using WidgetBoard.ViewModels;

namespace WidgetBoard.Views;

public class ClockWidget : ContentView
{
    public ClockWidget()
    {
        BindingContext = new ClockWidgetViewModel();

        Content = new Label()
            .Font(size: 80)
            .CenterHorizontal()
            .CenterVertical()
            .Bind(Label.TextProperty,
                nameof(ClockWidgetViewModel.Time));
    }
}
```

This code performs the same steps as the plain C# example; however, the code is much easier to read. I am sure you can imagine that when the complexity of the UI increases, this fluent approach can really start to benefit you.

Chosen Architecture for This Book

Throughout this book, we will be using the MVVM-based architecture while building the UI through XAML.

My reasons for choosing MVVM are as follows:

- I have spent the last 10+ years using this architecture so it certainly feels natural to me.

- It has been a very common way of building applications over the past decade so there is an abundance of resources online to assist in overcoming issues around it.

- It is a common pattern in all Microsoft products and has a proven track record.

Now that I have covered the various architecture options and decided on using MVVM, let's proceed to adding in the specific Views and ViewModels so that it can be used inside the application. Then I will show how to start simplifying the implementation so that the code really only needs to include the core logic by avoiding having to add a lot of the boilerplate code.

Adding the ViewModels

First, add a new folder to your project.

- Right-click the *WidgetBoard* project.

- Select **Add ➤ New Folder.**

- Enter the name *ViewModels*.

- Click **Add.**

This folder will house your application's view models. Let's proceed to adding the first one.

Adding IWidgetViewModel

The first item you need to add is an interface. It will represent all widget view models that you create in your application.

- Right-click the ViewModels folder.

- Select **Add ➤ New Item.**

- Select the **Interface** type.

- Enter the name *IWidgetViewModel.*

- Click **Add.**

Modify this file to the following:

```
namespace WidgetBoard.ViewModels;

public interface IWidgetViewModel
{
    int Position { get; set; }

    string Type { get; }
}
```

Adding BaseViewModel

This will serve as the base class for all of your view models so that you only have to write some boilerplate code once. Don't worry; you will see how to optimize this even further!

- Right-click the ViewModels folder.

- Select **Add ➤ Class.**

- Enter the name *BaseViewModel.*

- Click **Add.**

You can replace the contents of the class file with the following code:

```
using System.ComponentModel;
using System.Runtime.CompilerServices;

namespace WidgetBoard.ViewModels;

public abstract class BaseViewModel : INotifyPropertyChanged
{
    public event PropertyChangedEventHandler PropertyChanged;

    protected void OnPropertyChanged([CallerMemberName] string
    propertyName = "")
    {
        PropertyChanged?.Invoke(this, new PropertyChangedEventA
        rgs(propertyName));
    }

    protected bool SetProperty<TValue>(ref TValue backingField,
    TValue value, [CallerMemberName] string propertyName = "")
    {
        if (Comparer<TValue>.Default.Compare(backingField,
        value) == 0)
        {
            return false;
        }

        backingField = value;

        OnPropertyChanged(propertyName);

        return true;
    }
}
```

You should be familiar with the first line inside the class:

```
public event PropertyChangedEventHandler PropertyChanged;
```

This is the event definition that you must add as part of implementing the INotifyPropertyChanged interface and it serves as the mechanism for your view model to update the view.

The next method provides a mechanism to easily raise the PropertyChanged event:

```
protected void OnPropertyChanged([CallerMemberName] string
propertyName = "")
{
    PropertyChanged?.Invoke(this, new PropertyChangedEventArgs(
    propertyName));
}
```

The OnPropertyChanged method can be called with or without passing in a value for propertyName. By passing a value in, you are indicating which property name on your view model has changed. If you do not, then the [CallerMemberName] attribute indicates that the name of caller will be used. Don't worry if this is a little unclear right now; it will become much clearer when you add your property into your ClockWidgetViewModel so just bear with me.

The final method adds a lot of value:

```
protected bool SetProperty<TValue>(
    ref TValue backingField,
    TValue value,
    [CallerMemberName] string propertyName = "")
{
    if (Comparer<TValue>.Default.Compare(backingField,
    value) == 0)
    {
```

```
        return false;
    }
    backingField = value;
    OnPropertyChanged(propertyName);
    return true;
}
```

The SetProperty method does the following:

- Allows you to call it from a property setter, passing in the field and value being set

- Checks whether the value is different from the backing field, basically determining whether the property has really changed

- If it has changed, it fires the PropertyChanged event using your new OnPropertyChanged method

- Returns a Boolean indicating whether the value did really change. This can be really useful when needing to update other properties or commands!

This concludes the base view model implementation. Let's proceed to using it as the base for the ClockWidgetViewModel to really appreciate the value it is providing.

Adding ClockWidgetViewModel

Let's add a new class file into your ViewModels folder as you did for the BaseViewModel.cs file. Call this file ClockWidgetViewModel and modify the contents to the following:

```
using System;
```

```csharp
using System.ComponentModel;

namespace WidgetBoard.ViewModels;

public class ClockWidgetViewModel : BaseViewModel,
IWidgetViewModel
{
    private readonly Scheduler scheduler = new();
    private DateTime time;

    public DateTime Time
    {
        get => time;
        set => SetProperty(ref time, value);
    }

    public int Position { get; set; }

    public string Type => "Clock";

    public ClockWidgetViewModel()
    {
        SetTime(DateTime.Now);
    }

    public void SetTime(DateTime dateTime)
    {
        Time = dateTime;

        scheduler.ScheduleAction(
            TimeSpan.FromSeconds(1),
            () => SetTime(DateTime.Now));
    }
}
```

The above code should be familiar. You saw it when reviewing MVVM. The optimization made here is to reduce the size of the Time property down to just 5 lines where the original example was 16 lines of code.

Adding Views

First, add a new folder to your project.

- Right-click the *WidgetBoard* project.

- Select **Add ➤ New Folder.**

- Enter the name *Views*.

- Click **Add.**

This folder will house your application's views. Let's proceed to adding your first one.

Adding IWidgetView

The first item you need to add is an interface to represent all widget view models that you create in your application.

- Right-click the Views folder.

- Select **Add ➤ New Item.**

- Select the **Interface** type.

- Enter the name *IWidgetView.*

- Click **Add.**

Modify the contents of this file to the following:

```
using WidgetBoard.ViewModels;

namespace WidgetBoard.Views;

public interface IWidgetView
{
    int Position { get => WidgetViewModel.Position; set =>
    WidgetViewModel.Position = value; }

    IWidgetViewModel WidgetViewModel { get; set; }
}
```

Adding ClockWidgetView

The next item you need to add is a ContentView. This is the first time you are doing this, so use the following steps:

- Right-click the Views folder.

- Select **Add ➤ New Item.**

- Select the **.NET MAUI** tab.

- Select the **.NET MAUI ContentView (XAML)** option.

- Enter the name *ClockWidgetView.*

- Click **Add.**

Observe that two new files have been added to your project: ClockWidgetView.xaml and ClockWidgetView.xaml.cs. You may notice that the ClockWidgetView.xaml.cs file is hidden in the Solution Explorer panel and that you need to expand the arrow to the left of the ClockWidgetView.xaml file.

Let's update both files to match what was in the original examples.

Open the ClockWidgetView.xaml file and modify the contents to the following:

```xml
<?xml version="1.0" encoding="utf-8" ?>
<Label
    xmlns="http://schemas.microsoft.com/dotnet/2021/maui"
    xmlns:x="http://schemas.microsoft.com/winfx/2009/xaml"
    xmlns:viewmodels="clr-namespace:WidgetBoard.ViewModels"
    x:Class="WidgetBoard.Views.ClockWidgetView"
    FontSize="60"
    VerticalOptions="Center"
    HorizontalOptions="Center"
    x:DataType="viewmodels:ClockWidgetViewModel"
    Text="{Binding Time}">

</Label>
```

Open the ClockWidgetView.xaml.cs file and modify the contents to the following:

```csharp
using WidgetBoard.ViewModels;

namespace WidgetBoard.Views;

public partial class ClockWidgetView : Label, IWidgetView
{
    public ClockWidgetView()
    {
        InitializeComponent();

        WidgetViewModel = new ClockWidgetViewModel();
        BindingContext = WidgetViewModel;
    }

    public IWidgetViewModel WidgetViewModel { get; set; }
}
```

This completes the work to add the `ClockWidget` into your codebase. Now you need modify your application so that you can see this widget in action!

Viewing Your Widget

In order to view your widget in your application, you need to make some changes to the `MainPage.xaml` and `MainPage.xaml.cs` files that were generated when you first created your project.

Modifying MainPage.xaml

Simply replace the contents of the file with the following.

```xml
<?xml version="1.0" encoding="utf-8" ?>
<ContentPage xmlns="http://schemas.microsoft.com/
dotnet/2021/maui"
        xmlns:x="http://schemas.microsoft.com/
        winfx/2009/xaml"
        xmlns:views="clr-namespace:WidgetBoard.Views"
        x:Class="WidgetBoard.MainPage">

    <views:ClockWidgetView />

</ContentPage>
```

The original file had a basic example that ships with the .NET MAUI template, but it wasn't of much use in this application.

Modifying MainPage.xaml.cs

You need to modify the contents of this file because you deleted some controls from the `MainPage.xaml` file. If you don't update this file, Visual Studio will report compilation errors. You can replace the entire contents of the `MainPage.xaml.cs` file with the following to remove references to the controls you deleted from XAML file:

```
namespace WidgetBoard;

public partial class MainPage : ContentPage
{
    public MainPage()
    {
        InitializeComponent();
    }
}
```

This concludes the changes that you need to make in your application. Let's see what your application looks like now!

Taking the Application for a Spin

If you build and run your application just like you learned to in Chapter 2, you can see that it renders the `ClockWidget` just as I originally designed. Figure 4-4 shows the clock widget rendered in the application running on macOS.

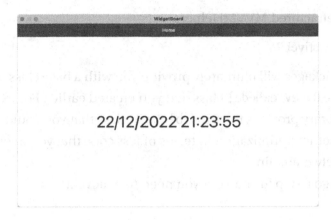

Figure 4-4. *The clock widget rendered in the application running on macOS*

You have looked at ways to optimize your codebase when using MVVM but I would like to provide some further details on how you can leverage the power of the community in order to further improve your experience.

MVVM Enhancements

There are two key parts I will cover regarding how you can utilize existing packages to reduce the amount of code you are required to write.

MVVM Frameworks

There are several MVVM frameworks that can expand on this by providing a base class implementation for you with varying levels of other extra features. To list a few,

- CommunityToolkit.Mvvm

- MVVMLight

- FreshMVVM

- Prism

- Refractored.MVVMHelpers

- ReactiveUI

These packages will ultimately provide you with a base class very similar to the `BaseViewModel` class that you created earlier. For example, the Prism library provides the `BindableBase` class that you could use. It offers yet another optimization in terms of less code that you need to write and ultimately maintain.

You can go a step further, but you need to believe…

Magic

Yes, that's right: magic is real! These approaches involve auto generating the required boilerplate code so that we as developers do not have to do it. There are two main packages that offer this functionality. They provide it through different mechanisms, but they work equally well.

- Fody: IL generation, `https://github.com/Fody/Home`

- CommunityToolkit.Mvvm: Source generators (yes, this gets a second mention), `https://learn.microsoft.com/dotnet/communitytoolkit/mvvm/`

In the past, I was skeptical of using such packages. I felt like I was losing control of parts that I needed to hold on to. Now I can appreciate that I was naïve, and this is impressive.

Let's look at how these packages can help to further reduce the code. This example uses CommunityToolkit.Mvvm, which provides the `ObservableObject` base class and a wonderful way of adding attributes (`[ObservableProperty]`) to the fields you wish to trigger `PropertyChanged` events when their value changes. This will then generate a property with the same name as the field but with a capitalized first character, so `time` becomes `Time`.

```
public partial class ClockWidgetViewModel : ObservableObject
{
    [ObservableProperty]
    private DateTime time;

    public ClockWigetViewModel()
    {
        SetTime(DateTime.Now);
    }

    public void SetTime(DateTime dateTime)
    {
        Time = dateTime;

        scheduler.ScheduleAction(
            TimeSpan.FromSeconds(1),
            () => SetTime(DateTime.Now));
    }
}
```

That's 17 lines down to 2 from the original example! The part that I really like is that it reduces all the noise of the boilerplate code so there is a bigger emphasis on the code that we need to write as developers.

You may have noticed that you are still referring to the Time property in the code but you haven't supplied the definition for this property. This is where the magic comes in! If you right-click the Time property and select *Go to Definition...* it will open the following source code so you can view what the toolkit has created for you:

```
// <auto-generated/>
#pragma warning disable
#nullable enable
namespace WidgetBoard.ViewModels
```

```
{
    partial class ClockWidgetViewModel
    {
        /// <inheritdoc cref="time"/>
        [global::System.CodeDom.Compiler.
        GeneratedCode("CommunityToolkit.Mvvm.SourceGenerators.
        ObservablePropertyGenerator", "8.0.0.0")]
        [global::System.Diagnostics.CodeAnalysis.
        ExcludeFromCodeCoverage]
        public global::System.DateTime Time
        {
            get => time;
            set
            {
                if (!global::System.Collections.Generic.
                EqualityComparer<global::System.DateTime>.
                Default.Equals(time, value))
                {
                    OnTimeChanging(value);
                    OnPropertyChanging(global::CommunityToo
                    lkit.Mvvm.ComponentModel.__Internals.__
                    KnownINotifyPropertyChangingArgs.Time);
                    time = value;
                    OnTimeChanged(value);
                    OnPropertyChanged(global::CommunityTool
                    kit.Mvvm.ComponentModel.__Internals.__
                    KnownINotifyPropertyChangedArgs.Time);
                }
            }
        }
```

```
/// <summary>Executes the logic for when <see
cref="Time"/> is changing.</summary>
[global::System.CodeDom.Compiler.
GeneratedCode("CommunityToolkit.Mvvm.SourceGenerators.
ObservablePropertyGenerator", "8.0.0.0")]
partial void OnTimeChanging(global::System.
DateTime value);
/// <summary>Executes the logic for when <see
cref="Time"/> just changed.</summary>
[global::System.CodeDom.Compiler.
GeneratedCode("CommunityToolkit.Mvvm.SourceGenerators.
ObservablePropertyGenerator", "8.0.0.0")]
partial void OnTimeChanged(global::System.
DateTime value);
    }
}
```

You can see that the generated source code looks a little noisy, but it does in fact generate the property you need. View the section highlighted in **bold** above.

I have only really scratched the surface regarding the functionality that the CommunityToolkit.Mvvm offers. I strongly urge you to refer to the documentation at https://learn.microsoft.com/dotnet/communitytoolkit/mvvm/ to learn how it can further aid your application development.

Summary

I hope I have made it clear that there is no single right way to do things or build applications. You should pick and choose what approaches will best suit your environment. With this point in mind, the goal of this chapter was to give you a good overview of several different approaches to architecting your application. There are always a lot of opinions floating around to indicate which architectures people prefer but I strongly urge you to evaluate which will help you to achieve your goals best.

In this chapter, you have

- Learned about the different possibilities you have to architect your applications

- Decided on what architecture to use

- Walked through a concrete example by creating the `ClockWidget`

- Learned how to further optimize your implementation using NuGet packages

In the next chapter, you will

- Create and apply an icon in your application

- Add some placeholder pages and view models

- Fill your first page with some UI and set up bindings to the view model

- Explore data binding and its many uses

- Gain an understanding of XAML

- Learn about the possible layouts you can use to group other controls

- Gain an understanding of Shell and apply this to building your application's structure

- Apply the Shell navigation to allow you to navigate

- Build your flyout menu

Source Code

The resulting source code for this chapter can be found on the GitHub repository at `https://github.com/Apress/Introducing-MAUI/tree/main/ch04`.

PART II

User Interface

CHAPTER 5

User Interface Essentials

In this chapter, you are going to investigate the fundamental parts of building a .NET MAUI application. You are going to apply an icon and splash screen, add in some pages and their associated view models, and configure some bindings between your page and the view model. You will also gain an understanding of what XAML is and what it has to offer as you build the pages and the Shell of your application. You will also learn how Shell allows you to navigate between pages in your application.

Prerequisites

You need to do some setup before you can jump into using Shell. If Shell is still feeling like an unknown concept, fear not. I will be covering it a little bit later in this chapter under the "Shell" section.

Let's go ahead and add the following folders to your project.

Models

This will house all of your Model classes. If you recall from Chapter 4, these are where some of your business logic is located. In your Models folder, you need to create three classes.

© Shaun Lawrence 2023
S. Lawrence, *Introducing .NET MAUI*, https://doi.org/10.1007/978-1-4842-9234-1_5

BaseLayout.cs

This will serve as a base class for the layout options you provide. During this book you will only be building fixed layout boards, but I wanted to lay some groundwork so if you are feeling adventurous you can go off and build alternative layout options without having to restructure the application. In fact, I would love to hear where you take it!

```
namespace WidgetBoard.Models;

public abstract class BaseLayout
{
}
```

FixedLayout.cs

This will represent the fixed layout, as I mentioned in the previous section. Your fixed layout will offer the user of the app the ability to choose a number of rows and columns and then position their widgets in them.

```
namespace WidgetBoard.Models;

public class FixedLayout : BaseLayout
{
    public int NumberOfColumns { get; init; }

    public int NumberOfRows { get; init; }
}
```

Board.cs

Your final model represents the overall board.

```
namespace WidgetBoard.Models;

public class Board
```

```
{
    public string Name { get; init; }

    public BaseLayout Layout { get; init; }
}
```

Pages

This will house the pages in your application. I am distinguishing between a page and a view because they do behave differently in .NET MAUI. You can think of a page as a screen that you are seeing whereas a view is a smaller component. A page can contain multiple views.

Let's go ahead and create the following files under the Pages folder. The following steps show how to add the new pages.

- Right-click the *Pages* folder.

- Select **Add ➤ New Item.**

- Select the **.NET MAUI** tab.

- Select **.NET MAUI ContentPage (XAML).**

- Click **Add.**

BoardDetailsPage

This is the page that lets you both create and edit your boards. For now, you will not touch the contents of this file. Note that you should see BoardDetailsPage.xaml and BoardDetailsPage.xaml.cs files created.

You also need to jump over to the MauiProgram.cs file and register this page with the Services inside the CreateMauiApp method.

```
builder.Services.AddTransient<BoardDetailsPage>();
```

FixedBoardPage

This is the page that will render the boards you create in the previous page. For now, you will not touch the contents of this file. Note that you should see FixedBoardPage.xaml and FixedBoardPage.xaml.cs files created.

You will also need to jump over to the MauiProgram.cs file and register this page with the Services inside the CreateMauiApp method.

```
builder.Services.AddTransient<FixedBoardPage>();
```

ViewModels

This houses your ViewModels that are the backing for both your Pages and Views. You created this folder in the previous chapter, but you need to add a number of classes. The following steps show how to add the new pages.

- Right-click the *ViewModels* folder.
- Select **Add ➤ New Class.**
- Click **Add.**

AppShellViewModel

This serves as the view model for the AppShell file that is created for you by the tooling.

```
namespace WidgetBoard.ViewModels;

public class AppShellViewModel : BaseViewModel
{
}
```

You also need to jump over to the MauiProgram.cs file and register this page with the Services inside the CreateMauiApp method.

```
builder.Services.AddTransient<AppShellViewModel>();
```

BoardDetailsPageViewModel

This serves as the view model for the BoardDetailsPage file you created.

```
namespace WidgetBoard.ViewModels;
public class BoardDetailsPageViewModel : BaseViewModel
{
}
```

You also need to jump over to the MauiProgram.cs file and register this page with the Services inside the CreateMauiApp method.

```
builder.Services.AddTransient<BoardDetailsPageViewModel>();
```

FixedBoardPageViewModel

This serves as the view model for the FixedBoardPage file you created.

```
namespace WidgetBoard.ViewModels;
public class FixedBoardPageViewModel : BaseViewModel
{
}
```

You also need to jump over to the MauiProgram.cs file and register this page with the Services inside the CreateMauiApp method.

```
builder.Services.AddTransient<FixedBoardPageViewModel>();
```

You should have noticed a common pattern with the creation of these files and the need to add them to the MauiProgram.cs file. This is to allow you to fully utilize the dependency injection provided by the framework, which you learned about in Chapter 3.

App Icons

Every application needs an icon, and for many people this will be how they obtain their first impression. Thankfully these days device screens allow for bigger icon sizes and therefore more detail to be included in them.

As with general image resources, each platform requires different sizes and many more combinations to be provided. For example, iOS expects the following:

- Five different sizes of the app icon

- Three different sizes for the Spotlight feature

- Three different sizes for Notifications

- Three different sizes for Settings

That's up to 14 different image sizes required just for your application icon on iOS alone. See `https://developer.apple.com/design/human-interface-guidelines/ios/icons-and-images/app-icon/`.

.NET MAUI manages the process of generating all the required images for you. All you need to do is provide an SVG image file. Since SVGs are vector-based, they can scale to each required size.

Adding Your Own Icon

Figure 5-1 shows the icon that you will be using for your application. You can grab a copy of the files that you will be using from `https://github.com/bijington/introducing-dotnet-maui/tree/main/chapter05` and place them in the `Resources/AppIcon` folder. You should notice that they replace two existing files.

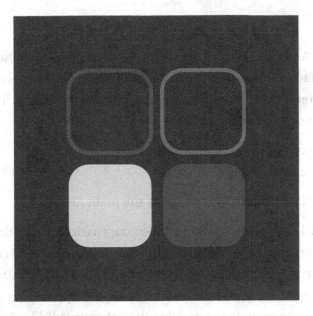

Figure 5-1. *Your application icon*

If you look in the contents of your project file, you will see the following entry:

```
<MauiIcon Include="Resources\AppIcon\appicon.svg" />
```

This tells the tooling to use the file `appicon.svg` and convert it into all the required sizes for each platform when building. Note you only want one `MauiIcon` in your project file. If you have multiple, the first one will be used.

You do not need to replace the above entry as the file you should have downloaded should have the name `appicon.svg`. If the file name is different, either rename it or update the name in the project file.

Platform Differences

It is worth noting that some platforms apply different rules to app icons and also can provide rather different outputs.

Android

App icons on Android can take many different shapes due to the different device manufacturers and their own flavor of the Android operating system. To cater for this, Google introduced the *adaptive icon*. This allows a developer to define two layers in their icon:

- The background: This is typically a single color or consistent pattern.

- The foreground: This includes the main detail.

.NET MAUI allows you to support the adaptive icon using the `IncludeFile` and the `ForegroundFile` properties on the `MauiIcon` element. You can see the `IncludeFile` is already defined in your project. This represents the background. You can split your application icon into two parts and then provide the detail to the `ForegroundFile`. Note that this can be applied to all platforms and is my recommended way to ship an application icon.

iOS and macOS

Apple does not allow for any transparency in an app icon. You can either make sure that you supply an image with no transparent pixels or you can use the `Color` property on the `MauiIcon` element, which will fill in any transparent pixels with that defined color.

Splash Screen

A splash screen is the first thing a user sees when they start your application. It gives you as a developer a way of showing the user something while the application is launching. Once everything has finished loading, the splash screen will be hidden and your main page will be shown.

In a similar manner to how the app icon is managed, the splash screen also has an entry in the project file and can generate a screen based on an SVG file. In fact, you will be using the same image to save effort.

```
<MauiSplashScreen Include="Resources\Splash\splash.svg"
Color="#512BD4" BaseSize="128,128" />
```

Note that splash screens built in this manner must be static. You can't have any animations running to show progress.

The Color property enables you to define a background color for the splash screen.

XAML

As a .NET MAUI developer, you will hear XAML be mentioned many times, XAML stands for *eXtensible Application Markup Language*. It is an XML-based language used for defining user interfaces. It originates from WPF and Silverlight, but the .NET MAUI version has its differences.

There are two different types of XAML files that you will encounter when building your application:

- A ResourceDictionary: This is a single file that contains resources that can easily be used throughout your application. Resources/Styles/Styles.xaml is a perfect example of this. The Styles.xaml file is a default set of styles that is provided when you create a new .NET MAUI application. If you wish to modify some in-built styling, this is a very good place to do so.

- A View-based file: This contains both a .xaml and .xaml.cs file. They are paired together using the partial class keyword.

When dealing with this second item, you have to make sure that the InitializeComponent line is called inside the constructor; otherwise the XAML will not be interpreted correctly, and you will see an exception thrown.

It is worth noting that XAML does not provide a rich set of features like C# does and for this reason there is almost always a xaml.cs file that goes alongside the XAML file. This C# file provides the ability to use the rich-feature set of the C# language when XAML does not. For example, handling a button interaction event would have to be done within the C# code file.

Dissecting a XAML File

In the prerequisites section of this chapter, you created the BoardDetailsPage.xaml file. Now you are going to modify it and add some meaningful content so you can start to see your application take shape. The code you should see in this file is shown below.

```xml
<?xml version="1.0" encoding="utf-8" ?>
<ContentPage xmlns="http://schemas.microsoft.com/
dotnet/2021/maui"
             xmlns:x="http://schemas.microsoft.com/winfx/2009/xaml"
             x:Class="WidgetBoard.Pages.BoardDetailsPage"
             Title="BoardDetailsPage">
    <VerticalStackLayout>
        <Label
            Text="Welcome to .NET MAUI!"
            VerticalOptions="Center"
            HorizontalOptions="Center" />
    </VerticalStackLayout>
</ContentPage>
```

If you break this down into small chunks, you can start to understand not only what makes up the UI of your application but also some of the fundamentals of how XAML represents it.

The root element is a `ContentPage`. As mentioned, a typical view in .NET MAUI is either a `ContentPage` or `ContentView`. As the name implies, it is a page that presents its content, and this will be a single view as its content.

As mentioned, XAML is an XML-based language and there are the following key parts to understanding XAML:

1. Properties are set by attributes on your element, so

    ```
    <Label Text="Welcome to .NET MAUI!" />
    ```

    is effectively the same as writing

    ```
    new Label
    {
        Text ="Welcome to .NET MAUI!"
    };
    ```

2. XAML represents the visual hierarchy in the file structure. You can work out that `ContentPage` has a child of `VerticalStackLayout` and it has a child of `Label`. This can be especially helpful. A complex XAML file will result in a complex visual tree and you want to try your best to avoid this.

3. The `xmlns` tag works like a `using` statement in C#. This allows you to refer to other functionality that might not be available out of the box. For example, you can add the line `xmlns:views="clr-namespace:WidgetBoard.Views"` and it is the equivalent of adding `using WidgetBoard.Views;` in a C# file. This allows you to refer to the views in your codebase.

The content of your ContentPage in your XAML is a
VerticalStackLayout. I will cover layouts a little bit later in this chapter
but as a very brief overview they allow you to have multiple child views as
content and therefore open up the possibilities of creating your UIs. It is
worth noting that a ContentPage can only have a single child, which makes
layouts really important controls for use when building user interfaces.

Now that you have covered some of the key concepts around XAML,
let's go ahead and start building your application's first page.

Building Your First XAML Page

I always like to work with a clear definition of what needs to be achieved so
let's define what your page needs to do. It needs to do the following:

- Allow the user to create a new board.

- Fit on a variety of screen sizes.

- Allow the user to provide a name for the board.

- Allow the user to choose the layout type.

- Apply any valid properties for the specific layout
  type chosen.

Now that you know what needs to be achieved, let's go ahead and do
it. You need to delete the existing contents of the page and replace them
with a Border. A Border is similar to a ContentView in that it can only have
a single child, but it offers you some extra properties that allow you to
provide a nice looking UI. In particular, you care about the StrokeShape
and Stroke properties. You may notice that you are not actually setting
these properties in the XAML and you would be correct! There are two
main reasons for this:

- You have suitable defaults defined in the `Resources/Styles/Styles.xaml` file that was created for you. Note that if you want to override these, it's perfectly fine. I will be covering this a little bit later in this chapter in the "Styling" section.

- It is considered good practice to only define the properties that you need to supply, which is basically anything that changes from the defaults. While the XAML compiler does a decent job of generating a UI that is defined at compile time, some bits are still potentially interpreted at runtime and this has a performance impact.

```xml
<?xml version="1.0" encoding="utf-8" ?>
<ContentPage
    xmlns="http://schemas.microsoft.com/
    dotnet/2021/maui"
    xmlns:x="http://schemas.microsoft.com/
    winfx/2009/xaml"
    x:Class="WidgetBoard.Pages.BoardDetailsPage">

    <Border
        MinimumWidthRequest="300"
        HorizontalOptions="Center"
        VerticalOptions="Center"
        Padding="0">

    </Border>

</ContentPage>
```

The most important part of the properties that you are setting are the `HorizontalOptions` and `VerticalOptions`. They allow you to define where in the parent this view will be displayed. By default, a view will `Fill` its parents content, but you are going to make it float in the Center. The main reason is so it will stay there regardless of the screen size it is running on. Of course, there are more in-depth ways of handling different screen sizes and you will explore them in the coming chapters.

While you have much more content to add to this XAML, file you are going to do so in the context of the following topics. Your next step is to add multiple child views. For this, you are going to need to choose a suitable Layout.

Layouts

.NET MAUI provides you with a set of prebuilt layout classes that allow you to group and arrange views in your application. The aim of this section is to explore each layout control and how it might be used for your application. I strongly recommend playing around with each of the layouts to see what will fit best for each individual use case and always remember to keep the visual tree as simple as possible.

AbsoluteLayout

As the name suggests, the AbsoluteLayout allows the positioning of its children with absolute values. The x, y, width, and height of a child is controlled through the LayoutBounds attached property. This means you use as follows:

```
<AbsoluteLayout>

    <Label
        AbsoluteLayout.LayoutBounds="0,0,600,200"/>
</AbsoluteLayout>
```

Figure 5-2 shows how a control is positioned inside an AbsoluteLayout.

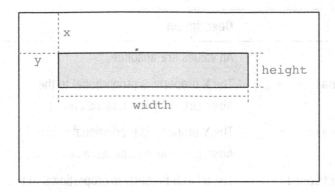

Figure 5-2. *Absolute layout overview*

There is also the option to define layout bounds that are proportional to the AbsoluteLayout itself. You can control this with the AbsoluteLayout.LayoutFlags attached property.

```
<AbsoluteLayout>
    <Label
        AbsoluteLayout.LayoutBounds="0,0,0.5,0.2"
        AbsoluteLayout.LayoutFlags="All"/>
</AbsoluteLayout>
```

This will result in the Label being positioned at 0,0 but the width will be 50% of the AbsoluteLayout and the height will be 20%,. This provides a lot of power when defining a user interface that can grow as the size of a device also increases.

The LayoutFlags option provides you with a lot of power. You can choose which part of the LayoutBounds are applied absolutely and which are applied proportionally. Here are the possible values for LayoutFlags and what they impact:

Value	Description
None	All values are absolute.
XProportional	The X property is proportional to the AbsoluteLayout dimensions.
YProportional	The Y property is proportional to the AbsoluteLayout dimensions.
WidthProportional	The Width property is proportional to the AbsoluteLayout dimensions.
HeightProportional	The Height property is proportional to the AbsoluteLayout dimensions.
PositionProportional	The X and Y properties are proportional to the AbsoluteLayout dimensions.
SizeProportional	The Width and Height properties are proportional to the AbsoluteLayout dimensions.
All	All properties are proportional to the AbsoluteLayout dimensions.

The AbsoluteLayout can be an incredibly powerful layout when used in the right scenario. For your scenario, it offers more complexities than I really think you need to handle.

FlexLayout

The FlexLayout comes with a large number of properties to configure how its children are positioned. If you want your controls to wrap, this is the control for you! A good example for using the FlexLayout is a media gallery.

Figure 5-3 shows how controls can be positioned inside a FlexLayout.

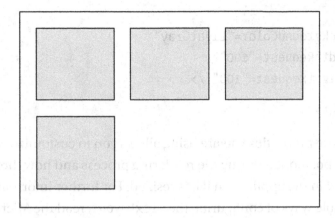

Figure 5-3. *FlexLayout overview*

The above layout can be achieved with the following code example:

```
<FlexLayout
    AlignItems="Start"
    Wrap="Wrap"
    Margin="30"
    JustifyContent="SpaceEvenly">

    <Border
        BackgroundColor="LightGray"
        WidthRequest="100"
        HeightRequest="100" />

    <Border
        BackgroundColor="LightGray"
        WidthRequest="100"
        HeightRequest="100" />

    <Border
        BackgroundColor="LightGray"
        WidthRequest="100"
        HeightRequest="100" />
```

```
<Border
    BackgroundColor="LightGray"
    WidthRequest="100"
    HeightRequest="100" />

</FlexLayout>
```

Each of the properties you are using allows you to customize where each item is positioned during the rendering process and how they will move around in the application if it is resized. For further information on the possible ways of configuring the FlexLayout, read the Microsoft documentation at https://learn.microsoft.com/dotnet/maui/user-interface/layouts/flexlayout.

Your BoardDetailsPage only needs controls positioned vertically so a FlexLayout feels like an overly complicated layout for this purpose.

Grid

I love Grids. They are usually my go-to layout option, mainly because I have become used to thinking about how they lay out controls and because they tend to allow you to keep your visual tree depth shallow. The layout essentially works by allowing you to define a set of rows and columns and then define which control should be displayed in which row/column combination.

Figure 5-4 shows how controls can be positioned inside a Grid.

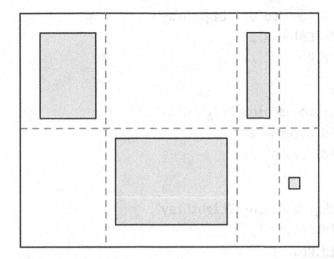

Figure 5-4. *Grid layout overview*

Controls inside a Grid are allowed to overlay each other, which can provide an extra tool in a developers toolbelt when needing to show/hide controls. Controls in the Grid are arranged by first defining the ColumnDefinitions and RowDefinitions. Let's take a look at how to create the above layout with a Grid.

```
<Grid
    ColumnDefinitions ="*,2*,250,Auto"
    ColumnSpacing="20"
    Margin="30"
    RowDefinitions="*,*"
    RowSpacing="20">

    <Border
        BackgroundColor="LightGray"
        Grid.Column="0"
        Grid.Row="0" />

    <Border
```

```
        BackgroundColor="LightGray"
        Grid.Column="1"
        Grid.Row="1" />

    <Border
        BackgroundColor="LightGray"
        Grid.Column="2"
        Grid.Row="0" />

    <Border
        BackgroundColor="LightGray"
        Grid.Column="3"
        Grid.Row="1"
        WidthRequest="30"
        HeightRequest="30" />

</Grid>
```

You can see that you have created columns using a variety of different options:

- 250: This is a fixed width of 250

- Auto: This means that the column will grow in width based on its contents. It is recommended to use this option sparingly as it will result in the Grid control having to measure its children and force a rerender of itself and the other children

- *: This is proportional and will result in the leftover space being allocated out. In this example, two columns use the * notation. This results in those two columns being allocated 1/3 and 2/3 of the remaining width respectively. This is because * is actually considered 1*.

In your scenario, you are going to need multiple groups of controls. For this reason, I believe grids will just make it slightly more complicated for you.

HorizontalStackLayout

The name really gives this away. It positions its children horizontally. The HorizontalStackLayout is not responsible for providing sizing information to its children, so the children are responsible for calculating their own size.

Figure 5-5 shows how controls can be positioned inside a HorizontalStackLayout.

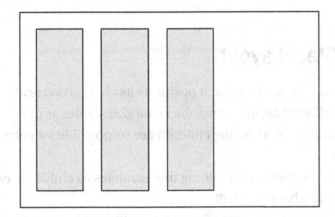

Figure 5-5. *HorizontalStackLayout overview*

The above layout can be achieved with the following code example:

```
<HorizontalStackLayout
    Spacing="20"
    Margin="30">

    <Border
        BackgroundColor="LightGray"
```

```
        WidthRequest="100" />

    <Border
        BackgroundColor="LightGray"
        WidthRequest="100" />

    <Border
        BackgroundColor="LightGray"
        WidthRequest="100" />

</HorizontalStackLayout>
```

You wish to layout your controls vertically so you can guess where this is going, although you will actually use one to group some of your inner controls.

VerticalStackLayout

The name really gives this away. It positions its children vertically. The VerticalStackLayout follows the same sizing rules as the HorizontalStackLayout, so the children are responsible for calculating their own size.

And there you have it: something that arranges its children vertically, which is exactly what you need!

Figure 5-6 shows how controls can be positioned inside a VerticalStackLayout.

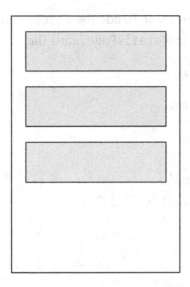

Figure 5-6. *VerticalStackLayout overview*

The above layout can be achieved with the following code example:

```
<VerticalStackLayout
    Spacing="20"
    Margin="30">

    <Border
        BackgroundColor="LightGray"
        HeightRequest="100" />

    <Border
        BackgroundColor="LightGray"
        HeightRequest="100" />

    <Border
        BackgroundColor="LightGray"
        HeightRequest="100" />

</VerticalStackLayout>
```

Let's go ahead and create it. Inside the Border you added earlier, add the following to your BoardDetailsPage.xaml file.

```
<VerticalStackLayout>

    <VerticalStackLayout
        Padding="20">

        <Label
            Text="Name"
            FontAttributes="Bold" />

        <Entry />

        <Label
            Text="Layout"
            FontAttributes="Bold" />

        <HorizontalStackLayout>
            <RadioButton
                x:Name="FixedRadioButton"
                Content="Fixed" />

            <!--<RadioButton
                Content="Freeform" />-->
        </HorizontalStackLayout>

        <VerticalStackLayout>
            <Label
                Text="Number of Columns"
                FontAttributes="Bold" />

            <Entry Keyboard="Numeric" />

            <Label
                Text="Number of Rows"
                FontAttributes="Bold" />
```

```
        <Entry Keyboard="Numeric" />
    </VerticalStackLayout>
</VerticalStackLayout>

<Button
    Text="Save"
    HorizontalOptions="End" />

</VerticalStackLayout>
```

Yes, I know! I spoke about keeping the visual tree simple and here you are nesting quite a few layouts. I find there is typically some level of pragmatism that needs to be applied. This page is still relatively simple in terms of what is being rendered on screen so I will argue that it is fine. If you were to repeat this layout multiple times, you would need to be a little more strict and find the best way to lay it all out. Quite often you will find that there can be a balancing act between defining something to give the best performance vs. making it easier to maintain as a developer.

So you have now built your UI but you will notice that it doesn't do anything other than let the user type in the entry fields. You need to bind the view up to your view model.

This is not strictly part of layouts but it is worth noting how you apply the Keyboard property to your Entry controls. This allows you to inform the operating system what soft keyboard to display and therefore limit the type of data the user can enter. Note that this only applies to mobile applications.

Data Binding

UI-based applications, as their name suggests, involve presenting an interface to the users. This UI is rarely ever just a static view and therefore needs to be updated, drive updates into the application, or both. This process is typically an event-driven one as either side of this synchronization needs to be notified when the other side changes. .NET MAUI wraps this process up for you through a concept called *data binding*. Data binding provides the ability to link the properties from two objects so that changes in one property are automatically updated in the second.

Binding

The most common type of bindings that you create are between a single value at source and a single value at the target. The target is the owner of the bindable property. I use the terms *target* and *source* because you do not have to solely bind between a view and a view model. There are scenarios where you may wish to bind one control to another.

Before you jump in to creating your first binding, you need to first create something to bind to. Open your `BoardDetailsPageViewModel` class, which is the view model for your view, and add the following:

```
private string boardName;

public string BoardName
{
    get => boardName;
    set => SetProperty(ref boardName, value);
}
```

It is worth noting that a `Binding` must be created against a property (e.g., the `BoardName` definition from the code above). Binding to a field (e.g., `boardName`) will not work.

BindingContext

And finally the crucial step is to set the `BindingContext` of your page to this view model. In Chapter 4, you did this by setting it in the XAML directly, but because you have registered your view model with the DI layer, you can make the most of that and have it create the view model and whatever dependencies it has for you. Open your BoardDetailsPage. xaml.cs file and change the constructor to

```
public BoardDetailsPage(BoardDetailsPageViewModel
boardDetailsPageViewModel)
{
    InitializeComponent();

    BindingContext = boardDetailsPageViewModel;
}
```

The above code allows you to rely on the constructor injection functionality that .NET MAUI and Shell provides.

The act of setting the BindingContext property means that any bindings created in the page/view and any child views will be by default against this BindingContext.

Now if you jump into the BoardDetailsPage.xaml file, you can apply the binding to your new BoardName property in your view model. You want to modify the first Entry that you added to look like

```
<Entry
    Text="{Binding BoardName}" />
```

This is a relatively small change and will look like the bindings you created back in Chapter 4 when exploring the MVVM pattern. There isn't much detail to this but there is a fair amount of implicit behavior that I feel I must highlight. Let's cover what it tells you first and then what it doesn't.

You are creating a binding between the BoardName property (which exists on your BoardDetailsPageViewModel) and the Text property on the Entry control.

Now on to what this code doesn't tell you.

Path

The binding could also be written as

```
Text="{Binding Path=BoardName}"
```

The `Path` element of the binding is implied if you do not explicitly provide it but only as the first part of the binding definition. Why am I telling you this? There are times when you will need to supply the `Path=` part.

Mode

I mentioned that bindings keep two properties in sync with each other. When you create a binding, you can define which direction the updates flow. In your example, you have not provided one, which then relies on the default `Mode` for the bindable property that you are binding to. In this case, it is the `Text` property of the `Entry`, which has a default binding mode of `TwoWay`. I strongly urge you to make sure you are aware of both these defaults and your expectation when creating a binding. Choosing the correct `Mode` can also boost performance. For example, the `OneTime` binding mode means that no updates need to be monitored for. In your scenario, you don't currently need to allow the view model to update the `Entry Text` property; however, as you progress, this page will also allow for the editing of a board so you will leave it alone. If you didn't need to edit, you could in theory modify your binding to be `Text="{Binding Path=BoardName, Mode=OneWay}"`.

There are several variations for binding modes:

- **Default**: As the name suggests, it uses the default, which is defined in the target property.

- **TwoWay**: It allows for updates to flow both ways between source and target. A typical example is binding to the `Text` property of an `Entry` where you want to both receive input from the user and update the UI, such as your scenario that you just added with the Entry and its Text property as Text="{Binding Path=BoardName}".

- **OneWay**: It allows for updates to flow from the source to the target. An example of this is your ClockWidget where you only want updates to flow from your source to your target.

- **OneWayToSource**: It allows for updates to flow from the target to the source. An example of this is binding the SelectedItem property on the ListView to a value in your view model.

- **OneTime**: It only updates the target once when the binding context changes.

Source

As mentioned, a binding does not have to be created against something defined in your code (e.g., a property on a view model). It can, in fact, be created against another control. If you look back at the XAML you created for this page, you will notice that you gave one of the RadioButtons a name of FixedRadioButton. This was actually setting you up for this moment: you can now bind your innermost VerticalStackLayouts visibility to the value of this RadioButton.

If you just wanted to allow the user to optionally turn a setting on in your UI, you could use a Switch control instead. I opted for the RadioButton as this will play very well with your extra assignment at the end of this chapter.

```
<VerticalStackLayout
    IsVisible="{Binding IsChecked, Source={x:Reference
    FixedRadioButton}}">
```

Bindings can start to look complicated quickly and this is a good example, but if you break it down, it can become much easier to follow. You are binding the `IsVisible` property on your `VerticalStack Layout` to the `IsChecked` property from the `Source`, which is a `Reference` to the RadioButton called `FixedRadioButton`.

Applying the Remaining Bindings

Let's apply the remaining bindings to your page and view model so that all fields now update your view model.

In your `BoardDetailsPageViewModel` class, you need to add the backing fields and properties to bind to

```
private bool isFixed = true;
private int numberOfColumns = 3;
private int numberOfRows = 2;

public bool IsFixed
{
    get => isFixed;
    set => SetProperty(ref isFixed, value);
}

public int NumberOfColumns
{
    get => numberOfColumns;
    set => SetProperty(ref numberOfColumns, value);
}
```

```
public int NumberOfRows
{
    get => numberOfRows;
    set => SetProperty(ref numberOfRows, value);
}
```

Then in your BoardDetailsPage.xaml file you need to bind to those new properties with the bold sections below highlighting your additions.

Change the first RadioButton to be

```
<RadioButton
    Content="Fixed"
    x:Name="FixedRadioButton"
    IsChecked="{Binding IsFixed}" />
```

Then change the Entry that follows after the RadioButton to be

```
<Entry
    Text="{Binding NumberOfColumns}"
    Keyboard="Numeric" />
```

And finally change the Entry that follows that to be

```
<Entry
    Text="{Binding NumberOfRows}"
    Keyboard="Numeric" />
```

MultiBinding

There can be occasions when you wish to bind multiple source properties to a single target property in a view. To take a minor detour, let's rework your ClockWidgetViewModel to have two properties: one with the date and one with the time. You should end up with the following code (the **bold** highlights the new parts):

141

```
namespace WidgetBoard.ViewModels;

public class ClockWidgetViewModel : ViewModelBase
{
    private readonly Scheduler scheduler = new();
    private DateOnly date;
    private TimeOnly time;

    public ClockWidgetViewModel()
    {
        SetTime(DateTime.Now);
    }

    public DateOnly Date
    {
        get => date;
        set => SetProperty(ref date, value);
    }

    public TimeOnly Time
    {
        get => time;
        set => SetProperty(ref time, value);
    }

    private void SetTime(DateTime dateTime)
    {
        Date = DateOnly.FromDateTime(dateTime);
        Time = TimeOnly.FromDateTime(dateTime);

        scheduler.ScheduleAction(
            TimeSpan.FromSeconds(1),
            () =>
            {
```

```
        SetTime(DateTime.Now);
    });
  }
}
```

The change in the view model actually opens up a number of possibilities for you. You could

- Add separate Labels to render the information in different locations.

- Make use of a MultiBinding and render both pieces of information in a single Label.

It is the latter you will be using here. Open your ClockWidgetView.xaml file and make the changes you see in **bold**.

```
<?xml version="1.0" encoding="utf-8" ?>
<Label
    xmlns="http://schemas.microsoft.com/dotnet/2021/maui"
    xmlns:x="http://schemas.microsoft.com/winfx/2009/xaml"
    xmlns:viewmodels="clr-namespace:WidgetBoard.ViewModels"
    x:Class="WidgetBoard.Views.ClockWidgetView"
    FontSize="80"
    VerticalOptions="Center"
    HorizontalOptions="Center">

    <Label.BindingContext>
        <viewmodels:ClockWidgetViewModel />
    </Label.BindingContext>

    <Label.Text>
        <MultiBinding StringFormat="{}{0} {1}">
            <Binding Path="Date" />
            <Binding Path="Time" />
```

```
    </MultiBinding>
  </Label.Text>
```

```
</Label>
```

To list what you have done here, you have

- Removed the `Text="{Binding Time}"` line

- Moved the above functionality into the
  `MultiBinding` section

You should notice a slightly different syntax to the single binding approach. In fact, you can write a single binding in a similar way, such as

```
<Label.Text>
  <Binding Path="Time" />
</Label.Text>
```

However, I am sure you can appreciate that the original `Text="{Binding Time}"` is a lot more concise and easier to read. Each of the properties that you covered under the "Binding" section apply to each of the `Binding` elements under `MultiBinding`.

You must supply either a `StringFormat` or a `Converter` in a `MultiBinding` or an exception will be thrown. The reason for this is to allow for the multiple values to be mapped down to the single value on the target.

Command

Very often you will need your applications to respond to user interaction. This can be by tapping or clicking on a button or selecting something in a list. This interaction is recorded in your view, but you usually require that the logic to handle this interaction to be performed in the view model. This comes in the form of a Command and an optional associated CommandParameter set of properties. The Command property itself can be bound from the view to the view model and allows the view model to not only handle the interaction but also to determine whether the interaction can be performed in the first place. You already added a Button to your BoardDetailsPage.xaml file but you didn't hook it, so let's do exactly that!

You just need to modify your button to be (changes in **bold**)

```
<Button
    Text="Save"
    HorizontalOptions="End"
    Command="{Binding SaveCommand}" />
```

Based on the binding content that you have explored, you can say that this Buttons Command property is now bound to a property on your view model called SaveCommand. You haven't actually created this property yet. If you are thinking it would be great if the tooling could know this and report it to me, then the next section has got you covered. "Compiled Bindings" will show you how to inform the tooling of how to report it to you. First, though, open your BoardDetailsPageViewModel.cs file and add your command implementation.

Your implementation comes in multiple parts.

1. You define the property itself:

    ```
    public Command SaveCommand { get; }
    ```

    You typically define a command as a read-only property as you rarely want it to change. You will likely come across commands being defined with the use of the ICommand interface rather than the Command class. The reason you are using the latter is so that you can make use of a specific method (see part 3) to update some of your view.

2. You define what action will be performed when the
    command is executed (basically when the Button is
    tapped/clicked in this scenario).

```
public BoardDetailsPageViewModel()
{
    SaveCommand = new Command(
        () => Save(),
        () => !string.IsNullOrWhiteSpace(BoardName));
}

private void Save()
{
    var board = new Board
    {
        Name = BoardName,
        Layout = new FixedLayout
        {
            NumberOfColumns = NumberOfColumns,
            NumberOfRows = NumberOfRows
        }
    };
}
```

The Command class takes two parameters. The first
is the action to perform when the command is
executed and the second, which is optional, is
a way of defining whether the command can be
executed. A good use case for this is if you wish to
make sure that the user has entered all the required
information. In your scenario, you will make sure
that the user has entered a name for the board.

3. You notify the view when the status of whether the command can be executed changes. To be clear, you don't have to know that the status has changed; you can simply inform the view that it should requery the status. This is where the Command class and its ChangeCanExecute method come in. For this, you need to tweak your BoardName property to the following:

```
public string BoardName
{
    get => boardName;
    set
    {
        SetProperty(ref boardName, value);
        SaveCommand.ChangeCanExecute();
    }
}
```

This change means that every time the BoardName property changes (and this will be done via the binding from the view), the Button that is bound to the SaveCommand will requery to check whether the command can be executed. If it can, the Button will be enabled and the user can interact with it; if not, it will be disabled.

Compiled Bindings

Compiled bindings are a great feature that you should in almost all cases turn on! They help to speed up your applications because they help the compiler know what the bindings will be set to and reduce the amount of reflection that is required. Reflection is notoriously bad for performance so wherever possible it is highly recommended to avoid using it. Bindings by default do use an amount of reflection in order to handle the value changes between source and target. Compiled bindings, as just discussed, help to reduce this so let's learn how to turn them on.

Compiled bindings also provide design-time validation. If you set a binding to a property on your view model that doesn't exist (imagine you made a typo, which I do a lot!), without compiled bindings the application would still build but your binding won't do anything. With a compiled binding, the application will fail to build and the tooling will report that the property you mistyped doesn't exist.

```
<ContentPage
    xmlns="http://schemas.microsoft.com/dotnet/2021/maui"
    xmlns:x="http://schemas.microsoft.com/winfx/2009/xaml"
    xmlns:viewmodels="clr-namespace:WidgetBoard.ViewModels"
    x:Class="WidgetBoard.Pages.BoardDetailsPage"
    x:DataType="viewmodels:BoardDetailsPageViewModel">
```

Now that you have set up your BoardDetailsPage to allow user entry and even perform an action when the Save button is interacted with, you need to structure your application so that you can see this happen.

Shell

Shell in .NET MAUI enables you to define how your application will be laid out, not in terms of actual visuals but by defining things like whether you want your pages viewed in tabs or just a single page at a time. It also enables you to define a flyout, which is a side menu in your application. You can choose to have it always visible or toggle it to slide in/out, and this can also vary based on the type of device you are running on. Typically a desktop has more visual real estate so you may wish to keep the flyout always open then.

For your application, you are going to make use of the flyout to allow you to define multiple boards that you can configure and load. I really like the idea of having one board for when I work and then swapping to something else when working on a side project or even for gaming.

To save having to return to this area and change bits, you are going to jump straight into the more in-depth option and feature-rich outcome. Don't worry, though; as you discover each new concept, you will dive into some detail to cover what it is and why you are using along with then applying that concept to your application.

ShellContent

If you take a look at your `AppShell.xaml` file, you should see very little inside. Currently it has the following line:

```
<ShellContent
    Title="Home"
    ContentTemplate="{DataTemplate local:MainPage}"
    Route="MainPage" />
```

This code sets the main content on the application to be an instance of the `MainPage`. In fact, you want to delete this line and replace it with

```
<ShellContent
    ContentTemplate="{DataTemplate pages:BoardDetailsPage}" />
```

There isn't too much difference here but you should explore what it means.

Your application's main content will now be an instance of your recently created `BoardDetailsPage`. You don't need the `Title` or `Route` options anymore as you will be controlling them in different ways.

The `Title` property will be set based on the page that is shown so you will learn about this a little later on.

The Route property you will control as part of the next section, "Navigation."

Finally, you will need to add xmlns:pages="clr-namespace:WidgetBoard.Pages" to the top of the file.

Navigation

I am personally a fan of simplifying the code I write so long as it continues to make it easy to read. With this in mind I would like to suggest you improve on the registration of your pages and their view models already.

Registering Pages for Navigation

Therefore I suggest that you create a new method into your MauiProgram.cs file.

```
private static IServiceCollection AddPage<TPage, TViewModel>(
    IServiceCollection services,
    string route)
    where TPage : Page
    where TViewModel : BaseViewModel
{
    services
        .AddTransient(typeof(TPage))
        .AddTransient(typeof(TViewModel));

    Routing.RegisterRoute(route, typeof(TPage));

    return services;
}
```

Notice the line Routing.RegisterRoute(route, typeof(TView));. This serves as a very important part in this topic of navigation. It means that when you tell Shell to navigate to a specific route, it will create a new instance of the TPage type you passed in and navigate to it. Of course, because you have registered these types with the dependency injection layer, it means that any dependencies that are defined as parameters to the constructor will be created and passed in for you.

The above then means that rather than writing

```
services.AddTransient<BoardDetailsPage>()
services.AddTransient<BoardDetailsPageViewModel>()

Routing.RegisterRoute(route, typeof(TPage));
```

you can now write

```
AddPage<BoardDetailsPage, BoardDetailsViewModel>(builder.
Services, "boarddetails");
```

with the added change that you now define this route. So let's go and delete your old registrations and replace with

```
AddPage<BoardDetailsPage, BoardDetailsPageViewModel>(builder.
Services, "boarddetails");
AddPage<FixedBoardPage, FixedBoardPageViewModel>(builder.
Services, "fixedboard");
```

I also recommend defining the routes as constant strings somewhere in your codebase to avoid typos when wanting to navigate to them.

This means you can save one line of code per page and view model pair that you had registered as well as the code to register the route for navigation.

Now that you have registered your pages, let's take a look at how you can actually perform navigation.

Performing Navigation

There are multiple ways to specify the route for navigation but they all use the Shell.Current.GoToAsync method.

So, for example, you could navigate to your FixedBoardPage with the following:

```
await Shell.Current.GoToAsync("fixedboard");
```

This will result in a FixedBoardPage being created and pushed onto the navigation stack. This is precisely the behavior that you need at the end of your SaveCommand execution in your BoardDetailsPagesViewModel class.

Navigating Backwards

You can also pop pages off the navigation stack by navigating backward. This can be achieved by the following:

```
await Shell.Current.GoToAsync("..");
```

with the .. component telling Shell that it needs to go backward. In fact, backwards and forwards navigation can be performed together:

```
await Shell.Current.GoToAsync("../board");
```

Passing Data When Navigating

One key thing that you really need to do as part of creating your board and navigating to the page that will render the board is to pass the context across to that page so it knows what to render. There are multiple ways to both send the data and also to receive it.

Let's start with sending.

- You can pass primitive data through the query string itself, for example

  ```
  await Shell.Current.GoToAsync("fixedboard?board
  id=1234");
  ```

By providing the boardid, you put the responsibility on
the receiving page (or page view model) to retrieve the
right board by using the specified ID.

- More complex data can be sent as an
  IDictionary<string, object> parameter in the
  GoToAsync method, such as

```
await Shell.Current.GoToAsync(
    "fixedboard",
    new Dictionary<string, object>
    {
        { "Board", board}
    });
```

You can also send a complex object like the above, which means the
originating page (or page view model) is responsible for retrieving or
constructing the board and you send the whole thing to the receiving page.

Then, to receive data, you can implement the IQueryAttributable
interface provided with .NET MAUI. Shell will either call this on
the page you are navigating to, or if the BindingContext (your view
model) implements the interface, it will call it there. Add this to your
FixedBoardPageViewModel class because you are going to need to process
the data. You will be going with the complex object option because you
have already loaded the Board in your AppShellViewModel class.

```
public void ApplyQueryAttributes(IDictionary<string,
object> query)
{
    var board = query["Board"] as Board;
}
```

You aren't going to do anything with this data just yet but it is ready for when you start to build your board layout view in the next chapter. For now, you will continue on with the theme of Shell and define your flyout menu.

You will also need to make your `FixedBoardPageViewModel` implement the `IQueryAttributable` interface. Change the class definition from

```
public class FixedBoardPageViewModel : BaseViewModel
```

to the following (changes in **bold**):

```
public class FixedBoardPageViewModel : BaseViewModel,
IQueryAttributable
```

Flyout

A flyout is a menu for a Shell application that is accessible through an icon or by swiping from the side of the screen. The flyout can consist of an optional header, flyout items, optional menu items, and an optional footer.

For your application, you are going to provide a basic header and then the main content will be a dynamic list of all the boards your user creates. This means that you are going to have to override the main content but thankfully Shell makes this an easy task.

The first thing I like to do when working on a new XAML file is to turn on compiled bindings, which I covered earlier. If you recall, this is by specifying the `x:DataType` attribute to tell the compiler the type that your view will be binding to. Let's do that now (in **bold**):

```
<?xml version="1.0" encoding="UTF-8" ?>
<Shell
    x:Class="WidgetBoard.AppShell"
    xmlns="http://schemas.microsoft.com/dotnet/2021/maui"
    xmlns:x="http://schemas.microsoft.com/winfx/2009/xaml"
    x:DataType="viewmodels:AppShellViewModel">
```

This helps you as you build the view to see what doesn't exist in your view model. Of course, if you prefer to build the view model first then this also helps.

Finally, you need to add `xmlns:viewmodels="clr-namespace:WidgetBoard.ViewModels"` to the top of the file.

FlyoutHeader

The `FlyoutHeader` can be given any control or layout and therefore you can build a really good looking header option. For your application, you are just going to add a title Label.

Below your `ShellContent` element you want to add the following:

```
<Shell.FlyoutHeader>
    <Label
        Text="My boards"
        FontSize="20"
        HorizontalTextAlignment="Center" />
</Shell.FlyoutHeader>
```

Hopefully the above is self-explanatory but to cover the parts I haven't already covered, you have the ability to specify different layout information in a Label so you can make the text centered. It is usually recommended that you use the `HorizontrolOptions` property over the `HorizontalTextAlignment` property; however, if you try that here, you will see that it doesn't center the `Label`.

Now let's add in the main part of your menu.

FlyoutContent

First, if you want to use a static set of items in your menu, you can simply add `FlyoutItems` to the content. This can work well when you have a fixed set of pages such as Settings, Home, and so on. You will be showing the boards that the user creates, so you will need something dynamic. For this you need to supply the FlyoutContent. More importantly, it's your first introduction to the CollectionView control.

The CollectionView allows you to define how an item will look and then have it repeated for each item in a collection that is bound to it. Additionally, the CollectionView provides the ability to allow the user to select items in the collection and you can define behavior that will be performed when that selection happens. Let's add the following to your Shell:

```
<Shell.FlyoutContent>
    <CollectionView
        ItemsSource="{Binding Boards}"
        SelectionMode="Single"
        SelectedItem="{Binding CurrentBoard}">

        <CollectionView.ItemTemplate>
            <DataTemplate x:DataType="models:Board">
                <Label
                    Text="{Binding Name}"
                    FontSize="20"
                    Padding="10,0,0,0" />
            </DataTemplate>
        </CollectionView.ItemTemplate>
    </CollectionView>
</Shell.FlyoutContent>
```

You also need to add xmlns:models="clr-namespace:WidgetBoard. Models" to the top of the file.

Your FlyoutContent will display a Label set to the Name of each Board instance in the collection of Boards in your view model. Additionally, the CurrentBoard property on your view model will be updated when the user selects one of the Labels in this collection.

If you have added all of the parts I have discussed, you will likely notice that the tooling is reporting that you haven't added any of the properties that you are binding to over in your view model. Let's jump over to your AppShellViewModel.cs file and add the following

Collection of Boards

```
public ObservableCollection<Board> Boards { get; } = new
ObservableCollection<Board>();
```

The ObservableCollection is a special type of collection that implements INotifyCollectionChanged. This means that anything bound to it will monitor changes to the collection and update its contents on screen.

Additionally, for now you will add a fixed entry into this Boards collection to make it possible to interact with. Later you will be saving to and loading from a database.

```
public AppShellViewModel()
{
    Boards.Add(
        new Board
        {
            Name = "My first board",
            Layout = new FixedLayout
            {
                NumberOfColumns = 3,
                NumberOfRows = 2
            }
        });
}
```

Selected Board

You bind the SelectedItem property from the CollectionView to your CurrentBoard property. When your property changes, you can navigate to the board that was selected.

```
private Board currentBoard;

public Board CurrentBoard
{
    get => currentBoard;
    set
    {
        if (SetProperty(ref currentBoard, value))
        {
            BoardSelected(value);
        }
    }
}
```

You may recall that I discussed in Chapter 4 the potential value of SetProperty returning a Boolean value. You have finally found a use for it! You only want to handle a board selection change if the CurrentBoard property really has changed.

Navigation to the Selected Board

Following on from the "Navigation" section earlier, you will navigate to the route "fixedboard" which your FixedBoardPage is configured to. You will also pass in the selected board so that it can be presented on screen.

```
private async void BoardSelected(Board board)
{
    await Shell.Current.GoToAsync(
```

```
"fixedboard",
new Dictionary<string, object>
{
    { "Board", board}
});
}
```

Before your bindings will work you, need to make some further changes.

Setting the BindingContext of Your AppShell

Let's change the constructor of your AppShell.xaml.cs file to set the BindingContext.

```
public AppShell(AppShellViewModel appShellViewModel)
{
    InitializeComponent();

    BindingContext = appShellViewModel;
}
```

You should recall that you added the AppShellViewModel as a transient in the MauiProgram.cs file, meaning that you will be provided with a new instance when your AppShell class is created for you.

Register AppShell with the MAUI App Builder

Let's register AppShell in your MauiProgram.cs file.

```
builder.Services.AddTransient<AppShell>();
```

Resolve the AppShell Instead of Creating It

Change the constructor in your App.xaml.cs file to be as follows:

```
public App(AppShell appShell)
{
    InitializeComponent();

    MainPage = appShell;
}
```

All of the above changes allow you to use AppShell just like any other page and not have to create an instance manually.

Tabs

It is worth noting that Shell offers you more functionality than you really need in building this application.

Shell allows you to design tab bars into your application. You can have bottom, top, or both to give flexibility on how you lay out your content. You have control over the styling and navigation within each of the tabs also.

I won't be covering tabs but I thoroughly recommend checking out the documentation provided by Microsoft at https://learn.microsoft.com/dotnet/maui/fundamentals/shell/tabs.

Search

Search is another useful feature that comes as part of Shell but again it is not something that you need in this application. Shell allows you to create your own SearchHandler, which means you can define how the results are met with the values entered in the search box that is automatically provided. You can even define the layout of the search results and the behavior for when an item in the search results is selected.

I won't be covering search but I thoroughly recommend checking out the documentation provided by Microsoft at https://learn.microsoft.com/dotnet/maui/fundamentals/shell/search.

Taking Your Application for a Spin

If you run the application, you will see that you are first presented with the screen to create a new board. You can enter the details and press Save.

Figure 5-7 shows how your application looks when it is first loaded.

Figure 5-7. *The application home page*

Or you can slide out the menu from the left-hand side. Figure 5-8 shows the flyout menu in your application.

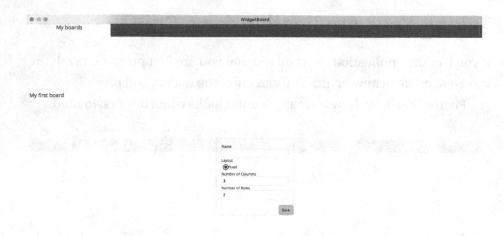

Figure 5-8. *The application flyout menu*

By either selecting the board or pressing Save you will be navigated to your `FixedBoardPage`. Figure 5-9 shows your `FixedBoardPage` displaying with the default content. This is because you haven't wired up the board object that you are receiving but it proves that your navigation and Shell setup is working.

Figure 5-9. The fixed board page after navigating

Summary

In this chapter, you

- Created and applied an icon for your application

- Added some placeholder pages and view models

- Filled your first page with some UI and setup bindings to the view model

- Covered data binding and its many uses

- Gained an understanding of XAML

- Learned about the possible layouts you can use to group other controls

- Gained an understanding of Shell and applied this to building your applications structure

- Applied the Shell navigation to allow you to navigate to your next page and the next chapter

- Built your flyout menu using all the learnings in this chapter

In the next chapter, you will

- Create your own layout.

- Make use of a variety of options when adding bindable properties.

- Provide command support from your layout.

- Use your layout in your application.

Source Code

The resulting source code for this chapter can be found on the GitHub repository at `https://github.com/Apress/Introducing-MAUI/tree/main/ch05`.

Extra Assignment

As an extra assignment, I would like you to consider how you might add a second layout type given that you

- Have a single layout type on your `BoardDetailsPage`

- Have options displayed when this type is selected

- Pass a `FixedLayout` instance over as data to your `FixedBoardPage`

I would love to see what concepts you come up with.

CHAPTER 6

Creating Our Own Layout

In the previous chapter, you learned a lot of the fundamentals of building and binding your user interfaces. In this chapter, you will create your own layout, make use of a variety of options when adding bindable properties, provide command support from your layout, and make use of your layout in your application. This will serve as the basis for adding much more functionality as we cover a variety of different topics in future chapters.

Let's recap what you achieved in the last chapter: you provided the ability for a user to create a board and supply a number of columns and rows. You now need to lay out your board with the number of columns and rows the user has configured and populate widgets onto the board. Figure 6-1 is a mock-up of what you will achieve by the end of this chapter.

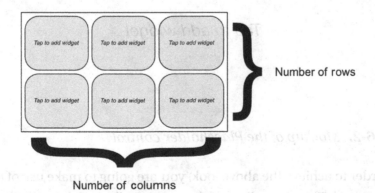

Figure 6-1. Mockup of a board

At the end of the last chapter, I discussed the idea of having a second type of layout in the "Extra Assignment" section. To continue with this theme, I have structured the architecture of the layout to aid in this journey. I am a fan of taking an approach like this because it allows you to potentially replace one part of the implementation without impacting the others.

BoardLayout will be responsible for displaying the widgets. It will be assigned an ILayoutManager implementation, which will decide where to place the widgets. You will be adding a FixedLayoutManager to decide this part.

Placeholder

The first item that you need to create is the placeholder to show where a widget will be placed. There isn't too much to this control but creating it allows you to group all of the related bits and pieces together. Figure 6-2 shows what your Placeholder control will look like when rendered inside the application.

Tap to add widget

Figure 6-2. *Mockup of the Placeholder control*

In order to achieve the above look, you are going to make use of the Border control. This is a really useful control. It allows you to provide borders, custom corner radius, shadows, and other styling options. It also behaves much like the ContentView in that it can contain a single child control.

Create a folder called Controls in your main project. It will house the Placeholder control and potentially more as you build your application.

Next, add a new class to the folder and call it Placeholder. Note that you are opting to create the control purely in C# without XAML; the main reason is that it results in less code. I always find there is never a single way to build things, and even if you like XAML, at times it doesn't add any value, just like in this scenario. Of course, if you prefer to build your UI with XAML, you can do so.

```
namespace WidgetBoard.Controls;

public class Placeholder : Border
{
    public Placeholder()
    {
        Content = new Label
        {
            Text = "Tap to add widget",
            FontAttributes = FontAttributes.Italic,
            HorizontalOptions = LayoutOptions.Center,
            VerticalOptions = LayoutOptions.Center
        };
    }

    public int Position { get; set; }
}
```

As discussed, there isn't too much to this implementation but let's still break it down. Here you have

- Created a control that inherits from Border

- Set the content of your control to be a Label showing fixed text in an italic font and the text is centered both horizontally and vertically

- Added a Position property to know where in the layout it will be positioned

Now you can start building the layout that will display the placeholders and ultimately your widgets.

ILayoutManager

You have a slight chicken-and-egg scenario here. You need to create a board and a layout manager, both of which need to know about the other; therefore, let's add in the LayoutManager parts first.

The purpose of the ILayoutManager interface is to define how the BoardLayout will interact with a layout manager implementation.

Create a folder called Layouts in your main project. It will house the ILayoutManager interface and more as you build your application.

Next, add a new class to the folder and call it ILayoutManager.

```
namespace WidgetBoard.Layouts;

public interface ILayoutManager
{
    object BindingContext { get; set; }

    BoardLayout Board { get; set; }

    void SetPosition(BindableObject bindableObject, int
    position);
}
```

Let's break it down so you have a clear definition of what you just created:

- The BindingContext property allows you to pass the context down from the BoardLayout later. This is important for allowing bindings on the layout manager.

- The Board property allows the manager to interact directly with the board it is intended to assist.

- The SetPosition method allows the manager to use the position parameter and set the appropriate layout settings on the widget/placeholder.

BoardLayout

Your BoardLayout will be the parent of your widgets. Create the layout inside your Layouts folder.

- Right-click the Layouts folder.

- Select Add ➤ New Item.

- Select the **.NET MAUI** tab.

- Select the **.NET MAUI ContentView (XAML)** option.

- Enter the name *BoardLayout*.

- Click **Add**.

This will give you two files. You'll modify each one individually.

BoardLayout.xaml

Modify the existing contents to the following:

```
<?xml version="1.0" encoding="utf-8" ?>
```

```
<Grid
    xmlns="http://schemas.microsoft.com/dotnet/2021/maui"
    xmlns:x="http://schemas.microsoft.com/winfx/2009/xaml"
    x:Class="WidgetBoard.Layouts.BoardLayout"
    x:Name="self">

    <Grid
        x:Name="PlaceholderGrid" />

    <Grid
        x:Name="WidgetGrid"
        ChildAdded="Widgets_ChildAdded"
        BindableLayout.ItemsSource="{Binding ItemsSource,
        Source={x:Reference self}}"
        BindableLayout.ItemTemplateSelector="{Binding
        ItemTemplateSelector, Source={x:Reference self}}"
        InputTransparent="True"
        CascadeInputTransparent="False" />
</Grid>
```

You have added quite a bit to this that might not feel familiar, so again let's break it down.

Your main layout is a Grid and inside of it are two more Grids.

The first inner Grid (PlaceholderGrid) is where you add the Placeholder control you created earlier in this chapter.

The second inner Grid (WidgetGrid) is where you add widgets. The reason you have built the control this way is mainly so you can utilize a really impressive piece of functionality that drastically reduces the amount of code you have to write: BindableLayout.

You have not supplied a `Grid.Row` or `Grid.Column` to either of your inner `Grids`. This results in both controls filling the space of the parent `Grid` and the second one overlapping the first. This behavior can provide some real power when building rather complex UIs.

BindableLayout

`BindableLayout` allows you to turn a layout control into a control that can be populated by a collection of data. `BindableLayout` is not a control itself, but it provides the ability to enhance layout controls by adding an `ItemsSource` property for bindings. This means that all of the layouts you learned about in the previous chapter (e.g., `Grid`, `AbsoluteLayout`, `FlexLayout`, `HorizontalStackLayout`, `VerticalStackLayout`) can be turned into a layout that can show a specific set of controls for each item that is provided. For this, you need to set two properties:

- `BindableLayout.ItemsSource`: This is the collection of items that you wish to represent in the UI.

- `BindableLayout.ItemTemplate` or `BindableLayout.ItemTemplateSelector`: This allows you to define how the item will be represented. In most scenarios, `ItemTemplate` is enough but this only works when you have one type of item to display in your collection. If you have multiple types, each widget will be a separate type in your application, so you need to use the `ItemTemplateSelector`.

I won't actually be providing the source for these bindings just yet; this will be done in Chapter 8. For now, you just need to make it possible to bind them.

BoardLayout.xaml.cs

Now that you have created your XAML representation, you need to add in the code-behind, which will work with it. We are going to follow a slightly different approach for this and the next section; you have a lot of code to add now so you will add it in stages and we will talk around what you are adding.

The initial code should look as follows:

```
namespace WidgetBoard.Layouts;

public partial class BoardLayout
{
    public BoardLayout()
    {
        InitializeComponent();
    }
}
```

Adding the LayoutManager Property

You want to allow the consumer of your BoardLayout control to be able to supply a LayoutManager that will control where the widgets are placed. For this, you need to add the following:

```
private ILayoutManager layoutManager;

public ILayoutManager LayoutManager
{
    get => layoutManager;
    set
    {
        layoutManager = value;
```

```
        layoutManager.Board = this;
    }
}
```

The key detail of this implementation is how it assigns the Board property on the LayoutManager to your BoardLayout control. This is to allow the manager to interact with the layout.

One very important thing to consider is that when you create properties that can be set in XAML, their setters can be called before your control has its BindingContext property set. Therefore, you usually need to handle both scenarios when relying on both pieces of functionality. To give a concrete example of this, you have your LayoutManager property that you have added. It will allow you to set bindings on it also, but it won't have a BindingContext passed down. For this, you need to override the OnBindingContextChanged method in your BoardLayout class and assign the value to your LayoutManager.

```
protected override void OnBindingContextChanged()
{
    base.OnBindingContextChanged();

    layoutManager.BindingContext = this.BindingContext;
}
```

In the past, I have found when building controls in this way, even if you do not need to use this method for an actual implementation, it can be really handy to debug what is going on when things don't behave as expected. For example, you can stick a breakpoint in to make sure that you are being assigned a BindingContext and that it is of the correct type.

Adding the ItemsSource Property

Your BoardLayout also needs to accept a collection of widgets that will ultimately be displayed on screen. For controls that support

displaying multiple items, the common name used for such a property is
ItemsSource. So, add a property with that name. You will need to add the
following to the top of the file:

```
using System.Collections;
```

This is to allow you to use the IEnumerable type.

```
public static readonly BindableProperty ItemsSourceProperty =
    BindableProperty.Create(
        nameof(ItemsSource),
        typeof(IEnumerable),
        typeof(BoardLayout));
 public IEnumerable ItemsSource
{
    get => (IEnumerable)GetValue(ItemsSourceProperty);
    set => SetValue(ItemsSourceProperty, value);
}
```

In the majority of scenarios, you bind an ObservableCollection to
an ItemsSource property, which is of a different type to IEnumerable. By
choosing to use IEnumerable, it allows the consumers of your layout to
provide any type that supports holding multiple items. This means that
you can supply an ObservableCollection or you can supply a List.

Finally, you need to add the using statement into your BoardLayout.
xaml.cs file at the top.

```
using System.Collections;
```

Adding the ItemTemplateSelector Property

Now that you have a collection of items to display on screen, you
need to know how to display them. It can be common to see controls
that have an ItemsSource property also have an ItemTemplate or an

ItemTemplateSelector or even both properties. An ItemTemplate allows
a developer to define how each item in the ItemsSource will be rendered
on screen. The reason you aren't using this approach is because you can
only define one template for all items. You will be binding your widget
view models to the ItemsSource property, which means you will have
several different views that you will want to display. This is where the
ItemTemplateSelector property comes in.

```
public static readonly BindableProperty
ItemTemplateSelectorProperty =
    BindableProperty.Create(
        nameof(ItemTemplateSelector),
        typeof(DataTemplateSelector),
        typeof(BoardLayout));
public DataTemplateSelector ItemTemplateSelector
{
    get => (DataTemplateSelector)GetValue(ItemTemplateSelector
    Property);
    set => SetValue(ItemTemplateSelectorProperty, value);
}
```

You make use of the DataTemplateSelector type for your property
here. You will create an implementation a little later in this chapter but for
now it allows you to override the OnSelectTemplate method and provide a
suitable template for the item that is passed in.

Handling the ChildAdded Event

I discussed earlier how the BindableLayout feature allows you to populate
a control with multiple views based on bindings. You need to hook into
the ChildAdded event so that your LayoutManager implementation can
determine where the new child should be positioned.

```
private void Widgets_ChildAdded(object sender,
ElementEventArgs e)
{
    if (e.Element is IWidgetView widgetView)
    {
        LayoutManager.SetPosition(e.Element, widgetView.
        Position);
    }
}
```

This handler checks to see if the new child being added is of the
IWidgetView type, and if it is, it delegates out to the LayoutManager
implementation to set the widget's position.

Adding Remaining Bits

You have a few extra methods and properties to add in that will be used
by the FixedLayoutManager. Let's add them and discuss their purpose
as you go.

Add the using statement at the top of the file.

```
using WidgetBoard.Controls;
```

Then add the first new method.

```
public void AddPlaceholder(Placeholder placeholder) =>
PlaceholderGrid.Children.Add(placeholder);
```

This method allows the caller to pass a placeholder that will be added
to PlaceholderGrid. This is useful when first loading a board or when
dealing with a widget being removed from a specific position.

```
public void RemovePlaceholder(Placeholder placeholder) =>
PlaceholderGrid.Children.Remove(placeholder);
```

This method allows the caller to pass a placeholder that will be removed from the `PlaceholderGrid`. This is useful for when dealing with a widget being added to a specific position.

```
public void AddColumn(ColumnDefinition columnDefinition)
{
    PlaceholderGrid.ColumnDefinitions.Add(columnDefinition);
    WidgetGrid.ColumnDefinitions.Add(columnDefinition);
}
```

This method allows for the board's columns to be defined on both the `PlaceholderGrid` and `WidgetGrid`.

```
public void AddRow(RowDefinition rowDefinition)
{
    PlaceholderGrid.RowDefinitions.Add(rowDefinition);
    WidgetGrid.RowDefinitions.Add(rowDefinition);
}
```

This method allows for the board's rows to be defined on both the `PlaceholderGrid` and `WidgetGrid`.

```
public IReadOnlyList<Placeholder> Placeholders =>
PlaceholderGrid.Children.OfType<Placeholder>().ToList();
```

This property provides all children from the `PlaceholderGrid` that are of type `Placeholder`. This is to allow for determining which placeholder needs to be removed when adding a widget.

FixedLayoutManager

The final part for you to create is the `FixedLayoutManager` class. This will provide the logic to

- Accept the number of rows and columns for a board.

- Provide tap/click support through a command.

- Build the board layout.

- Set the correct row/column position for each widget.

Create the file and then you can work through adding each of the above pieces of functionality. Let's add a new class file and call it FixedLayoutManager.cs. Add the following content:

```
namespace WidgetBoard.Layouts;

public class FixedLayoutManager
{
}
```

To start, you are going to want to add the following using statements:

```
using System.Windows.Input;
using WidgetBoard.Controls;
```

And also make your class inherit from BindableObject and implement your ILayoutManager interface. Your class should now look as follows:

```
using System.Windows.Input;
using WidgetBoard.Controls;

namespace WidgetBoard.Layouts;

public class FixedLayoutManager : BindableObject,
ILayoutManager
{
}
```

The reason for inheriting from BindableObject is down to the fact that you need to add some bindable properties onto this class so that developers using this implementation can bind values to the properties.

Accepting the Number of Rows and Columns for a Board

You need to add the ability to set the number of rows and columns to be displayed in your fixed layout board. For this, you are going to add two bindable properties to your FixedLayoutManager class.

Adding the NumberOfColumns Property

```
public static readonly BindableProperty
NumberOfColumnsProperty =
    BindableProperty.Create(
        nameof(NumberOfColumns),
        typeof(int),
        typeof(FixedLayoutManager),
        defaultBindingMode: BindingMode.OneWay,
        propertyChanged: OnNumberOfColumnsChanged);

public int NumberOfColumns
{
    get => (int)GetValue(NumberOfColumnsProperty);
    set => SetValue(NumberOfColumnsProperty, value);
}

static void OnNumberOfColumnsChanged(BindableObject bindable,
object oldValue, object newValue)
{
    var manager = (FixedLayoutManager)bindable;

    manager.InitialiseGrid();
}
```

179

The key difference with this implementation over the previous bindable properties that you created is the use of the propertyChanged parameter. It allows you to define a method (see OnNumberOfColumnsChanged) that will be called whenever the property value changes.

The property changed method will only be called when the value changes. This means that it may not be called initially if the value does not change from the default value.

Adding the NumberOfRows Property

```
public static readonly BindableProperty NumberOfRowsProperty =
    BindableProperty.Create(
        nameof(NumberOfRows),
        typeof(int),
        typeof(FixedLayoutManager),
        defaultBindingMode: BindingMode.OneWay,
        propertyChanged: OnNumberOfRowsChanged);

public int NumberOfRows
{
    get => (int)GetValue(NumberOfRowsProperty);
    set => SetValue(NumberOfRowsProperty, value);
}

static void OnNumberOfRowsChanged(BindableObject bindable,
object oldValue, object newValue)
{
    var manager = (FixedLayoutManager)bindable;

    manager.InitialiseGrid();
}
```

This is virtually identical to the NumberOfColumns property that you just added, except for the NumberOfRows value.

Providing Tap/Click Support Through a Command

The next item on your list is to provide the ability to handle tap/click support. This is your first time providing command support; you used commands in your bindings, but that was on the source side rather than the target side like here.

First, you need to add the bindable property, which should start to feel rather familiar.

```
public static readonly BindableProperty
PlaceholderTappedCommandProperty =
    BindableProperty.Create(
        nameof(PlaceholderTappedCommand),
        typeof(ICommand),
        typeof(FixedLayoutManager));

public ICommand PlaceholderTappedCommand
{
    get => (ICommand)GetValue(PlaceholderTappedCommand
    Property);
    set => SetValue(PlaceholderTappedCommandProperty, value);
}
```

Next, you need to add the code that will execute the command. You will be relying on the use of a TapGestureRecognizer by adding one to your Placeholder control inside your InitialiseGrid method that you will be adding in the next section. For now, you can add the method that will be used so that you can focus on how to execute the command. Let's add the code and then look over the details.

```
private void TapGestureRecognizer_Tapped(object sender,
EventArgs e)
{
    if (sender is Placeholder placeholder)
    {
        if (PlaceholderTappedCommand?.CanExecute(placeholder.
        Position) == true)
        {
            PlaceholderTappedCommand.Execute(placeholder.
            Position);
        }
    }
}
```

You can see from the implementation that there are three main parts to the command execution logic:

- First, you make sure that command has a value.

- Second, you check that you can execute the command. If you recall back in Chapter 5 you provided a method to prevent the command from executing if the user hadn't entered a BoardName.

- Finally, you execute the command and pass in the command parameter. For this scenario, you will be passing in the current position of the placeholder so when a widget is added, it can be placed in the same position.

Building the Board Layout

Now you can focus on laying out the underlying Grids so that they display as per the user's entered values for rows and columns.

First, add in a property to store the current Board because you need to use it when building the layout. You also need to record whether you have built the layout to prevent any unnecessary updates rebuilding the user interface.

```
private BoardLayout board;
private bool isInitialised;

public BoardLayout Board
{
    get => board;
    set
    {
        board = value;

        InitialiseGrid();
    }
}
```

Your method to build the grid layout has several parts, so let's add them as you go and discuss their value. You initially need to make sure that you have valid values for the Board, NumberOfRows and NumberOfColumns properties plus you haven't already built the UI.

```
private void InitialiseGrid()
{
    if (Board is null ||
        NumberOfColumns == 0 ||
        NumberOfRows == 0 ||
        isInitialised == true)
    {
        return;
    }

    isInitialised = true;
}
```

The next step is to use the NumberOfColumns value and add them to your Board. Let's add this to the end of the InitialiseGrid method.

```
for (int i = 0; i < NumberOfColumns; i++)
{
    Board.AddColumn(new ColumnDefinition(new GridLength(1,
    GridUnitType.Star)));
}
```

The GridUnitType.Star value means that each column will have an even share of the width of the grid. So, if the Grid is 300 pixels wide and you have 3 columns, then each column has a resulting width of 100 pixels.

The next step is to use the NumberOfRows value and add them to your Board. Let's add this to the end of the InitialiseGrid method.

```
for (int i = 0; i < NumberOfRows; i++)
{
    Board.AddRow(new RowDefinition(new GridLength(1,
    GridUnitType.Star)));
}
```

The final step in your InitialiseGrid method is to populate each cell (row and column) combination with a Placeholder control.

```
for (int column = 0; column < NumberOfColumns; column++)
{
    for (int row = 0; row < NumberOfRows; row++)
    {
        var placeholder = new Placeholder();

        placeholder.Position = row * NumberOfColumns + column;
        var tapGestureRecognizer = new TapGestureRecognizer();
```

```
   tapGestureRecognizer.Tapped += TapGestureRecognizer_Tapped;
   placeholder.GestureRecognizers.Add(tapGesture
   Recognizer);

   Board.AddPlaceholder(placeholder);

   Grid.SetColumn(placeholder, column);
   Grid.SetRow(placeholder, row);
  }
}
```

In the above code, you

- Looped through the combinations of rows/columns

- Created a Placeholder control

- Set its position for use later

- Added a TapGestureRecognizer to handle user interaction

- Added the Placeholder to the Board

- Positioned the Placeholder to the correct column and row position

Setting the Correct Row/Column Position for Each Widget

The final part in building the board layout is to provide the method required by the ILayoutManager interface that your FixedLayoutManager is implementing. This method will

- Calculate the column/row value based on the position parameter passed in.

185

- Position the bindableObject parameter passed into the calculated column and row position.

- Remove any existing Placeholder in the position.

```
public void SetPosition(BindableObject bindableObject, int
position)
{
    if (NumberOfColumns == 0)
    {
        return;
    }

    int column = position % NumberOfColumns;
    int row = position / NumberOfColumns;

    Grid.SetColumn(bindableObject, column);
    Grid.SetRow(bindableObject, row);

    var placeholder = Board.Placeholders.Where(p => p.Position
== position).FirstOrDefault();

    if (placeholder is not null)
    {
        Board.RemovePlaceholder(placeholder);
    }
}
```

Now that you have completed the work of providing a BoardLayout and managing its layout with your FixedLayoutManager class, you should go ahead and use it in your application.

Using Your Layout

Before you can jump in and start using the BoardLayout you have created, there is a little bit more work to be done. You need to

- Add a factory that will create instances of your widgets.

- Add in the DataTemplateSelector that I referred to earlier on.

- Update your FixedBoardPageViewModel so your bindings will work.

Adding a Factory That Will Create Instances of Your Widgets

For this, you are going to create a new class called WidgetFactory in the root of your project.

```
using WidgetBoard.ViewModels;
using WidgetBoard.Views;

namespace WidgetBoard;

public class WidgetFactory
{
}
```

There are three main purposes for this factory:

- Allows for the registration of widget views and view models

- Creation of a widget view

- Creation of a widget view model

So, let's support these three requirements.

187

Allowing for the Registration of Widget Views and View Models

You need to add the following code:

```
private static IDictionary<Type, Type> widgetRegistrations =
new Dictionary<Type, Type>();
private static IDictionary<string, Type>
widgetNameRegistrations = new Dictionary<string, Type>();

public static void RegisterWidget<TWidgetView,
TWidgetViewModel>(string displayName) where TWidgetView :
IWidgetView where TWidgetViewModel : IWidgetViewModel
{
    widgetRegistrations.Add(typeof(TWidgetViewModel),
    typeof(TWidgetView));
    widgetNameRegistrations.Add(displayName,
    typeof(TWidgetViewModel));
}

public IList<string> AvailableWidgets =>
widgetNameRegistrations.Keys.ToList();
```

The above may look a little complicated but if you break it down, hopefully it should become clear. You have added two fields that will store the type information and name information needed for when you create the instances of widgets.

The RegisterWidget method takes a display name parameter and two types:

- TWidgetView: This must implement your IWidgetView interface.

- TWidgetViewModel: This must implement your IWidgetViewModel interface.

You then store a mapping between the view model type and the view type (`widgetRegistrations`). This allows you to create a view when you pass in a view model. This really helps you to keep a clean separation between your view and view model.

You also store a mapping between the display name and the view model type (`widgetNameRegistrations`). This will allow you to present an option on screen to the user. Once they choose the name of the widget they would like to add, the factory will create an instance of it.

Creation of a Widget View

You first need to add a dependency to your constructor.

```
private readonly IServiceProvider serviceProvider;

public WidgetFactory(IServiceProvider serviceProvider)
{
    this.serviceProvider = serviceProvider;
}
```

The `IServiceProvider` will allow you to create a new instance of your widgets and make sure that they are provided with all of their dependencies. Don't worry about needing to register the `IServiceProvider` implementation with your `MauiAppBuilder` as you have done with other dependencies that you require. This is automatically provided by .NET MAUI.

Now let's add the ability to create the widget view.

```
public IWidgetView CreateWidget(IWidgetViewModel
widgetViewModel)
{
    if (widgetRegistrations.TryGetValue(widgetViewModel.
    GetType(), out var widgetViewType))
    {
```

```
    var widgetView = (IWidgetView)serviceProvider.GetRequir
    edService(widgetViewType);

    widgetView.WidgetViewModel = widgetViewModel;

    return widgetView;
}

return null;
}
```

Breaking this down,

- You check whether the supplied widgetViewModels type has been registered with the factory.

- If it has, you use the IServiceProvider to get an instance of the associated widget view.

- You assign the widgetViewModel parameter value to the WidgetViewModel property on the widget view. This is to allow for the setting of the widgets BindingContext property.

Creation of a Widget View Model

You also need to provide the ability to create the widget view model because this is required in your view model.

```
public IWidgetViewModel CreateWidgetViewModel(string
displayname)
{
    if (widgetNameRegistrations.TryGetValue(displayname, out
    var widgetViewModelType))
    {
```

```
    return (IWidgetViewModel)serviceProvider.GetRequiredSer
    vice(widgetViewModelType);
}

  return null;
}
```

Breaking this down,

- You check whether the supplied displayname has been registered with the factory.

- If it has, you use the IServiceProvider to get an instance of the associated widget view model.

Registering the Factory with MauiAppBuilder

Inside your MauiProgram.cs file, you need to register your WidgetFactory with the MauiAppBuilder to make sure any dependencies can resolve it. Open that file and add the following line into the CreateMauiApp method:

```
builder.Services.AddSingleton<WidgetFactory>();
```

Registering Your ClockWidget with the Factory

Now that you have your WidgetFactory, you need to modify it so that the factory can create the widget for you. This requires a number of steps, so let's walk through it.

First, open the ClockWidgetView.xaml.cs file and change it to the following:

```
using WidgetBoard.ViewModels;

namespace WidgetBoard.Views;

public partial class ClockWidgetView : Label, IWidgetView
{
```

```
public ClockWidgetView(ClockWidgetViewModel
clockWidgetViewModel)
{
    InitializeComponent();

    WidgetViewModel = clockWidgetViewModel;
    BindingContext = clockWidgetViewModel;
}

public IWidgetViewModel WidgetViewModel { get; set; }
}
```

This results in your `ClockWidgetView` taking a dependency on `ClockWidgetViewModel`.

Next, you need to register your widget with the factory. Open your `MauiProgram.cs` file and add the following lines to the `CreateMauiApp` method:

```
WidgetFactory.RegisterWidget<ClockWidgetView, ClockWidgetView
Model>("Clock");

builder.Services.AddTransient<ClockWidgetView>();
builder.Services.AddTransient<ClockWidgetViewModel>();
```

This will enable the `WidgetFactory` to return the clock widget as an option when presented in your overlay.

WidgetTemplateSelector

The main purpose of this implementation is to provide a conversion between the widget view models that you will be storing on your FixedBoardPageViewModel and something that can actually be rendered on the screen. You are going to depend on the WidgetFactory you have just created. Create the class under the root project folder.

```
using WidgetBoard.ViewModels;

namespace WidgetBoard.Views;

public class WidgetTemplateSelector : DataTemplateSelector
{
    private readonly WidgetFactory widgetFactory;

    public WidgetTemplateSelector(WidgetFactory widgetFactory)
    {
        this.widgetFactory = widgetFactory;
    }

    protected override DataTemplate OnSelectTemplate(object
    item, BindableObject container)
    {
        if (item is IWidgetViewModel widgetViewModel)
        {
            return new DataTemplate(() => widgetFactory.Create
            Widget(widgetViewModel));
        }

        return null;
    }
}
```

The main part you need to focus on here is the `OnSelectTemplate` method. I did discuss the purpose of this method briefly earlier on; let's take a deeper look now. Its main purpose is to provide a `DataTemplate` and something that can be rendered on screen. This is a great way to keep the separation between view and view model.

In your implementation, you can see that

- You check whether the item passed in implements your `IWidgetViewModel` interface.

- If so, then you create a new `DataTemplate` and rely on the `WidgetFactory` to return the widget view that is mapped to the view models type.

Registering the Template Selector with MauiAppBuilder

Inside your `MauiProgram.cs` file you need to register your `WidgetTemplateSelector` with the `MauiAppBuilder` to make sure any dependencies can resolve it. Open that file and add the following line into the `CreateMauiApp` method:

```
builder.Services.AddSingleton<WidgetTemplateSelector>();
```

Updating FixedBoardPageViewModel

You need to add in the properties that you can bind to in your view.

```
private string boardName;
private int numberOfColumns;
private int numberOfRows;

public string BoardName
{
    get => boardName;
```

```
    set => SetProperty(ref boardName, value);
}

public int NumberOfColumns
{
    get => numberOfColumns;
    set => SetProperty(ref numberOfColumns, value);
}

public int NumberOfRows
{
    get => numberOfRows;
    set => SetProperty(ref numberOfRows, value);
}

public ObservableCollection<IWidgetViewModel> Widgets { get; }

public WidgetTemplateSelector WidgetTemplateSelector { get; }
```

Notice that the Widgets and WidgetTemplateSelector properties do not call the SetProperty method to notify the UI of changes. This is a perfectly valid scenario. You know that the value will be set in the constructor and therefore the value will be set before the binding is applied.

You also need to add in the remaining code to your ApplyQueryAttributes method that you added in the last chapter. It should now look like the following:

```
public void ApplyQueryAttributes(IDictionary<string,
object> query)
{
    var board = query["Board"] as Board;

    BoardName = board.Name;
```

```
NumberOfColumns = ((FixedLayout)board.Layout).
NumberOfColumns;
NumberOfRows = ((FixedLayout)board.Layout).NumberOfRows;
}
```

Finally, you need to add the WidgetTemplateSelector as a dependency in your constructor. It should now look like the following:

```
public FixedBoardPageViewModel(
    WidgetTemplateSelector widgetTemplateSelector
)
{
    WidgetTemplateSelector = widgetTemplateSelector;

    Widgets = new ObservableCollection<IWidgetViewModel>();
}
```

You are now ready to add the layout to your page.

Finally Using the Layout

Now that you have built your layout, you should go ahead and use it. You previously added the FixedBoardPage so you can go ahead and change it to the following:

```
<?xml version="1.0" encoding="utf-8" ?>
<ContentPage
    xmlns="http://schemas.microsoft.com/dotnet/2021/maui"
    xmlns:x="http://schemas.microsoft.com/winfx/2009/xaml"
    xmlns:layouts="clr-namespace:WidgetBoard.Layouts"
    xmlns:viewmodels="clr-namespace:WidgetBoard.ViewModels"
    x:Class="WidgetBoard.Pages.FixedBoardPage"
    Title="FixedBoardPage"
    x:DataType="viewmodels:FixedBoardPageViewModel">
```

```
<layouts:BoardLayout
    ItemsSource="{Binding Widgets}"
    ItemTemplateSelector="{Binding Widget
    TemplateSelector}">
    <layouts:BoardLayout.LayoutManager>
        <layouts:FixedLayoutManager
            NumberOfColumns="{Binding NumberOfColumns}"
            NumberOfRows="{Binding NumberOfRows}" />
    </layouts:BoardLayout.LayoutManager>
</layouts:BoardLayout>

</ContentPage>
```

This now includes your shiny new BoardLayout complete with all the bindings you have created to make it functional.

Summary

In this chapter, you

- Created your own layout

- Made use of a variety of options when adding bindable properties

- Provided command support from your layout

- Used your layout in your application

In the next chapter, you will

- Gain an understanding of what accessibility is

- Learn why it is important to build inclusive applications

197

- Look at how you can make use of .NET MAUI functionality

- Consider other scenarios and how to support them

- Look over some testing options to support your journey to building accessible applications

Source Code

The resulting source code for this chapter can be found on the GitHub repository at `https://github.com/Apress/Introducing-MAUI/tree/main/ch06`.

Extra Assignment

You will have noticed how a lot of the naming includes the word Fixed. Let's continue the extra assignment from the previous chapter and build a board that is a variation of this approach. I really like the idea of a freeform board where the user can position their widgets wherever they like. This is a little more involved but if you consider how the `BoardLayout` can use `AbsoluteLayouts` rather than `Grids`, then a new `ILayoutManager` implementation should hopefully be where the alternative logic will need to be applied. If you do embark on this journey, please feel free to share your experience and findings.

CHAPTER 7

Accessibility

In this chapter, you will be taking a break from adding new parts to the user interface in order to gain an understanding of what accessibility is, why you should make your applications accessible, and how .NET MAUI makes this easier. You will also cover some testing options to support your journey to building accessible applications.

I wanted this chapter to appear earlier on in this book. I feel it is such an important topic and one that you really do need to consider early on in your projects. It has come to settle nicely in the middle of the book now because you needed some UI to apply the concepts to.

What Is Accessibility?

The definition of accessibility according to the Cambridge Dictionary (https://dictionary.cambridge.org/dictionary/english/accessibility) is

> *"the quality of being easy to understand."*

By considering the scenarios where your application might be less easy to understand for a large percentage of the world's population that have some form of disability, you can learn to provide ways to break down the complexities in understanding the content. This might be through the use of assistive technologies such as voice-over assistants or screen readers, or even providing the ability to increase the font size to make the content easier to read.

All of this can help you as a developer learn how to build applications that are much more inclusive of the entire population of the world.

Why Make Your Applications Accessible?

I heard an excellent quote recently and sadly I have been unable to discover the original author of the quote, but it is *"if you don't know whether your application is accessible, then you can safely say that is it not."* Essentially, if you are not putting any effort into making it accessible, then you can almost guarantee that it is not.

According to the World Health Organization, *globally at least 2.2 billion people have a near or distance vision impairment* (www.who.int/news-room/fact-sheets/detail/blindness-and-visual-impairment).

You want to build your applications and make them as successful as possible. Imagine immediately ruling out up to 27% of your potential market purely based on not making your application more inclusive for that population.

What to Consider When Making Your Applications Accessible

There is a whole heap of things you can do in order to make your applications more inclusive. To aid you on your journey to building accessible applications, there is a fantastic set of guidelines known as the *Web Content Accessibility Guidelines (WCAG)*. There are four main principles to consider:

- **Perceivable**: Making sure that you provide information that can be perceived by the user. This can be by providing text-based alternatives to images, suitable contrast ratios, adaptive text sizing, and much more.

- **Operable**: Making sure that you provide the user with the ability to use the application. This can be by providing keyboard navigation, making sure they have enough time to read and use the content, and much more.

- **Understandable**: Making sure that you provide a user interface that is understandable to the user. This can be making sure that the content is readable, predictable (appear and behave as expected), and helps the user avoid making mistakes.

- **Robust**: Making sure the content is robust enough that it can be interpreted by a wide variety of user agents, including assistive technologies. This can be by providing suitable support for assistive technologies.

To read more on these guidelines, I thoroughly recommend checking out the Quick Reference Guide at `www.w3.org/WAI/WCAG21/quickref/`.

How to Make Your Application Accessible

There are several things to consider when building an application that is inclusive. This section will not provide a complete set of tools for building applications inclusive for all. However, it will provide some insights to what .NET MAUI offers and some other concepts to consider to set you off on a journey of discovery to building much more accessible applications.

Screen Reader Support

.NET MAUI provides great tools to provide explicit support for the screen readers on each of the supported platforms. I feel it is worth highlighting that point again: **.NET MAUI utilizes the screen readers on each platform**. This means that they will need to be enabled by the user for the settings to take effect. You will dive into each concept and how it enables you to expose information to those screen readers so you can provide a much more informative experience for your users.

As a starting exercise, pick up your phone and turn on your screen reader assistant. Try navigating around to get an understanding of what the experience is like and, most importantly, try an application you built. Does it provide a good experience?

Let's see how you can make the WidgetBoard application more accessible with the screen readers available. Thankfully you haven't built too much UI already, so you are in a good position to start. I urge you to consider applying concepts like this as early on in the development phase as possible.

SemanticProperties

The `SemanticProperties` class offers a set of attached properties that can be applied to any visual element. .NET MAUI applies these property values on the platform-specific APIs that provide accessibility.

Let's look through each of the properties and apply them to your `BoardDetailsPage`.

SemanticProperties.Description

The `SemanticProperties.Description` property allows you to define a short string that will be used by the screen reader to announce the element to the user when it gains focus.

As I type this chapter, I am testing the application. The first `Entry` added on the `BoardDetailsPage` currently results in the macOS VoiceOver assistant announcing *"edit text, is editing, blank."*

You can change the `Entry` to the following:

```
<Entry
```

```
Text="{Binding BoardName}"
SemanticProperties.Description="Enter the board name"/>
```

This now results in *"Enter the board name, is editing, blank"* being announced, which is much more useful to the user.

You can take this a step further. You have a label above that just has the Text of "Name." If you change this to use your new descriptive text, then you can set the SemanticProperties.Description value to its text. Let's do that now; the changes are highlighted in **bold:**

```
<Label
    Text="Enter the board name"
    x:Name="EnterBoardNameLabel"
    FontAttributes="Bold" />

<Entry
    Text="{Binding BoardName}"
    SemanticProperties.Description="{Binding Text,
Source={x:Reference EnterBoardNameLabel}}" />
```

The resulting code may look less appealing but it provides a number of benefits:

- The text description is more informative on the Label.

- When you add in localization support, you will have only one text field to update.

The macOS screen reader does provide a second announcement following the announcement you have been improving. This follow-up is *"You are currently on a text field. To enter text in this field, type."* This isn't the most informative, so let's provide a better hint to the user.

The act of setting the `SemanticProperties.Description` property will automatically make a visual element be announced by the screen reader. By default, an `Image` control is not announced but by setting this property, the text will be announced when the control gains semantic focus.

SemanticProperties.Hint

The `SemanticProperties.Hint` property allows you to provide a string that the screen reader will announce to the user so that they have a better understanding of the purpose of the control.

Let's add a hint to `Entry` with the addition in **bold**:

```
<Entry
    Text="{Binding BoardName}"
    SemanticProperties.Description="{Binding Text,
    Source={x:Reference EnterBoardNameLabel}}"
    SemanticProperties.Hint="Provides a name that will be
    used to identify your widget board. This is a required
    field." />
```

This change results in *"Provides a name that will be used to identify your widget board. This is a required field. You are currently on a text field. To enter text in this field, type"* being announced. I think you can agree that this adds yet more context to the user and this is a good thing.

SemanticProperties.HeadingLevel

The `SemanticProperties.HeadingLevel` property allows you to mark an element as a heading to help organize the UI and make it easier for users to navigate. Some screen readers enable users to quickly jump between headings and thus providing a far more friendly navigation for those users that rely on screen readers. Headings have a level from 1 to 9 and are represented by the SemanticHeadingLevel enumeration.

SemanticScreenReader

.NET MAUI provides the SemanticScreenReader that enables you to instruct a screen reader to announce some text to the user. This can work especially well if you wish to present instructions to a user or to prompt them if they have paused their interaction.

The SemanticScreenReader provides a static Announce method to perform the announcements, it also provides a Default instance. I personally like to make use of the scenarios where .NET MAUI provides you with a Current or a Default instance and register this with the app builder to make full use of the dependency injection support. To do this, write the following line of code in your MauiProgram.cs file:

```
builder.Services.AddSingleton(SemanticScreenReader.Default);
```

With the screen reader registered, you can announce that the new board was created successfully once the user has tapped on the Save button. You need to open the BoardDetailsPageViewModel.cs file and make the following changes.

Add the read-only field.

```
private readonly ISemanticScreenReader semanticScreenReader;
```

Assign a value in your constructor, just applying the **bold code** to your existing content.

```
public BoardDetailsPageViewModel(ISemanticScreenReader
semanticScreenReader)
{
    this.semanticScreenReader = semanticScreenReader;
```

```
    SaveCommand = new Command(
        () => Save(),
        () => !string.IsNullOrWhiteSpace(BoardName));
}
```

Call Announce in your Save method, just applying the **bold code** to your existing content.

```
private async void Save()
{
    var board = new Board
    {
        Name = BoardName,
        Layout = new FixedLayout
        {
            NumberOfColumns = NumberOfColumns,
            NumberOfRows = NumberOfRows
        }
    };

    semanticScreenReader.Announce($"A new board with the name
    {BoardName} was created successfully.");

    await Shell.Current.GoToAsync(
        "fixedboard",
        new Dictionary<string, object>
        {
            { "Board", board}
        });
}
```

If you run your application and save a new board called "My work board," you will observe that the screen reader will announce *"A new board with the name My work board was created successfully."* This gives the user some valuable audible feedback. If you expect the save process to take some time, you can also perform an announcement at the start of the process to keep the user informed.

AutomationProperties

AutomationProperties are the old Xamarin.Forms way of exposing information to the screen readers on each platform. I won't cover all of the options because some have been replaced by the SemanticProperties section that you just learned about. The following are the important ones that provide a different set of functionality.

AutomationProperties.ExcludedWithChildren

The AutomationProperties.ExcludeWithChildren property allows developers to exclude the element supplied and all its children from the accessibility tree. Setting this property to true will exclude the element and all of its children from the accessibility tree.

AutomationProperties.IsInAccessibleTree

The AutomationProperties.IsInAccessibleTree property allows developers to decide whether the element is visible to screen readers. A common scenario for this feature is to hide controls such as Label or Image controls that serve a purely decorative purpose (e.g., a background image). Setting this property to true will exclude the element from the accessibility tree.

Suitable Contrast

WCAG states in guideline *1.4.3 Contrast (Minimum) – Level AA* that the visual presentation of text and images of text has a contrast ratio of at least 4.5:1, except for the following:

- **Large Text:** Large-scale text and images of large-scale text have a contrast ratio of at least 3:1.

- **Incidental:** Text or images of text that are part of an inactive user interface component, that are pure decoration, that are not visible to anyone, or that are part of a picture that contains significant other visual content, have no contrast requirement.

- **Logotypes:** Text that is part of a logo or brand name has no contrast requirement.

This all boils down to calculating the difference between the lighter and darker colors in your application when displaying text. If that contrast ratio is 4.5:1 or higher, it's suitable. Let's look at how this is calculated:

```
(L1 + 0.05) / (L2 + 0.05)
```

where L1 is the relative luminance of the lighter color and L2 is the relative luminance of the darker color. Relative luminance is defined as *the relative brightness of any point in a colorspace, normalized to 0 for darkest black and 1 for lightest white*. Relative luminance can be further be calculated as

For the sRGB colorspace, the relative luminance of a color is defined as L = 0.2126 * R + 0.7152 * G + 0.0722 * B where R, G and B are defined as:

```
if RsRGB <= 0.03928 then R = RsRGB/12.92 else R =
((RsRGB+0.055)/1.055) ^ 2.4
```

if GsRGB <= 0.03928 then G = GsRGB/12.92 else G =
((GsRGB+0.055)/1.055) ^ 2.4
if BsRGB <= 0.03928 then B = BsRGB/12.92 else B =
((BsRGB+0.055)/1.055) ^ 2.4
and RsRGB, GsRGB, and BsRGB are defined as:

RsRGB = R8bit/255
GsRGB = G8bit/255
BsRGB = B8bit/255
The "^" character is the exponentiation operator.

These formulas are taken from www.w3.org/TR/WCAG21/#dfn-relative-luminance. Let's turn this into some C# to make it a little easier to follow and something that you can use to test your color choices.

```
private static double GetContrastRatio(Color lighterColor,
Color darkerColor)
{
    var l1 = GetRelativeLuminance(lighterColor);
    var l2 = GetRelativeLuminance(darkerColor);

    return (l1 + 0.05) / (l2 + 0.05);
}

private static double GetRelativeLuminance(Color color)
{
    var r = GetRelativeComponent(color.Red);
    var g = GetRelativeComponent(color.Green);
    var b = GetRelativeComponent(color.Blue);

    return
        0.2126 * r +
        0.7152 * g +
        0.0722 * b;
}
```

209

```
private static double GetRelativeComponent(float component)
{
    if (component <= 0.03928)
    {
        return component / 12.92;
    }

    return Math.Pow(((component + 0.055) / 1.055), 2.4);
}
```

If you take a look at the colors you are using for your text controls and the background colors, you can work out whether you need to improve on the contrast ratio. You can see by checking in your Styles.xaml file that your Label control uses Gray900 for the text color. Checking in the Colors. xaml file, you can see that this Gray900 color has a value of #212121. Therefore, you can use your methods to calculate the contrast ratio with

```
GetContrastRatio(Colors.White, Color.FromArgb("#212121");
```

This gives you a contrast ratio of 16.10:1, which means this is providing a very good contrast ratio. The best possible contrast is black on white, which gives a contrast ratio of 21:1. Therefore, you do not need to make any changes to your color scheme, which shows that .NET MAUI ships with default color options that are suitable for building accessible applications.

Dynamic Text Sizing

WCAG states in guideline *1.4.4 Resize text – Level AA* that except for captions and images of text, text can be resized without assistive technology up to 200 percent without loss of content or functionality.

This guideline mainly focuses on highlighting the fact that there is still a large percentage of users that do not rely on accessibility features such as screen readers or screen magnification when they could benefit from them. The guideline further states that, as a developer, you should provide the ability to scale the text in your application up to 200% without relying on the operating system to perform the scaling.

In this section, I am not going to focus on adding that specific feature; however, I will be discussing some approaches that will aid this feature as well as using the assistive technology options.

Avoiding Fixed Sizes

Wherever possible you want to avoid setting the `WidthRequest` and `HeightRequest` properties for any control that can contain text.

Imagine you set `WidthRequest="200"` and `HeightRequest="30"` on the `Label` controls in your `BoardDetailsPage.xaml` file. What you would initially see is that the text fits nicely using the standard font scaling options. Figure 7-1 shows your application with fixed size controls and a small font size.

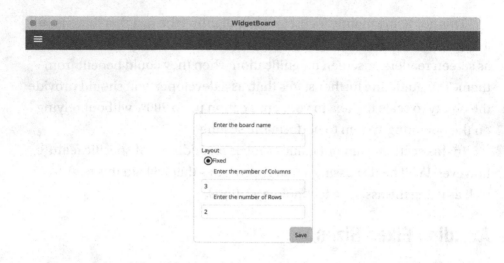

Figure 7-1. *Your application with fixed sizing and a small font size*

However, if you up the scaling to 200%, you will see a rather unpleasant screen. Figure 7-2 shows your application with fixed size controls and a large font size, highlighting that the text becomes clipped and unreadable.

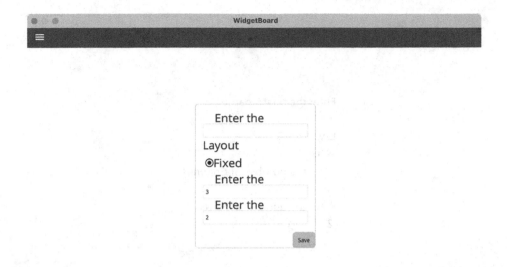

Figure 7-2. *Your application with fixed sizing and a large font size*

It actually appears that your initial changes without the `WidthRequest` and `HeightRequest` values on the `Label` controls gives the best experience. Figure 7-3 shows your application responding to font size changes when control sizes are not fixed.

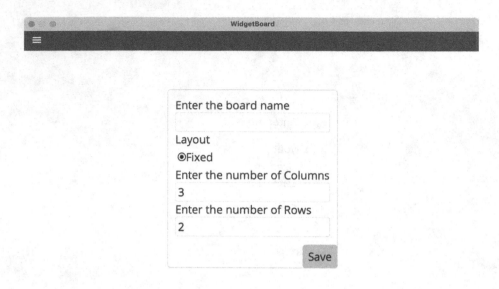

Figure 7-3. Your application showing responsiveness to font scaling

Preferring Minimum Sizing

Where possible, you should use MinimumWidthRequest and
MinimumHeightRequest over WidthRequest and HeightRequest,
respectively. This allows for controls to grow. There may be scenarios
where a combination of Minimum and Maximum property values will give
a good experience when scaling is introduced.

Font Auto Scaling

By default, all controls that render text in a .NET MAUI application have
the FontAutoScalingEnabled property set to true. This means that the
controls automatically scale their font size accordingly when the operating
systems font scaling settings are changed.

214

There can be scenarios when disabling this feature can provide a more accessible experience. One example is in a wordsearch application I built. The application made the letters appear as big as possible, so any additional scaling by the operating system would result in parts of the text being cut off. I advise using this option sparingly.

Testing Your Application's Accessibility

Each platform supported by .NET MAUI has its own set of guidelines around testing for accessibility and even tools to aid that journey. In this section, you are going to take a brief look at what each platform provider offers.

Android

Google, much like each of the other platform providers, does recommend that you perform a manual test, such as turning on TalkBack and verifying that the user experience is as you have designed.

Google also offers some analysis tools to detect whether any accessibility guidelines are not being met. There is a good list provided by Google with a breakdown of the functionality provided by each tool at `https://developer.android.com/guide/topics/ui/accessibility/testing#analysis`.

iOS

Apple doesn't offer as much as Google on this front. There is the Accessibility Inspector but it only focuses on allowing you to view the information that the screen reader will be provided. I don't feel this is as good as taking a dry run through your application with the VoiceOver assistant turned on. Further information on

Apple's offering can be found at `https://developer.apple.com/
library/archive/technotes/TestingAccessibilityOfiOSApps/
TestAccessibilityiniOSSimulatorwithAccessibilityInspector/
TestAccessibilityiniOSSimulatorwithAccessibilityInspector.html`.

macOS

Apple provides a little extra functionality when testing on macOS. It
does provide the Accessibility Inspector as per iOS and well as the
Accessibility Verifier. This tool allows you to run tests against your
application to verify items like the accessibility description have been
defined on all required elements. Further information on these features
can be found at `https://developer.apple.com/library/archive/
documentation/Accessibility/Conceptual/AccessibilityMacOSX/
OSXAXTestingApps.html`.

Windows

Microsoft offers the biggest amount of options when it comes to testing the
accessibility of your applications. The Windows Software Development Kit
(SDK) provides several tools such as the ability to inspect an application
and view all related properties as plus automation tests that verify the
state of accessibility. All details of the tools can be found at `https://docs.
microsoft.com/windows/apps/design/accessibility/accessibility-
testing`.

Accessibility Checklist

The following checklist is provided by Microsoft on their documentation
site at `https://docs.microsoft.com/dotnet/maui/fundamentals/
accessibility#accessibility-checklist`. I haven't added to it or

reworded because I believe it provides an excellent breakdown of the possible ways to provide accessible support.

Follow these tips to ensure that your .NET MAUI apps are accessible to the widest audience possible:

- Ensure your app is perceivable, operable, understandable, and robust for all by following the Web Content Accessibility Guidelines (WCAG). WCAG is the global accessibility standard and legal benchmark for web and mobile. For more information, see Web Content Accessibility Guidelines (WCAG) Overview.

- Make sure the user interface is self-describing. Test that all the elements of your user interface are screen reader accessible. Add descriptive text and hints when necessary.

- Ensure that images and icons have alternate text descriptions.

- Support large fonts and high contrast. Avoid hardcoding control dimensions, and instead prefer layouts that resize to accommodate larger font sizes. Test color schemes in high-contrast mode to ensure they are readable.

- Design the visual tree with navigation in mind. Use appropriate layout controls so that navigating between controls using alternate input methods follows the same logical flow as using touch. In addition, exclude unnecessary elements from screen readers (for example, decorative images or labels for fields that are already accessible).

- Don't rely on audio or color cues alone. Avoid situations where the sole indication of progress, completion, or some other state is a sound or color change. Either design the user interface to include clear visual cues, with sound and color for reinforcement only, or add specific accessibility indicators. When choosing colors, try to avoid a palette that is hard to distinguish for users with color blindness.

- Provide captions for video content and a readable script for audio content. It's also helpful to provide controls that adjust the speed of audio or video content, and ensure that volume and transport controls are easy to find and use.

- Localize your accessibility descriptions when the app supports multiple languages.

- Test the accessibility features of your app on each platform it targets. For more information, see Testing accessibility.

Summary

In this chapter, you have

- Gained an understanding of what accessibility is

- Learned why it is important to build inclusive applications

- Looked at how you can make use of .NET MAUI functionality

- Considered other scenarios and how to support them

- Looked over some testing options to support your journey to building accessible applications

In the next chapter, you will

- Add a widget to a board.

- Explore the different options available when showing an overlay.

- Explore how you can define styling information for your application.

- Learn how to handle devices running in light and dark modes.

- Learn how to apply triggers to enhance your UI.

- Explore how to animate parts of your application.

- Explore what happens when you combine triggers and animations together.

Source Code

The resulting source code for this chapter can be found on the GitHub repository at `https://github.com/Apress/Introducing-MAUI/tree/main/ch07`.

Extra Assignment

Take one of your favorite applications that you are completely familiar with because you know the layout and how to use it. Then proceed to

- Turn on the screen reading assistant on your phone.

- Try to navigate your way around this application.

- Better still, try to impact your vision with a blindfold or remove any glasses if you use them. Try to rely entirely on the screen reader.

- Perhaps try the same but modify the device font scaling and see if the application is able to handle increases in text size, or if it even allow this option.

The objective is to gain a sense of the experience users with limited vision have when using the same application. Take notes on how well applications do things and how poorly they do other things. This can be a really great learning exercise for you all!

CHAPTER 8

Advanced UI Concepts

In this chapter, you will provide the user of your application with the ability to add a widget to the boards they create through the use of an overlay. You will further enhance this overlay by defining common styling techniques and handling the differences between light and dark mode devices.

You will then take a journey into discovering how you can build an application that feels natural and organic to your human user base. Finally, you will look at how you can keep the animations driving the organic look and feel cleanly separated from your business logic code.

Adding the Ability to Add a Widget to a Board

In Chapter 6, you created your own `BoardLayout` and the associated `FixedLayoutManager` that enabled you to show a board and added in the ability to handle interaction events by the user. In this section, you are going to expand on that to handle the user tapping on a widget `Placeholder` and letting the user choose a widget to add to the board.

© Shaun Lawrence 2023
S. Lawrence, *Introducing .NET MAUI*, https://doi.org/10.1007/978-1-4842-9234-1_8

Possible Ways of Achieving Your Goal

There are several ways you can go about adding in this piece of functionality. Some are better suited to different scenarios and some simply come down to a personal preference. I encourage you to understand your goal before you embark on this journey of working out which option will best suit your need. If you only wish to report a message to the user or capture a choice or even a single piece of input, then you can utilize some underlying functionality provided by .NET MAUI. The Page class provides the ability to do each of the three items discussed; it doesn't solve your needs, but it really does have value in many applications. The Microsoft documentation provides a good set of reference examples on how to use these options at https://learn.microsoft.com/dotnet/maui/user-interface/pop-ups.

Let's discuss some of these options that do solve your needs and then make a decision on which you feel is the best candidate for your application.

Showing a Modal Page

So far in this book you have only considered how Shell offers the ability to navigate between ContentPages. This is the default and most common scenario. There can be times when you wish to show a page that is blocking and will require the user to engage with it to return to the previous page. This type of page or display is referred to as *modal*. The scenario of showing something to the user and requiring them to engage with it could be a perfect scenario.

In order to enable this functionality in .NET MAUI, you need to set the Shell.PresentationMode property on the ContentPage that you wish to display. For example,

```
<ContentPage ...
            Shell.PresentationMode="Modal">
    ...
</ContentPage>
```

You can then call the `Shell.Current.GoToAsync` method with the routing options configured for this page and it will be presented modally instead of being navigated to.

Pro

- Keeps specific code contained

Con

- Complicates flow of code when handling a return result

Overlaying a View

Sometimes the most straightforward way to achieve this approach is to add another view to your page and programmatically change its visibility to give the impression you have a modal page displaying.

Pro

- Reduces effort of page creation

Con

- Requires specific code in calling view/view model

Showing a Popup

There is currently no explicit support in .NET MAUI for displaying popups; however, the functionality does exist on the each of the platforms that .NET MAUI runs on. You can go to the lengths of implementing your own ability to display a popup but it would be rather involved. Instead, the .NET MAUI Community Toolkit provides a `Popup` class that makes it straightforward for you to display a popup in your application.

Pros

- Keeps specific code contained

- Provides easy return result handling

For further reading on how to use the toolkit and its Popup class, please refer to the documentation at https://learn.microsoft.com/dotnet/communitytoolkit/maui/views/popup.

The Chosen Approach

Given the pros and cons outlined above, you might guess that you will be using the Popup class. Nope. Let's use the overlaying-a-view approach. This is mainly because it will help to expose you to more .NET MAUI-specific concepts that I believe will be extremely valuable in building applications. However, for your own work, use the approach that best fits your scenario. I would like to emphasize that each of the above options will achieve the results needed. In fact, there could well be more options that I haven't covered, and if you find one, I would love to hear about it.

Adding Your Overlay View

You need to add a view to your FixedBoardPage.xaml file that will present the option to the user to add a new widget to the board. Let's open that file and add the following code inside the Grid and below the </layouts:BoardLayout> line:

```
<BoxView
    BackgroundColor="Black"
    Opacity="0.5"
    IsVisible="{Binding IsAddingWidget}" />

<Border
    IsVisible="{Binding IsAddingWidget}"
```

```
    HorizontalOptions="Center"
    VerticalOptions="Center"
    Padding="10">

    <VerticalStackLayout>
        <Label
            Text="Add widget"
            FontSize="20" />

        <Label
            Text="Widget" />

        <Picker
            ItemsSource="{Binding AvailableWidgets}"
            SelectedItem="{Binding SelectedWidget}"
            SemanticProperties.Description="{Binding Text,
            Source={x:Reference SelectTheWidgetLabel}}"
            SemanticProperties.Hint="Picker containing the
            possible widget types that can be added to the
            board. This is a required field." />

        <Label
            Text="Preview" />

        <ContentView
            WidthRequest="250"
            HeightRequest="250" />

        <Button
            Text="Add widget"
            Command="{Binding AddWidgetCommand}"
            SemanticProperties.Hint="Adds the selected widget
            to the board. Requires the 'Select the widget'
            field to be set." />
    </VerticalStackLayout>
</Border>
```

The code addition results in two new controls added to the parent Grids children collection: a BoxView and a Border. The BoxView is added to provide a semi-transparent overlay on top of the rest of the application and the Border presents the content for selecting a new widget. Adding them after the BoardLayout means it will be rendered on top of the BoardLayout. This ordering is referred to as Z-index and in the majority of .NET MAUI applications, layouts are determined by the order in which the children are added to their parent. This means that the later the controls are added, the higher they will appear visually. You can modify this default behavior by using the ZIndex property where the higher the value, the higher they will appear visually. With this knowledge, you can add a binding between the IsVisible property of your new controls and a property on your view model, so your view model can control whether you are adding a widget to the board.

Let's update your view model.

Updating Your View Model

Since you turned on compiled bindings in a previous chapter, you will now see that your code will not compile because you have not defined the properties you are binding to. So open the FixedBoardPageViewModel.cs file and make the following additions.

Add the new properties and associated backing fields into your FixedBoardPageViewModel class.

```
private int addingPosition;
private string selectedWidget;
private bool isAddingWidget;
private readonly WidgetFactory widgetFactory;

public IList<string> AvailableWidgets => widgetFactory.
AvailableWidgets;
```

```
public ICommand AddWidgetCommand { get; }

public ICommand AddNewWidgetCommand { get; }

public bool IsAddingWidget
{
    get => isAddingWidget;
    set => SetProperty(ref isAddingWidget, value);
}

public string SelectedWidget
{
    get => selectedWidget;
    set => SetProperty(ref selectedWidget, value);
}
```

Update the constructor with the new WidgetFactory dependency and set the new commands that you have added; changes are in **bold**.

```
public FixedBoardPageViewModel(
    WidgetTemplateSelector widgetTemplateSelector,
    WidgetFactory widgetFactory)
{
    WidgetTemplateSelector = widgetTemplateSelector;
    this.widgetFactory = widgetFactory;

    Widgets = new ObservableCollection<IWidgetViewModel>();

    AddWidgetCommand = new Command(OnAddWidget);

    AddNewWidgetCommand = new Command<int>(index =>
    {
        IsAddingWidget = true;
        addingPosition = index;
    });
}
```

In the previous code section, you set the IsAddingWidget property to true in order to show the overlay view and you also keep a record of the index variable, which is the Position property from the Placeholder that was tapped.

Provide the method implementation for the AddWidgetCommand.

```
private void OnAddWidget()
{
    if (SelectedWidget is null)
    {
        return;
    }

    var widgetViewModel = widgetFactory.CreateWidgetViewModel
    (SelectedWidget);

    widgetViewModel.Position = addingPosition;

    Widgets.Add(widgetViewModel);

    IsAddingWidget = false;
}
```

Hopefully the majority of what you just added should feel familiar. The part that most likely doesn't is the final OnAddWidget method. Let's take a deeper look at this implementation.

The SelectedWidget property is bound to your Picker in the view. You do some initial input validation to make sure that the user has chosen a type of widget to add; otherwise, you return out of the method.

Next, you use the new dependency (widgetFactory) to create a view model for you.

Then you set its Position based on which placeholder was tapped initially.

Then you add your newly created `widgetViewModel` to the collection of `Widgets` so that it can update the UI.

Finally, you set the `IsAddingWidget` property to false in order to hide the overlay view again.

Showing the Overlay View

Now you can add the ability to programmatically show the `Border` that allows your users to pick a widget and add it to the board. You already provided a large amount of this functionality inside your `Placeholder` and `FixedLayoutManager` classes, so you just need to hook up your view model to this functionality. You have also just set the groundwork in your view model, so let's hook the components up. Open the `FixedBoardPage.xaml` file again and add the following **bold** line:

```
<layouts:BoardLayout
    ItemsSource="{Binding Widgets}"
    ItemTemplateSelector="{Binding WidgetTemplateSelector}">
    <layouts:BoardLayout.LayoutManager>
        <layouts:FixedLayoutManager
            NumberOfColumns="{Binding NumberOfColumns}"
            NumberOfRows="{Binding NumberOfRows}"
            PlaceholderTappedCommand="{Binding
            AddNewWidgetCommand}" />
    </layouts:BoardLayout.LayoutManager>
</layouts:BoardLayout>
```

If you build and run your application, you can see that once you have created a board, you can now tap or click on the `Placeholder` and observe that your overlay displays. You will notice that there is no background to your overlay, though, so it is really difficult for a user to understand what to do. You can just set the `BackgroundColor` of your `Border` control; however, this can lead to a number of issues. For example, if you fixed the BackgroundColor to white and a user switches on dark mode on their device, they would have a rather unpleasant experience. Figure 8-1 shows how the application currently looks and highlights the issue.

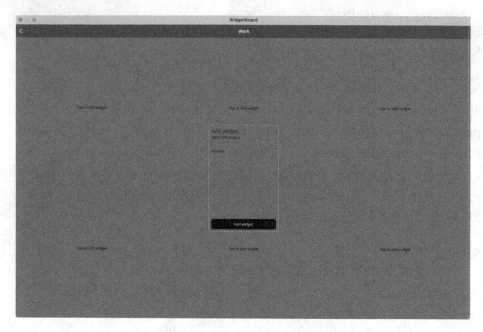

Figure 8-1. *The application showing the overlay with a poor user experience*

Let's look at how .NET MAUI provides the ability to style your applications, which includes supporting light and dark modes.

Styling

.NET MAUI provides the ability to style your applications. Styling in .NET MAUI offers many advantages:

- Central definition of look and feel

- Less verbosity in your XAML/code

- Style inheritance

  Styles in .NET MAUI can be defined at many different
  levels and where they are defined is extremely important
  when understanding what impact they will have. The two
  key distinctions between where they are defined can be
  considered as

- **Globally** : These styles are added to the application's
  resources. You can see an example of this if you open
  the App.xaml file. The line in bold shows that another
  file (Styles.xaml) containing the styles is loaded into
  the Application.Resources property. These styles
  apply to all controls in the application unless otherwise
  explicitly overridden.

```xml
<Application xmlns="http://schemas.microsoft.com/
dotnet/2021/maui"

           xmlns:x="http://schemas.microsoft.com/
           winfx/2009/xaml"
           xmlns:local="clr-namespace:WidgetBoard"
           x:Class="WidgetBoard.App">
<Application.Resources>
    <ResourceDictionary>
        <ResourceDictionary.MergedDictionaries>
            <ResourceDictionary
            Source="Resources/Styles/Colors.
            xaml" />
            <ResourceDictionary Source="Resources/
            Styles/Styles.xaml" />
        </ResourceDictionary.MergedDictionaries>
    </ResourceDictionary>
</Application.Resources>
</Application>
```

- **Locally**: These styles are added to a view or page
  resources property. Styles defined in this way will apply
  to all controls that are children of the view or page they
  are defined in.

Your global example refers to the Styles.xaml file. This is a file that
comes with a new .NET MAUI project.

Examining the Default Styles

You can view this file under Resources/styles.xaml. Let's take a look at
the style for Border in this file:

```
<Style TargetType="Border">
    <Setter Property="Stroke" Value="{AppThemeBinding
    Light={StaticResource Gray200}, Dark={StaticResource
    Gray500}}" />
    <Setter Property="StrokeShape" Value="Rectangle"/>
    <Setter Property="StrokeThickness" Value="1"/>
</Style>
```

The XAML syntax used to define a style looks rather different to
the XAML you have written so far. Let's break it down to gain a better
understanding of what it all means.

TargetType

To start, when defining a Style, you must define the TargetType. This
property defines which type of control the style definition targets and
therefore applies to. Defining a Style with only the TargetType property
set will apply to all controls of that type within the scope it is defined. This
is referred to as *implicit styling*.

If you wish to explicitly style a control, you can also add the x:Key property. This is referred to as *explicit styling*. You are then required to set the Style property on any control that wishes to use this explicit style that you have created. You will be creating an explicit style in the "Creating a style" section following shortly.

ApplyToDerivedTypes

By default, styles created explicitly apply to the type defined in the TargetType property I just covered. If you wish to allow derived classes to also inherit this style, you need to set the ApplyToDerivedTypes property to true.

Setter

This is the part that looks and feels quite a bit different to the previous XAML you have written. Since you are not creating controls but defining how they will look, you must follow this syntax. Let's look at the following example:

```
<Style TargetType="Label">
    <Setter Property="TextColor" Value="Black" />
</Style>
```

The above is not a style you would include in an application; however, as an example it allows you to say

The Style for Label controls will set the TextColor property to Black.

Now that you have had a look at some of the key concepts that make up a style in .NET MAUI, let's create your own style for your overlay.

Creating a Style

Let's view this in action by adding the following to the `Styles.xaml` file. Add this just below the existing `<Style TargetType=="Border">` entry.

```xaml
<Style TargetType="Border" x:Key="OverlayBorderStyle">
    <Setter Property="BackgroundColor" Value="White"
/>    <Setter Property="Stroke" Value="{AppThemeBinding
Light={StaticResource Gray200}, Dark={StaticResource
Gray500}}" />
    <Setter Property="StrokeShape" Value="Rectangle"/>
    <Setter Property="StrokeThickness" Value="1"/>
</Style>
```

The above looks very similar to the default `Border` style already defined with the addition of the `BackgroundColor` setter.

It is also worth noting that you only need to set the values that you wish to change from the implicit style. Therefore, your explicit style can be reduced down to

```xaml
<Style TargetType="Border" x:Key="OverlayBorderStyle">
    <Setter Property="BackgroundColor" Value="White" />
</Style>
```

The `Stroke`, `StrokeShape`, and `StrokeThickness` properties will all be inherited from the implicit global style. This provides yet another great way to reduce the amount of code you need to write.

Now you can use this style in your application. Open the `FixedBoardPage.xaml` file and add the following line to your `Border` element (change in **bold**):

```xaml
<Border
    IsVisible="{Binding IsAddingWidget}"
    HorizontalOptions="Center"
```

```
VerticalOptions="Center"
Padding="10"
Style="{StaticResource OverlayBorderStyle}">
```

This will result in your overlay looking far better to the user now because it is no longer transparent. Also, consider moving the HorizontalOptions, VerticalOptions, and Padding properties over to the style definition. Figure 8-2 shows how much better the overlay now looks.

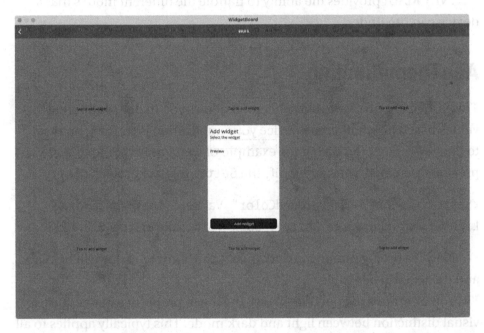

Figure 8-2. *The overlay with a much clearer background*

What you have done here is considered bad practice, though! You have hardcoded the BackgroundColor of your Border control in the style definition so your application will look great on a device running in light mode. However, as soon as the user switches to dark mode, they will have a glaring white border showing.

235

The repercussions of using fixed values can include text or content disappearing entirely from the application. Imagine that the text color switches to white in dark mode, with you having hardcoded to a white background of the overlay view, so the user would see no text on screen. This would result in a terrible user experience.

.NET MAUI provides the ability to handle the different modes that a device can run under.

AppThemeBinding

This is an extremely valuable concept. It allows you to define different values based on whether the device your application is running on is set to light or dark mode. Taking the example of the `OverlayBorderStyle` you previously created, you can modify the `Setter` for `BackgroundColor` to

```
<Setter Property="BackgroundColor" Value="{AppThemeBinding
Light={StaticResource White}, Dark={StaticResource Black}}" />
```

Now if a user is running in dark mode, the border overlay will be black and the text will be visible.

You only need to apply `AppThemeBinding` to properties that require a visual distinction between light and dark mode. This typically applies to all `Brush`/`Color` properties; however, you could conceivably decide to change the `StrokeThickness` of your `Border` control, for example.

Further Reading

It is worth noting that this book is limited to covering the styling options in XAML. However, .NET MAUI does provide support for CSS-based stylesheets. Go to `https://docs.microsoft.com/dotnet/maui/user-interface/styles/css`.

Triggers

.NET MAUI provides a concept called triggers. They enable you to further enhance how your views react to changes in the view model. You are given the ability to define actions that can modify the appearance of the UI based on event or data changes. Triggers provide us with another way of changing the visibility of our border overlay for adding a new widget. The initial work will appear more verbose in the short term but do bear with me - it will result in a much better outcome!

There are a number of different types of triggers that can be attached to a control, each with a varying level of functionality. You will take a brief look at them and then dig into the one that you need for your scenario.

- **Trigger:** A `Trigger` represents a trigger that applies property values, or performs actions, when the specified property meets a specified condition.

- **DataTrigger:** A `DataTrigger` represents a trigger that applies property values, or performs actions, when the bound data meets a specified condition. The Binding markup extension is used to monitor for the specified condition.

- **EventTrigger:** An `EventTrigger` represents a trigger that applies a set of actions in response to an event. Unlike `Trigger`, `EventTrigger` has no concept of termination of state, so the actions will not be undone once the condition that raised the event is no longer true.

- **MultiTrigger:** A `MultiTrigger` represents a trigger that applies property values, or performs actions, when a set of conditions are satisfied. All the conditions must be true before the Setter objects are applied.

Creating a DataTrigger

In this chapter, you have added your overlay Border control and are currently changing its visibility through a binding direct to the IsVisible property. You can write this differently with a DataTrigger. Let's open the FixedBoardPage.xaml file and modify the Border control to the following:

```
<Border
    IsVisible="False"
    HorizontalOptions="Center"
    VerticalOptions="Center"
    Padding="10"
    Style="{StaticResource OverlayBorderStyle}">
    <Border.Triggers>
        <DataTrigger
            TargetType="Border"
            Binding="{Binding IsAddingWidget}"
            Value="True">

            <Setter
                Property="IsVisible"
                Value="True" />

        </DataTrigger>

    </Border.Triggers>
```

Notice that the syntax for a Trigger is very similar to a Style. You will also notice that it looks a lot more verbose than your original simple binding approach. If you simply want to control the IsVisible property of a control, a trigger is overkill, in my opinion. You will not be ending here, though, so bear with me. First, let's break down what you have added and then look to how you can enhance it.

First, you modify the `IsVisible` property binding to `false`. This is the initial state of the visibility of your view.

```
IsVisible="False"
```

Next, you add the `DataTrigger` to the `Border.Triggers` property.

```
<DataTrigger
    TargetType="Border"
    Binding="{Binding IsAddingWidget}"
    Value="True">
```

Much like with styles, you define the type of control the `DataTrigger` applies to. You also set the `Binding` property to bind to the `IsAddingWidget` property on your view model. Finally, you set the `Value` property of `true`. This all means that when the `IsAddingWidget` property value is set to `true`, the contents of the `DataTrigger` will be applied.

This leads you onto the final change, which is the setter.

```
<Setter
    Property="IsVisible"
    Value="True" />
```

To repeat myself, all of this is rather verbose up until you consider that you can define actions that can be performed when your state is entered/exited.

EnterActions and ExitActions

As an alternative to simply defining values for properties to be set when the `IsAddingWidget` property value becomes true, like in your previous example, you can define actions that will be performed when the value enters or exits a specific state. What exactly does this mean? Let's take a look at an example. You can rewrite the trigger usage from the previous example as

```
<DataTrigger
    TargetType="Border"
    Binding="{Binding IsAddingWidget}"
    Value="True">

    <DataTrigger.EnterActions>
        <!--action to perform-->
    </DataTrigger.EnterActions>

    <DataTrigger.ExitActions>
        <!--action to perform-->
    </DataTrigger.ExitActions>

</DataTrigger>
```

Given the above, you can state the following:

When the property (IsAddingWidget) in the Binding enters the state defined in Value (True), the EnterActions will be performed.

When the property (IsAddingWidget) in the Binding exits the state defined in Value (False), the ExitActions will be performed.

You need to define an action to be performed for these scenarios now.

Creating a TriggerAction

.NET MAUI provides the TriggerAction<T> base class that allows you to define an action that will be performed in the enter or exit scenario. This enables you to build a more complex behavior that can be performed when a value changes. When creating a trigger action, you can use the base class TriggerAction<T> provided by .NET MAUI and then you need to override the Invoke method. It is this method that defines what action will be performed when the value changes. Let's create your own action that you can use.

Creating ShowOverlayTriggerAction

First, you need to find a place to locate this action. Create a new folder in the root project called `Triggers` and then add a new class file called `ShowOverlayTriggerAction.cs`. Then you can adding the following code:

```
public class ShowOverlayTriggerAction :
TriggerAction<VisualElement>
{
    public bool ShowOverlay { get; set; }

    protected override void Invoke(VisualElement sender)
    {
        sender.IsVisible = ShowOverlay;
    }
}
```

This code doesn't do too much right now. It will just change the `IsVisible` property of the control it is attached to when the value changes.

Now you need to attach it to your `AddWidgetFrame` control.

Using ShowOverlayTriggerAction

You can now add in the action to perform sections that you left when first adding a `DataTrigger` to your control. Modify your code in the `FixedBoardPage.xaml` file, with the changes in **bold.**

```
<DataTrigger
    TargetType="Border"
    Binding="{Binding IsAddingWidget}"
    Value="True">

    <DataTrigger.EnterActions>
        <triggers:ShowOverlayTriggerAction ShowOverlay="True" />
    </DataTrigger.EnterActions>
```

```
    <DataTrigger.ExitActions>
        <triggers:ShowOverlayTriggerAction ShowOverlay="False" />
    </DataTrigger.ExitActions>

</DataTrigger>
```

This can now be interpreted as, when the IsAddingWidget property value changes to true, a ShowOverlayTriggerAction will be invoked with ShowOverlay set to true. This will result in the AddWidgetFrame control becoming visible. Then, when the IsAddingWidget property value changes to false, a ShowOverlayTriggerAction will be invoked with ShowOverlay set to false. This will result in the AddWidgetFrame control becoming invisible.

It is also worth noting that you can define triggers in styles, meaning this type of functionality can be reused multiple times without having to duplicate the code.

Let's take a break from triggers for now to take a look at how you can animate controls in .NET MAUI. Then you will return and combine triggers and animations together to really show off the power of the action you just created.

Further Reading

You have only scratched the surface on the functionality that can be achieved with triggers. I recommend checking out the Microsoft documentation to see more ways triggers can be useful: https://learn.microsoft.com/dotnet/maui/fundamentals/triggers.

Animations

This feels like it could be a challenging topic to show off in printed form given the dynamic nature of an animation but it is one of my favorite topics so I am going to show it off as best I can. Animations provide you with the building blocks to make your applications feel much more natural and organic.

.NET MAUI provides two main ways to perform an animation against any `VisualElement`. You will take a look at each approach and how some animations can be built using them.

Basic Animations

.NET MAUI ships with a set of prebuilt animations available via extension methods. These methods provide the ability to rotate, translate, scale, and fade a `VisualElement` over a period of time. Each of these methods have a *To* suffix, for example `ScaleTo`. It is worth noting that each of the methods for animating are asynchronous and will therefore need to be awaited if you wish to know when they have finished. The full list of animation methods are as follows:

Method	Description
FadeTo	Animates the `Opacity` property of a `VisualElement`
RelScaleTo	Applies an animated incremental increase or decrease to the `Scale` property of a `VisualElement`
RotateTo	Animates the `Rotation` property of a `VisualElement`
RelRotateTo	Applies an animated incremental increase or decrease to the `Rotation` property of a `VisualElement`
RotateXTo	Animates the `RotationX` property of a `VisualElement`
RotateYTo	Animates the `RotationY` property of a `VisualElement`
ScaleTo	Animates the `Scale` property of a `VisualElement`
ScaleXTo	Animates the `ScaleX` property of a `VisualElement`
ScaleYTo	Animates the `ScaleY` property of a `VisualElement`
TranslateTo	Animates the `TranslationX` and `TranslationY` properties of a `VisualElement`

The overlay view you added in the previous section just shows immediately and disappears immediately based on the IsVisible binding you created. What if you animate your overlay to grow from nothing up to the required size? Don't worry about adding this code to your application just yet. You will look over some examples and then add it to Visual Studio in the "Combining Triggers and Animations" section. The main reason for not adding it immediately is because the animations API relies on direct access to the view-related information, and this breaks the MVVM pattern. However, once you look over how to animate, you can take this learning and add it into your ShowOverlayTriggerAction implementation.

The code to animate a VisualElement is surprisingly small, as you can see in the following example:

```
AddWidgetFrame.Scale = 0;

await AddWidgetFrame.ScaleTo(1, 500);
```

First, you make sure that the AddWidgetFrame has a Scale of 0 and then you call ScaleTo, telling it to grow to a Scale of 1 (which is 100%) over a duration of 500 milliseconds.

All of the prebuilt animation methods apart from the ones that start with *Rel* perform the animation against the VisualElements existing value (e.g., for ScaleTo it will change from the existing Scale property value). This means that it is entirely possible that no animation will take place if both the existing property and the value provided to the method are the same.

Combining Basic Animations

It is entirely possible to combine the basic animations to provide much more complex animations. There are two main ways of achieving this.

Chaining Animations

You can chain animations together into a sequence. A common example here is to provide the appearance of a tile being flipped over and giving a 3D effect to the user. The key detail when chaining animations is that you await each animation method call to make sure that one animation has finished before the next one begins.

```
await frame.RotateXTo(90, 100);

frame.Content.IsVisible = tileViewModel.IsSelected;

await frame.RotateXTo(0, 100);
```

Concurrent Animations

In a similar way to chaining, you can perform multiple animations concurrently by simply not awaiting each method call or alternatively awaiting all of the calls.

```
AddWidgetFrame.Scale = 0;
AddWidgetFrame.IsVisible = true;
AddWidgetFrame.Opacity = 0;

await Task.WhenAll(
    AddWidgetFrame.FadeTo(1),
    AddWidgetFrame.ScaleTo(1, 500));
```

In fact, this animation looks like a very good contender for your actual implementation in the ShowOverlayTriggerAction implementation.

Cancelling Animations

Providing the ability to cancel an animation can be an extremely valuable feature for a user. Quite often in applications, and predominantly games, an animation will show when an action completes. Animations like this if blocking can become tiresome for users especially if the same animation repeats frequently. Therefore, a common pattern to follow is when the user taps on the control being animated, it cancels the animation.

If you wish to cancel an animation, you can call the `CancelAnimations` extension method on the `VisualElement` that you are animating.

```
AddWidgetFrame.CancelAnimations();
```

Easings

Animations in general will move mechanically as a computer changes a value over time. Easings allow you to move away from a linear update of those values in order to provide a much more organic and natural motion. .NET MAUI offers a whole host of prebuilt easings, plus there is even the ability to build your own if you really wish to do so. Let's take a look at the options that .NET MAUI provides out of the box:

Easing function	Description
BounceIn	Bounces the animation at the beginning
BounceOut	Bounces the animation at the end
CubicIn	Slowly accelerates the animation
CubicInOut	Accelerates the animation at the beginning and decelerates the animation at the end
CubicOut	Quickly decelerates the animation
Linear	Uses a constant velocity and is the default easing function

Easing function	Description
SinIn	Smoothly accelerates the animation
SinInOut	Smoothly accelerates the animation at the beginning and smoothly decelerates the animation at the end
SinOut	Smoothly decelerates the animation
SpringIn	Causes the animation to very quickly accelerate towards the end
SpringOut	Causes the animation to quickly decelerate towards the end

As a general guide, an easing ending with the *In* suffix will start the animation slowly and speed up as it comes to a finish. An easing ending with the *Out* suffix will start off quickly and slow down towards the end.

Complex Animations

.NET MAUI provides the Animation class. This enables you to define complex animation sequences. In fact, the prebuilt animations that you covered in the "Basic Animations" section are built using this class inside the .NET MAUI code. Using this class, it is possible to animate any visual property of a VisualElement; for example, you can animate a change in BackgroundColor or TextColor.

The Animation class provides the ability to define simple animations through to really quite complex animations. Take a quick look at how the ScaleTo animation can be implemented to understand what the class offers.

Recreating the ScaleTo Animation

You can also animate the scale of your AddWidgetFrame control with the following:

```
public void ScaleTo()
```

```
{
    var animation = new Animation(v => AddWidgetFrame.Scale =
    v, 0, 1);

    animation.Commit(AddWidgetFrame, "ScaleTo");
}
```

When creating an instance of the `Animation` class, you provide the following parameter:

```
v => AddWidgetFrame.Scale = v
```

This is the `callback` parameter and it allows you to define what property is set during the animation.

The next parameter is `start`. This is the starting value that will be passed into the callback lambda you defined in the first parameter. In your example, you set it to 0, meaning the `AddWidgetFrame` control will not be visible because it has a scale of 0.

The final parameter you pass in is `end`. This is the resulting value that will be passed into the callback lambda.

The animation will only begin when you call the `Commit` method. This method also allows you to define how long it should take as well as how often to call the callback parameter you defined.

```
animation.Commit(AddWidgetFrame, "ScaleTo", length: 2000);
```

This code shows the simplest type of animation you can create within .NET MAUI. It is entirely possible to create much more complex animations. To achieve this, you need to create an animation and then add child animations in order to define the changes for each property and different sequences in the animation.

Creating a Rubber Band Animation

As an example on how to build a complex animation, I would like to show you one of my favorite animations, the rubber band animation. This animation simulates the VisualElement being pulled horizontally, letting go, and then bouncing back to its original shape just like a rubber band would. Figure 8-3 shows what it would look like, albeit in motion.

Widget Board

Widget Board

Widget Board

Widget Board

Widget Board

Widget Board

Widget Board

Figure 8-3. *The distinguishing frames from the animation you will be building*

Let's build the animation with the Animation class using the understanding you gained in the previous section.

```
public void Rubberband(VisualElement view)
{
    var animation = new Animation();

    animation.Add(0.00, 0.30, new Animation(v =>
    view.ScaleX = v, 1.00, 1.25));
    animation.Add(0.00, 0.30, new Animation(v =>
    view.ScaleY = v, 1.00, 0.75));
```

```
animation.Add(0.30, 0.40, new Animation(v =>
view.ScaleX = v, 1.25, 0.75));
animation.Add(0.30, 0.40, new Animation(v =>
view.ScaleY = v, 0.75, 1.25));

animation.Add(0.40, 0.50, new Animation(v =>
view.ScaleX = v, 0.75, 1.15));
animation.Add(0.40, 0.50, new Animation(v =>
view.ScaleY = v, 1.25, 0.85));

animation.Add(0.50, 0.65, new Animation(v =>
view.ScaleX = v, 1.15, 0.95));
animation.Add(0.50, 0.65, new Animation(v =>
view.ScaleY = v, 0.85, 1.05));

animation.Add(0.65, 0.75, new Animation(v =>
view.ScaleX = v, 0.95, 1.05));
animation.Add(0.65, 0.75, new Animation(v =>
view.ScaleY = v, 1.05, 0.95));

animation.Add(0.75, 1.00, new Animation(v =>
view.ScaleX = v, 1.05, 1.00));
animation.Add(0.75, 1.00, new Animation(v =>
view.ScaleY = v, 0.95, 1.00));

animation.Commit(view, "RubberbandAnimation",
length: 2000);
}
```

Yes, I know this looks quite different to the previous animation you built. Let's deconstruct the parts that feel unfamiliar.

```
animation.Add(0.00, 0.30, new Animation(v => view.ScaleX = v,
1.00, 1.25));
animation.Add(0.00, 0.30, new Animation(v => view.ScaleY = v,
1.00, 0.75));
```

The two lines above define the first transition in your animation. You see that the ScaleX property will change from 1.00 (100%) to 1.25 (125%) and the ScaleY property will change from 1.00 (100%) to 0.75% (75%) of the control's current size. This provides the appearance that the view is being stretched. The key new part for you is the use of the Add method and the first two parameters. This allows you to add the animation defined as the third parameter as a child of the animation it is being added to. The result is that when you Commit the main animation, all of the child animations will be executed based on the sequence you defined in these two first parameters. Let's cover what these parameters mean.

The first parameter is the beginAt parameter. This determines when the child animation being added will begin during the overall animation sequence. So, in the example of your first line, you define 0.00, meaning it will begin as soon as the animation starts.

The second parameter is the finishAt parameter. This determines when the child being added will finish during the overall animation sequence. So, in the example of your first line, you define 0.30, meaning it will end 30% into the animation sequence.

Both the beginAt and finishAt parameters should be supplied as a value between 0 and 1 and considered a percentage in the overall animation sequence. You will also notice that I tend to include the decimal places even when they are 0; this really makes it easier to read the animation sequence as it ensures that all of the code is indented in the same way.

Finally, you call the Commit method as before to begin the animation sequence.

Now that you have covered building animations and some possible examples of using them, let's combine them with your trigger knowledge to really make your AddWidgetFrame look great when it becomes visible.

Combining Triggers and Animations

Animations are a really powerful tool but they require view knowledge. This is where having the ability to trigger them from a trigger allows you to keep with the MVVM approach and keep your view and view model cleanly separated.

Now that you have covered how to apply an animation to your overlay view and looked at separating view from view model through the use of triggers, you can combine the two together to trigger the animation and keep the separation.

Let's return to the ShowOverlayTriggerAction.cs file and add in the animation from the "Concurrent animations" section (changes are in **bold**).

```
namespace WidgetBoard.Triggers;

public class ShowOverlayTriggerAction :
TriggerAction<VisualElement>
{
    public bool ShowOverlay { get; set; }

    protected async override void Invoke(VisualElement sender)
    {
        if (ShowOverlay)
        {
            sender.Scale = 0;
            sender.IsVisible = true;
            sender.Opacity = 0;
```

```
        await Task.WhenAll(
            sender.FadeTo(1),
            sender.ScaleTo(1, 500, Easing.SpringOut));
    }
    else
    {
        await sender.ScaleTo(0, 500, Easing.SpringIn);

        sender.Opacity = 0;

        sender.IsVisible = false;
    }
    }
}
```

The trigger action now provides two key visual changes when the ShowOverlay property value changes. When the property becomes true, the AddWidgetFrame control will both fade in over 250ms and scale up from 0 to 1 over 500ms. You also make use of the Easing.SpringOut option to give a slightly more fluid feel to the changes in the animation.

When ShowOverlay becomes false, you just reverse the scale animation to show it shrink. Once the animation has completed, you then make sure that the control is no longer visible.

This concludes the sections on triggers and animations. You have seen how they can help to both simplify the views and view models you create while at the same time provide some really great functionality to make your applications feel alive. I would recommend taking the application for a spin and observing the animations in action, sadly we can't show that functionality off in printed form.

Summary

In this chapter, you have

- Provided the ability to add a widget to a board

- Covered the different options available when showing an overlay

- Explored how you can define styling information for your application

- Learned how to handle devices running in light and dark modes

- Learned how to apply triggers to enhance your UI

- Covered how to animate parts of your application

- Explored what happens when you combine triggers and animations

In the next chapter, you will

- Learn about the different types of local data.

- Discover what .NET MAUI offers in terms of local file storage locations and when to use each one.

- Gain an understanding of database technologies and apply two different options.

- Modify your application to save and load the boards your users create.

- Gain an understanding of the options for storing small bits of data or preferences.

- Add the ability to record the last opened board.

- Gain an understanding of the options for storing small bits of data securely or SecureStorage.

Source Code

The resulting source code for this chapter can be found on the GitHub repository at https://github.com/Apress/Introducing-MAUI/tree/main/ch08.

Extra Assignment

I think you can take these animations to another level and really make your application feel alive! Try the following possible extensions!

Animate the BoxView Overlay

You've added an animation to present your Border with the widget selection details inside. A nice further enhancement on this would be to also animate the BoxView that you are using as your semi-transparent overlay. I personally think a nice FadeTo animation would work well but I would love to hear what works best for you.

Animate the New Widget

To really make the application feel alive, you could consider animating each widget as it is added onto the board. You have the Widgets_ChildAdded method inside your BoardLayout.xaml.cs file where you set the Position. You could consider expanding this method implementation to also animate the new widget. Perhaps you could make the new widget scale up similar to how your Border presents.

PART III

Behind the Scenes

CHAPTER 9

Local Data

In this chapter, you will learn about the different types of local data, what they are best used for, and how to apply them in your application. The options will include understanding when and where to store data that needs to be kept secure.

You will modify your application to store the boards that your user creates so that they can be displayed in the slide-out menu and also be opened. You will also record the last opened board so that when returning to the application this board will be presented to the user.

What Is Local Data?

When building an application, whether it is targeted for a single or multiple platforms, you will very likely need to store some data about the state of the application. The types of data you will need to store can vary between storing "simple" settings, caching files/data, or even storing a full set of data inside a local database. These types of data are called *local data* since they live on the device that your application is running on. Data that comes from a remote endpoint is called *remote data* and this will be covered in Chapter 10.

.NET MAUI provides multiple options when you want to store data locally on a device. Each option is better suited to a specific purpose and size of data. Here is a brief overview of those options:

© Shaun Lawrence 2023
S. Lawrence, *Introducing .NET MAUI*, https://doi.org/10.1007/978-1-4842-9234-1_9

- **File system**: Stores loose files directly on the device through file system access

- **Database**: Stores data in a file optimized for access

- **Preferences**: Stores data in key-value pairs

- **Secure storage**: Stores data in key-value pairs like preferences but stores them in a secure location on the device

File System

.NET MAUI provides some helpful abstractions over the multiple platforms that it supports. One such abstraction is the `FileSystem` helper class. It comes from the old Xamarin.Essentials library and now is a core part of .NET MAUI. It allows you to obtain useful bits of information to help with common tasks involving the file system.

Let's take a look at the properties the `FileSystem` class offers you as it helps to know when they should be used and for what type of data.

Cache Directory

You have no need to cache anything as part of the application we're building in this book; however, I feel this is a valuable piece of information to mention. This property enables you to get the most appropriate location to store cache data. You can store any type of data in this directory. Typically you store it when you want to persist it longer than just holding it in memory. Your application should not rely on this data to function because the operating system can and will clear this storage down.

App Data Directory

The AppDataDirectory property provides the app's top-level directory for storing any files. These files are backed up with the operating system syncing framework.

This property is precisely what you are going to need to use when creating and opening your database files in the next section. So, let's set up the bits that you will need.

The FileSystem helper class provides a set of static properties, meaning you can simply write

```
var appDataDirectory = FileSystem.AppDataDirectory;
```

However, as you have discovered already in this book, it does not lend itself well to unit testing. Instead, you can rely on the IFileSystem interface and register the .NET MAUI implementation with your app builder. Let's open up your MauiProgram.cs file and add the following line into the CreateMauiApp method:

```
builder.Services.AddSingleton(FileSystem.Current);
```

This will register the FileSystem.Current property as the IFileSystem interface so whenever you state that your classes depend on IFileSystem, they will be provided with the FileSystem.Current instance.

Now that you have covered FileSystem and are ready to create your database files, you can learn about database access in .NET MAUI.

Database

A database is a collection of data that is organized. In a database, data is organized or structured into tables consisting of rows and columns. Databases are a much better approach than storing data in files. The ability to index the data makes it easier to query and manipulate. There are different kinds of databases, ranging from relational databases to distributed databases, cloud databases, and NoSQL databases. In this chapter, you will focus on relational and NoSQL databases.

Every application I have ever built has required some form of database, and I suspect that most of the applications that you will build will also require one. A database really provides value when you need to link data together or filter and sort the data in an efficient manner.

In your application, you are going to provide the ability to save a board and return a list of boards that the user has created. To abstract this slightly, you will be using the repository pattern. You will also provide the ability to store where the widgets have been placed so that they will be remembered when a user loads the board back up. Figure 9-1 shows the entity relationship diagram for the database you will be creating.

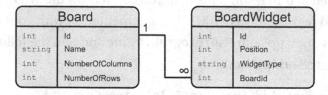

Figure 9-1. *The entity relationship diagram of your database models*

Repository Pattern

The repository pattern allows you to hide all the logic that deals with creating, reading, updating, and deleting (also known as CRUD) entities within your application. By using this pattern, it allows you to keep all the knowledge around how entities are loaded, saved, and more in a single place. This has the added benefit that if you want to completely change where your data is loaded from, you only need to change the implementation inside the repository. It also allows you to provide mock implementations when wanting to perform things like unit testing and you don't want to have to rely on an actual database existing.

Let's add a new folder called Data and then add an interface for your repository to that folder called IBoardRepository. Change the code to look as follows:

```
using WidgetBoard.Models;

namespace WidgetBoard.Data;

public interface IBoardRepository
{
    void CreateBoard(Board board);

    void CreateBoardWidget(BoardWidget boardWidget);

    void DeleteBoard(Board board);

    IReadOnlyList<Board> ListBoards();

    Board LoadBoard(int boardId);

    void UpdateBoard(Board board);
}
```

Now that you have defined your interface, you can update your application's codebase to use this interface when loading and saving your boards.

Creating a Board

The first place to update is your BoardDetailsPageViewModel class, which provides support for creating a new board. Open up the class and make the following modifications.

Add a new IBoardRepository field.

```
private readonly IBoardRepository boardRepository;
```

Assign a valid instance to the boardRepository field; the modifications are in **bold.**

```
public BoardDetailsPageViewModel(
    ISemanticScreenReader semanticScreenReader,
    IBoardRepository boardRepository)
{
    this.semanticScreenReader = semanticScreenReader;
    this.boardRepository = boardRepository;

    SaveCommand = new Command(
        () => Save(),
        () => !string.IsNullOrWhiteSpace(BoardName));
}
```

Use the boardRepository field when saving; the modifications are in **bold.**

```
private async void Save()
{
    var board = new Board
    {
        Name = BoardName,
        NumberOfColumns = NumberOfColumns,
        NumberOfRows = NumberOfRows
    };

    this.boardRepository.CreateBoard(board);

    semanticScreenReader.Announce($"A new board with the name
    {BoardName} was created successfully.");

    await Shell.Current.GoToAsync(
        "fixedboard",
```

```
new Dictionary<string, object>
{
    { "Board", board}
});
}
```

Listing Your Boards

In the previous chapters, you just added a fixed board and added it to the
Boards collection in your `AppShellViewModel` class. Now you are going to
modify it so that it can be populated by the boards the user creates and you
store in the database. Open the `AppShellViewModel.cs` file and make the
following changes.

Add a field for your `IBoardRepository`.

```
private readonly IBoardRepository boardRepository;
```

Modify your constructor to use the `IBoardRepository` as a
dependency.

```
public AppShellViewModel(
    IBoardRepository boardRepository)
{
    this.boardRepository = boardRepository;
}
```

Load the list of boards and populate your collection.

```
public void LoadBoards()
{
    var boards = this.boardRepository.ListBoards();

    foreach (var board in boards)
    {
```

```
      Boards.Add(board);
   }
}
```

There is a further change that you need to make in order to allow your AppShellViewModel class to actually load the board. You need to hook into some of the lifecycle events that apply to Pages in .NET MAUI. AppShell inherits from Page, which means you get full access to those lifecycle events. The specific event you care about now is the OnAppearing event. It is called when your page is displayed on screen.

The OnAppearing method can be called multiple times during the lifetime of the page, so it is recommended to make your method idempotent or check whether it has been called before in order to prevent odd behavior when called a second time.

OnAppearing is a great choice for your scenario because it will result in your code being executed every time the view appears; this can be every time your flyout menu is opened. This provides you with the ability to refresh your list of boards every time the user opens the flyout menu. The main reason it is fine for your scenario is because you will be loading data from a local database with a limited number of boards to load, so it will be pretty quick. In scenarios where you are loading from an external webservice, it can take much more time to perform it and therefore you may wish to maintain some level of caching and prevent calling the webservice every time the view appears. A better option under this scenario and probably most typical scenarios in .NET MAUI applications is to use the OnNavigatedTo method.

Let's open your AppShell.xaml.cs file and make use of this lifecycle method.

```
protected override void OnAppearing()
```

```
{
    base.OnAppearing();

    ((AppShellViewModel)BindingContext).LoadBoards();
}
```

When the method gets called, you use the newly added `LoadBoards` method on your view model. The main reason you hook into this lifecycle event is when you eventually try to navigate to the last used board in the `LoadBoards` method, you need to make sure the application has started rendering; otherwise the navigation will fail.

Loading a Board

Up until this point you have relied on passing the `Board` into the `FixedBoardPageViewModel` and displaying the details of that. The loading process would become rather inefficient if you were to load all boards and the associated `BoardWidgets` when listing all boards in the system, so you need to do this in a two-step process: first, list the boards as you did in the previous section and, second, load the board in the view model. This will be a slightly involved process so let's walk through it step-by-step. Open the `FixedBoardPageViewModel.cs` file and make the following changes

Add the following fields to store the board that is loaded and the repository to perform the load:

```
private Board board;
private readonly IBoardRepository boardRepository;
```

In your constructor, add the board repository dependency and assign to the newly created field. Changes are in **bold.**

```
public FixedBoardPageViewModel(
    WidgetTemplateSelector widgetTemplateSelector,
    WidgetFactory widgetFactory,
```

```
    IBoardRepository boardRepository)
{

    WidgetTemplateSelector = widgetTemplateSelector;
    this.widgetFactory = widgetFactory;
    this.boardRepository = boardRepository;

    Widgets = new ObservableCollection<IWidgetViewModel>();

    AddWidgetCommand = new Command(OnAddWidget);

    AddNewWidgetCommand = new Command<int>(index =>
    {
        IsAddingWidget = true;
        addingPosition = index;
    });
}
```

Now let's load the Board inside your ApplyQueryAttributes method. The changes are in **bold.**

```
public void ApplyQueryAttributes(IDictionary<string,
object> query)
{
    var boardParameter = query["Board"] as Board;

    board = boardRepository.LoadBoard(boardParameter.Id);

    BoardName = board.Name;
    NumberOfColumns = board.NumberOfColumns;
    NumberOfRows = board.NumberOfRows;

    foreach (var boardWidget in board.BoardWidgets)
    {
```

```
    var widgetViewModel = widgetFactory.CreateWidgetViewMod
    el(boardWidget.WidgetType);

    widgetViewModel.Position = boardWidget.Position;

    Widgets.Add(widgetViewModel);
  }
}
```

Next, add the ability to save a widget's position on the board.

```
private void SaveWidget(IWidgetViewModel widgetViewModel)
{
    var boardWidget = new BoardWidget
    {
        BoardId = board.Id,
        Position = widgetViewModel.Position,
        WidgetType = widgetViewModel.Type
    };

    boardRepository.CreateBoardWidget(boardWidget);
}
```

The above method will create a new BoardWidget model class and save it into the database for you.

Finally, you need to call the SaveWidget method. For the purpose of your application, you are going to provide an auto save feature, so each time a widget is added to the board, you will save it immediately to the database. In order to achieve this, you just need to add the **bold** line into your AddWidget method.

```
private void OnAddWidget()
{
    if (SelectedWidget is null)
```

```
{
    return;
}
var widgetViewModel = widgetFactory.CreateWidgetViewModel(S
electedWidget);

widgetViewModel.Position = addingPosition;

Widgets.Add(widgetViewModel);

SaveWidget(widgetViewModel);

IsAddingWidget = false;
}
```

You can't run your code yet because you don't have an implementation of your IBoardRepository interface so let's look at two different database options that will allow you to provide an implementation for your IBoardRepository.

SQLite

SQLite is a lightweight cross-platform database that has become the go-to option for providing database support in mobile applications. The database is stored locally in a single file on the device's file system.

SQLite is supported natively by Android and iOS; however, they require access via C++. There are several C# wrappers around the native SQLite engine that .NET developers can use. The most popular choice is the C# wrapper called SQLite-net.

Installing SQLite-net

In order to install and use Sqlite-net, you need to install the NuGet package called *Sqlite-net-pcl*. You may notice the extra *-pcl* suffix in the NuGet package name and find this confusing. This is an artifact of an old piece of technology used in Xamarin.Forms applications. The name has been retained but don't worry; this is the correct package for adding to a .NET MAUI project.

You can do this by following these steps.

1. Right-click the WidgetBoard project.

2. Click **Manage NuGet Packages**.

3. In the Search field, enter *Sqlite-net-pcl*.

4. Select the **Sqlite-net-pcl package** and select **Add Package**.

5. A confirmation dialog will show. Review and accept the license details if you are happy.

6. Repeat the above steps for the following packages:

   a. SQLitePCLRaw.bundle_green

   b. SQLitePCLRaw.provider.dynamic_cdecl

   c. SQLitePCLRaw.provider.sqlite3

Using Sqlite-net

The first step is to create your IBoardRepository implementation. Add a new class file called SqliteBoardRepository in your Data folder, and make it implement your IBoardRepository interface.

```
using SQLite;
using WidgetBoard.Models;
```

271

```
namespace WidgetBoard.Data;

public class SqliteBoardRepository : IBoardRepository
{
    public void CreateBoard(Board board)
    {
        throw new NotImplementedException();
    }

    public void CreateBoardWidget(BoardWidget boardWidget)
    {
        throw new NotImplementedException();
    }

    public void DeleteBoard(Board board)
    {
        throw new NotImplementedException();
    }

    public IReadOnlyList<Board> ListBoards()
    {
        throw new NotImplementedException();
    }

    public Board LoadBoard(int boardId)
    {
        throw new NotImplementedException();
    }

    public void UpdateBoard(Board board)
    {
        throw new NotImplementedException();
    }
}
```

You also need to register your implementation with the app builder in MauiProgram.cs. You can add the following line

```
builder.Services.AddTransient<IBoardRepository,
SqliteBoardRepository>();
```

Connecting to an SQLite database

As mentioned, an SQLite database is contained within a single file, so when connecting to the database you need to provide the path to that file. You can do this through the SqliteConnection class. Note that if you wish to make use of async/await, you can use the SqliteAsyncConnection class.

Let's edit your repository class to support opening a connection to your database.

Add a field for the database connection.

```
private readonly SQLiteConnection database;
```

Add a constructor to open the connection.

```
public SqliteBoardRepository(IFileSystem fileSystem)
{
    var dbPath = Path.Combine(fileSystem.AppDataDirectory,
    "widgetboard_sqlite.db");

    database = new SQLiteConnection(dbPath);
}
```

Here you make use of the IFileSystem implementation you registered in the previous section. Then you make use of it to determine where to store your database file. Finally, you open a connection using the path to your database file. Note that if the file does not exist, one will be created for you.

Mapping Your Models

Sqlite-net provides the ability to define mapping information in your model classes that will ultimately be used to create your table definition automatically for you. There is a rich set of options ranging from setting a PrimaryKey through to defining if a column has a MaxLength or even if it needs to be Unique. Open your Board.cs file and make the following modifications in **bold**:

using SQLite;

namespace WidgetBoard.Models;

public class Board
{
    [PrimaryKey, AutoIncrement]
    public int Id { get; set; }

    public string Name { get; init; }

    public int NumberOfColumns { get; init; }

    public int NumberOfRows { get; init; }
}

You add a new Id column, marking it as the PrimaryKey, and state that it will AutoIncrement, meaning that Sqlite will manage the id generation for you.

Your second model class is in the BoardWidget.cs file. This represents each widget that is placed on the board and where it is positioned.

using SQLite;

namespace WidgetBoard.Models;

```
public class BoardWidget
{
    [PrimaryKey, AutoIncrement]
    public int Id { get; set; }

    public int BoardId { get; set; }

    public int Position { get; set; }

    public string WidgetType { get; set; }
}
```

Creating Your Tables

You can inform the Sqlite-net connection to create a table for you. This can be done by calling the CreateTable<T> method and passing the appropriate model type. Note that CreateTable is idempotent, so unless you change your model, calling CreateTable a second time will have no impact. You can modify your SqliteBoardRepository to call the CreateTable method in its constructor as follows; changes in **bold**.

```
public SqliteBoardRepository(IFileSystem fileSystem)
{
    var dbPath = Path.Combine(fileSystem.AppDataDirectory,
    "widgetboard_sqlite.db");

    connection = new SQLiteConnection(dbPath);
    connection.CreateTable<Board>();
    connection.CreateTable<BoardWidget>();
}
```

Inserting into an SQLite Database

You can now add in the ability to insert a board into your database by supplying the following implementation into the CreateBoard method:

```
public void CreateBoard(Board board)
{
    connection.Insert(board);
}
```

Reading a Collection from an SQLite Database

You only need to return a list of the boards your user has created in the application.

```
public IReadOnlyList<Board> ListBoards()
{
    return connection.Table<Board>()
        .ToList();
}
```

Perhaps you should consider sorting these boards alphabetically. Sqlite-net offers a rich set of functionality when querying data in the database. You can make use of LINQ-based expressions, which gives you the following (the addition in **bold**):

```
public IReadOnlyList<Board> ListBoards()
{
    return connection.Table<Board>()
        .OrderBy(b => b.Name)
        .ToList();
}
```

Reading a Single Entity from an SQLite Database

When reading a Board from the database, you also need to load any
BoardWidgets that relate to it. For this you can write the following:

```
public Board LoadBoard(int boardId)
{
    var board = connection.Find<Board>(boardId);

    if (board is null)
    {
        return null;
    }

    var widgets = connection.Table<BoardWidget>().Where(w =>
    w.BoardId == boardId).ToList();

    board.BoardWidgets = widgets;

    return board;
}
```

The first line calling Find allows you to find an entity with the supplied
primary key value. This retrieves the Board. Next, you need to retrieve the
collection of BoardWidgets. This is performed in a very similar manner
to loading your collection of Boards. Finally, you assign the widgets you
loaded into the board before returning it to the caller.

It is worth noting that the *sqlite-net-pcl* package does not provide more
complex querying operations such as joins. If this is something that you
still require, it is possible to write the SQL directly and execute against
the connection. If you wish to join your Board and BoardWidget tables
together, you can achieve this as follows:

```
var board = connection.Query<Board>("SELECT B.* FROM Board B
JOIN BoardWidget BW ON BW.BoardId = B.BoardId WHERE B.BoardId =
?", boardId);
```

Note that the above query is purely aimed at showing how joins work, it does not provide you with any particularly useful in the context of your application.

Deleting from an SQLite Database

While I haven't focused on providing this functionality just yet, it is a very common use case.

```
public void DeleteBoard(Board board)
{
    connection.Delete(board);
}
```

Updating an Entity in an SQLite Database

While I haven't focused on providing this functionality just yet, it is a very common use case.

```
public void UpdateBoard(Board board)
{
    connection.Update(board);
}
```

LiteDB

LiteDB is a simple, fast, and lightweight embedded .NET document database. LiteDB was inspired by the MongoDB database and its API is very similar to the official MongoDB .NET API.

Installing LiteDB

In order to install and use LiteDB, you need to install the NuGet package called *LiteDB*. Don't worry; it is perfectly fine to install both the LiteDB and SQLite packages side by side into your project. In fact, that is precisely what you will do here.

You can do this by following these steps.

1.   Right-click the WidgetBoard project.

2.   Click **Manage NuGet Packages**.

3.   In the Search field, enter *LiteDB*.

4.   Select the **LiteDB package** and select **Add Package.**

5.   A confirmation dialog will show. Review and accept the license details if you are happy.

Using LiteDB

The first step is to create your IBoardRepository implementation. Add a new class file called LiteDBBoardRepository in your Data folder, and make it implement your IBoardRepository interface.

```
using LiteDB;
using WidgetBoard.Models;

namespace WidgetBoard.Data;

public class LiteDBBoardRepository : IBoardRepository
{
    public void CreateBoard(Board board)
    {
        throw new NotImplementedException();
    }
```

```
public void CreateBoardWidget(BoardWidget boardWidget)
{
    throw new NotImplementedException();
}
public void DeleteBoard(Board board)
{
    throw new NotImplementedException();
}

public IReadOnlyList<Board> ListBoards()
{
    throw new NotImplementedException();
}

public Board LoadBoard(int boardId)
{
    throw new NotImplementedException();
}

public void UpdateBoard(Board board)
{
    throw new NotImplementedException();
}
}
```

You also need to register your implementation with the app builder in MauiProgram.cs. You can add the following line. Just make sure that you have removed or commented out the line to register the SqliteBoardRepository implementation.

```
builder.Services.AddTransient<IBoardRepository,
LiteDBBoardRepository>();
```

Connecting to a LiteDB database

LiteDB stores all its data in a single file on disk, so your first task is to specify where this file exists so that you can create and open the file for users within your application. For this part, you will borrow a concept from a little further ahead in this chapter (the "File System" section).

Edit your repository class to support opening a connection to your database.

Add a field to hold the database access details.

```
private readonly LiteDatabase database;
```

Add a constructor to open the connection.

```
public LiteDBBoardRepository(IFileSystem fileSystem)
{
    var dbPath = Path.Combine(fileSystem.AppDataDirectory,
    "widgetboard_litedb.db");

    database = new LiteDatabase(dbPath);
}
```

The above should look very similar to the Sqlite way of accessing the database. Here you make use of the IFileSystem implementation you registered in the previous section. Then you make use of that to determine where to store your database file. Finally, you open a connection using the path to your database file. Note that if the file does not exist, one will be created for you.

Mapping Your Models

First, you need to add a field to hold a collection of boards and one for the collection of board widgets

```
private readonly ILiteCollection<Board> boardCollection;
```

```
private readonly ILiteCollection<BoardWidget>
boardWidgetCollection;
```

Then you need to get access to that collection in order to allow you to perform your operations against it.

```
boardCollection = database.GetCollection<Board>("Boards");
boardCollection = database.GetCollection<BoardWidget>("Board
Widgets");
```

The final part of your mapping setup is to define indexing information about your model. For this you use the EnsureIndex method.

```
boardCollection.EnsureIndex(b => b.Id, true);
```

In LiteDB, any property that you wish to be unique or want to query against needs to have a definition provided through the EnsureIndex method.

Creating Your Tables

You don't actually need to do anything to create your tables here. The key difference between LiteDB and other databases that you might use is that the schema of the data is held with the data.

Inserting into a LiteDB Database

You can now add in the ability to insert a board into your database by supplying the following implementation into the CreateBoard method:

```
public void CreateBoard(Board board)
{
    boardCollection.Insert(board);
}
```

Reading a Collection from a LiteDB Database

You only need to return a list of the boards your user created in the application.

```
public IReadOnlyList<Board> ListBoards()
{
    return boardCollection.Query()
        .ToList();
}
```

Perhaps you should consider sorting these boards alphabetically. LiteDB offers a similar set of functionality that you looked at with Sqlite-net. LINQ-based expressions can be used to order your boards, which gives you the following (the addition is in **bold**):

```
public IReadOnlyList<Board> ListBoards()
{
    return connection.Table<Board>()
        .OrderBy(b => b.Name)
        .ToList();
}
```

You also need to add the following line to your constructor to make sure querying is possible:

```
boardCollection.EnsureIndex(b => b.Name, false);
```

Reading a Single Entity from a LiteDB Database

When reading a Board from the database, you also need to load any BoardWidgets that relate to it. For this you can write the following:

```
public Board LoadBoard(int boardId)
{
```

```
var board = boardCollection.FindById(boardId);
var boardWidgets = boardWidgetCollection.Find(w =>
w.BoardId == boardId).ToList();

board.BoardWidgets = boardWidgets;

return board;
}
```

The first line calls FindById, which allows you to find an entity with
the supplied primary key value. This retrieves the Board. Next, you need
to retrieve the collection of BoardWidgets. This is performed in a very
similar manner to loading your collection of Boards. Finally, you assign the
widgets you loaded into the board before returning it to the caller.

Deleting from a LiteDB Database

While I haven't focused on providing this functionality, it is a very common
use case.

```
public void DeleteBoard(Board board)
{
    boardCollection.Delete(board.Id);
}
```

Updating an Entity in a LiteDB Database

While I haven't focused on providing this functionality, it is a very common
use case.

```
public void UpdateBoard(Board board)
{
    boardCollection.Update(board);
}
```

Database Summary

There is an abundance of options when it comes to choosing not only which database but then also the ORM layer on top of it. The aim of this section is to give a taste of what some options offer and to encourage you to decide which will benefit your application and team most.

Both options I covered provide support for encryption.

I strongly encourage you to evaluate which database will provide you with the best development experience and the users of your application with the best user experience. Some databases perform better in different scenarios.

Moving forward with this application you will continue to use LiteDB.

Application Settings (Preferences)

Quite often you will want to persist data about your application that you really do not need a database for. I like to refer to these bits of data as application settings. If you have previous experience with building .NET applications, this would be similar to an `app.config` or `appsettings.json` file. The .NET MAUI term is *Preferences*, though, and this is the API that you will look at accessing.

An item in Preferences is stored as a key-value pair. The key is a string and it is recommended to keep the name short in length.

As with all of the other APIs provided by .NET MAUI, you register the Preferences implementation with the app builder in the `MauiProgram.cs` file. You can add the following line into the `CreateMauiApp` method:

```
builder.Services.AddSingleton(Preferences.Default);
```

What Can Be Stored in Preferences?

There is a limitation on the type of data that can be stored in Preferences. The API provides the ability to store the following .NET types:

- Boolean
- Double
- Int32
- Single
- Int64
- String
- DateTime

Having the ability to provide a String value surely means you could in theory store anything in there, right? While this is technically possible it is highly recommended that you only store small amounts of text. Otherwise the performance of storing and retrieval can be impacted in your applications.

Setting a Value in Preferences

You can store a value in Preferences through the use of the Set method. You can provide a key, the value, and also an optional sharedName. The preferences stored in your application are only visible to that application. You can also create a shared preference that can be used by other extensions or a watch application.

A perfect use case for your application is to store the id of the last accessed board and open it the next time the application loads. Let's store the id initially. Inside your FixedBoardPageViewModel class you can make the following changes.

Add the preferences field.

```
private readonly IPreferences preferences;
```

Update the constructor to set the preferences field; changes in **bold.**

```
public FixedBoardPageViewModel(
    WidgetTemplateSelector widgetTemplateSelector,
    IPreferences preferences)
{
    WidgetTemplateSelector = widgetTemplateSelector;
    this.preferences = preferences;

    Widgets = new ObservableCollection<IWidgetViewModel>();
}
```

Finally, record the id of the board that was supplied when navigating to the page. You can do this by adding the **bold** line to your ApplyQueryAttributes method:

```
public void ApplyQueryAttributes(IDictionary<string,
object> query)
{
    var board = query["Board"] as Board;

    preferences.Set("LastUsedBoardId", board.Id);

    BoardName = board.Name;
    NumberOfColumns = board.NumberOfColumns;
    NumberOfRows = board.NumberOfRows;
}
```

This means that every time a user opens a board to view it, the id will be remembered in Preferences. When the application is opened again in the future, it will use that id to open the last viewed board.

A possible alternative way of achieving this type of functionality could be to maintain a last opened column in the database and always find the latest of that set.

Getting a Value in Preferences

You can retrieve a value from Preferences using the Get method. You are required to supply the key identifying the setting and a default value to be returned if the key does not exist. You can optionally provide a sharedName, much like with the Set method covered in the previous section.

You have already written the code to store your LastUsedBoardId in Preferences so let's read it back when loading your boards up to display. Open up your AppShellViewModel.cs file and make the following changes

Add the preferences field.

```
private readonly IPreferences preferences;
```

Set the preferences field in the constructor; changes in **bold**.

```
public AppShellViewModel(
    IBoardRepository boardRepository,
    IPreferences preferences)
{
    this.boardRepository = boardRepository;
    this.preferences = preferences;
}
```

Update your LoadBoards method to support navigating to the last used board; changes in **bold.**

```
public void LoadBoards()
{
    var boards = this.boardRepository.ListBoards();
```

```
var lastUsedBoardId = preferences.
Get("LastUsedBoardId", -1);
Board lastUsedBoard = null;

foreach (var board in boards)
{
    Boards.Add(board);

    if (lastUsedBoardId == board.Id)
    {
        lastUsedBoard = board;
    }
}

if (lastUsedBoard is not null)
{
    Dispatcher.GetForCurrentThread().Dispatch(() =>
    {
        BoardSelected(lastUsedBoard);
    });
}
}
```

There are a few new concepts here, so let's break them down in to understandable chunks.

Use of the preferences.Get method, as you learned about before writing the above code. You supply the key name and the default value to be returned if the key does not exist. You use -1 for the default because it is not a valid id for a database key.

The final new concept is the use of Dispatcher. This allows you to trigger a deferred action and make sure that it is dispatched onto the UI thread. Your method will be called on the UI thread, but you want the OnAppearing logic to finish before you attempt to navigate somewhere, by calling `Dispatcher.GetForCurrentThread().Dispatch` you are queuing up an action to be performed once the UI thread is no longer busy. .NET MAUI does handle a lot of dispatching for you when you trigger updates in bindings, but there are times when you need to make sure that you are updating things on the UI thread.

If you run your code now, you can create a new board and view it once saved. If you then close and reopen the application, you will see that the board you created is now shown for you. Providing an experience like this can go a long way to an enjoyable user experience (UX) as they are returning to where they were previously.

Checking if a Key Exists in Preferences

There can be times when you are unable to supply a suitable default value to the Get method in order to know whether a value has been set, for example using a Boolean. false is a valid value and therefore the default value would not be able to distinguish whether it was set as false or the default value of false. In this scenario, you can make use of the ContainsKey method. So instead of writing

```
var lastUsedBoardId = preferences.Get("LastUsedBoardId", -1);
```

you could have first checked whether the key existed, like

```
if (preferences.ContainsKey("LastUsedBoardId"))
{
    // Perform your logic
}
```

Removing a Preference

There may be times when you need to remove an option from the Preferences store or even remove all options. If you want to remove your LastUsedBoardId preference, you can write

```
Preferences.Remove("LastUsedBoardId");
```

If you want to remove all options, you can write

```
Preferences.Clear();
```

Secure Storage

When building an application, there will quite often be an occasion where you need to store an API token or some form of data that needs to be held securely. .NET MAUI provides another API that makes sure that the values you supply are held securely on each of the platforms' secure storage locations.

As always with a new API provided by .NET MAUI, you must register it with the MauiAppBuilder in your MauiProgram.cs file, so let's open up that file and add the following line into the CreateMauiApp method:

```
builder.Services.AddSingleton(SecureStorage.Default);
```

This will allow you to declare a dependency on ISecureStorage in your class constructors and have it provided for you.

Storing a Value Securely

You don't currently have a need to write a secure value just yet. It will follow in the next chapter, but to give a brief explanation of this type of local data, you can take a look at an example.

To save a value in secure storage with the key of apiToken and a value of 1234567890, you can write the following:

```
await SecureStorage.Default.SetAsync("apiToken", "1234567890");
```

Reading a Secure Value

It is also possible to retrieve the value you have stored securely by using the GetAsync method and passing in the key. It is worth noting that if the key does not exist, the method will return null.

To retrieve a value in secure storage with the key of apiToken, you can write the following:

```
string apiToken = await SecureStorage.Default.
GetAsync("apiToken");

if (apiToken is not null)
{

}
```

Removing a Secure Value

As with Preferences, you can remove and remove all secure values.

To remove a specific value, remove the key:

```
bool success = SecureStorage.Default.Remove("apiToken");
```

To remove all values, use the RemoveAll method:

```
SecureStorage.Default.RemoveAll();
```

Platform specifics

As mentioned, the SecureStorage API makes use of each of the platform-specific APIs to handle the actual storage of the data you pass in. It is worth noting that the implementations for each individual platform are different and may change in the operating systems but SecureStorage will leverage whatever is in the operating system and therefore will always be the most secure option. This section explains how.

Android

The data you pass in is encrypted with the Android EncryptedSharedPreferences class, from the Android Security library, which automatically encrypts keys and values using a two-scheme approach:

1. Keys are deterministically encrypted, so that the key can be encrypted and properly looked up.

2. Values are non-deterministically encrypted using AES-256 GCM.

The Android Security library provides an implementation of the security best practices related to reading and writing data at rest, as well as key creation and verification.

Since Google introduced Android 6.0 (API level 23), the operating system offers the ability to back up the user's data. This includes the Preferences and also the SecureStorage that .NET MAUI offers. It is entirely possible and in fact I recommend that you disable this backup functionality when using SecureStorage.

In order to disable the auto backup feature, you need to set the android:allowBackup to false in the AndroidManifest.xml file under the Platforms/Android folder. The resulting change should look something like the following:

```
<manifest ... >
    ...
    <application android:allowBackup="false" ... >
        ...
    </application>
</manifest>
```

iOS and macOS

Data passed into SecureStorage on iOS and macOS is encrypted through the Keychain API. To quote Apple,

> The keychain is the best place to store small secrets, like passwords and cryptographic keys. You use the functions of the keychain services API to add, retrieve, delete, or modify keychain items.

For further reading, refer to the Apple documentation at https://developer.apple.com/documentation/security/certificate_key_and_trust_services/keys/storing_keys_in_the_keychain.

In some cases, keychain data is synchronized with iCloud, and uninstalling the application may not remove the secure values from user devices. I have certainly observed this in some applications I have built, so it is best to plan around this possibility.

Windows

SecureStorage on Windows uses the DataProtectionProvider class to encrypt values securely. The .NET MAUI implementation allows for the data to be protected against the local user or computer account.

For further reading, refer to the Microsoft documentation at

https://docs.microsoft.com/uwp/api/windows.security.
cryptography.dataprotection.dataprotectionprovider?view=wi
nrt-22621.

Viewing the Result

Now when running your application you will see that not only does the last
board that you create get loaded back up but it also shows the widgets you
previously added. Figure 9-2 shows an example of the results.

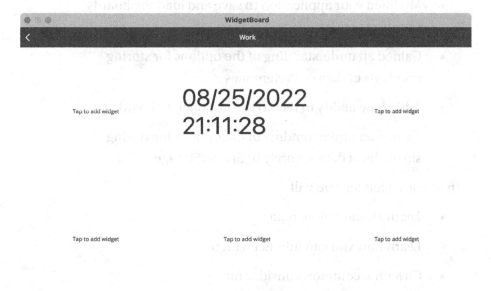

Figure 9-2. *The application loads back up and shows the previously
added widgets*

Summary

In this chapter, you

- Learned about the different types of local data

- Discovered what .NET MAUI offers in terms of local file storage locations and when to use each one

- Gained an understanding of database technologies and applied two different options

- Modified your application to save and load the boards your users create

- Gained an understanding of the options for storing small bits of data or Preferences

- Added the ability to record the last opened board

- Gained an understanding of the options for storing small bits of data securely or SecureStorage

In the next chapter, you will

- Learn about remote data.

- Learn how you can interact with it.

- Cover the common considerations.

- Look a concrete example with the Open Weather API.

- Build your own implementation to consume the Open Weather API.

- Cover how to consume the data returned.

- Talk through scenarios where things can go wrong.

- Provide implementations to handle those scenarios.

- Look at how you can reduce the complexity of your implementation with Refit.

- Add in your Weather Widget.

Source Code

The resulting source code for this chapter can be found on the GitHub repository at `https://github.com/Apress/Introducing-MAUI/tree/main/ch09`.

Extra Assignment

You have provided the ability to users to add widgets to their boards and automatically save them so when they next load the board it will be remembered for them. I would like to see if you can add the ability to remove the widgets from the board and the database.

CHAPTER 10

Remote Data

In this chapter, you will be exploring the topic of remote data, learning what exactly it is, types of it, how to interact with it, and what to consider when doing so. You will then build upon this learning by building a new widget:, the Weather Widget, to display the current weather. This will be done by interacting directly with the Open Weather API. You will get exposure to handling HTTP requests and responses with an API, how to handle the response being in a JSON format and the varying levels of flexibility when mapping to the JSON data. You will finish off by simplifying the implementation with a fantastic NuGet package that generates source code for you, simply from an interface you define to represent the web service.

What Is Remote Data?

Remote data is any data that is sourced from outside the device your application is running on. This can range from querying a web API in order to obtain data, utilizing a cloud-based database provider, images hosted online, streaming video or audio data, and more.

The vast majority of applications will interact with some form of remote endpoint in order to pull data. In this world of constantly changing data, this becomes an essential part of practically any application.

© Shaun Lawrence 2023
S. Lawrence, *Introducing .NET MAUI*, https://doi.org/10.1007/978-1-4842-9234-1_10

Considerations When Handling Remote Data

There can be quite a few concepts to consider when interacting with remote data. You will be explicitly addressing these as you build your new widget, but I want to draw your attention to them before you start.

Loading Times

One of the worst experiences for a user is to tap on a button or open a new page/application and just see the application lock up while it is loading data. The user will think that the application has crashed and, in fact, platforms like Android and Windows will likely indicate that the application has crashed/locked up if the load takes too long. Thankfully .NET offers you the `async` and `await` keywords. They are not essential but they really do make your life easier. There could be an entire chapter or even book on this topic; however, my good friend Brandon Minnick has already covered a lot of this in his AsyncAwaitBestPractices repository on GitHub. If you haven't checked it out before, I thoroughly recommend you do if you want to dig deeper; `https://github.com/brminnick/AsyncAwaitBestPractices`.

A common use case is to display to the user that the application is busy loading. This can be with a simple `ActivityIndicator`, which loads the platform-specific spinner/loading icon users should feel familiar with, or you can make use of the animation features I covered to show something more involved. With this loading display you then initiate your web service call. If you get a response, you display the result of that response in your application (e.g., items in a shopping list or, in your scenario, the user's current weather).

Failures

During the building of a recent application, some of the most valuable testing I did was to install the application and then ride the London Underground and observe just how flaky a mobile phone's data connection really can be.

There are two key questions to consider when dealing with network connectivity issues:

1.   What does the user need to know?

2.   How does the application need to recover?

Security

As a developer of applications, it is essential that you maintain the trust that your users put in you with regard to keeping their data safe. With this in mind, you should always choose HTTPS over HTTP. In fact, most platforms won't allow HTTP traffic by default to avoid it accidentally being used. There are ways to disable the prevention of HTTP traffic; however, I strongly advise against it, so I won't cover how to do so in this book.

I strongly recommend that as you build your applications you consider security as a top priority. The Open Web Application Security Project (OWASP) is a non-profit foundation that works to improve the security of software and it provides some really great resources and guidance on what you should really consider when building websites and mobile applications. As a good starting point, look at their Mobile Application Security Testing Guide repository on GitHub at `https://github.com/OWASP/owasp-mastg/`.

Quite often APIs will require levels of authentication that complicate the flow to pulling data from them. This typically happens when your application needs to consume data specific to a user and not just the API itself. I won't be covering this scenario in this book, but I recommend reading up on OAuth2.0 with a good initial resource at `www.oauth.com/oauth2-servers/mobile-and-native-apps/`. Additionally, specific APIs such as the GitHub API will likely provide good documentation on how to use their specific authentication mechanism. So with this in mind, I recommend referring to the documentation for the API that you wish to integrate with.

Webservices

Webservices act as a mechanism to query or obtain data from a remote server. They typically offer many advantages to developers building them because they provide the ability to charge based on usage, protect the developer's intellectual property, and other reasons.

The Open Weather API

You will be calling the Open Weather API and specifically version 2.5 of the OneCall API. The API is free to use with some usage limits. You can call it up to 60 times per minute and 1,000,000 calls per month, which will certainly be fine for this scenario.

For the initial work, you will be using a fixed latitude and longitude of 20.7984 and -156.3319, respectively, which if you look it up represents Maui, Hawaii. You will enabling the application to use the device's current location information in the next chapter.

Creating an Open Weather Account

You will be required to create an account. To do so, navigate to the website at https://home.openweathermap.org/users/sign_up and create the account. Note that you do not need to enter any billing details. You can use it entirely for free. If you breach the call limits, the API will simply fail instead of running into accidental charges.

Creating an Open Weather API key

Next, you need to create an API key, which can be done on the following page at https://home.openweathermap.org/api_keys. Keep a copy of this API key ready for when you eventually use it later in this chapter. Don't worry too much for now as you can return to the above web page and access the key.

Examining the Data

Before you dive into writing some code, you should take a look at the API and the data that it returns. In fact, the API offers a lot more detail than you really need. You can consume the details in case you want to use them in the future; however, this does bring in some possible drawbacks. It increases the complexity of reading through the data if you need to debug things, and it also increases the amount of data that needs to be retrieved by your application. In the mobile world, this can be expensive!

Given the above, you can make the following web service call which includes following details:

- Calls version 2.5 of the OneCall API

- Supplies latitude of 20.7984

- Supplies longitude of -156.3319

- Supplies units of metric, meaning you will receive degrees Celsius

- Supplies exclude of minutely, hourly, daily, alerts, meaning you will only receive the current weather data

- Supplies the api key you created in the previous section

The full URL that you need to call looks as follows:

```
https://api.openweathermap.org/data/2.5/onecall?lat=20.7984&
lon=-156.3319&units=metric&exclude=minutely,hourly,daily,alerts
&appid=APIKEY
```

You can open this in any web browser to view the following response back. You can see the key details that you will need for your application highlighted in **bold**.

```
{
    "lat": 20.7984,
    "lon": -156.3319,
```

```
    "timezone": "Pacific/Honolulu",
    "timezone_offset": -36000,
    "current": {
        "dt": 1663101650,
        "sunrise": 1663085531,
        "sunset": 1663129825,
        "temp": 20.77,
        "feels_like": 21.15,
        "pressure": 1017,
        "humidity": 86,
        "dew_point": 18.34,
        "uvi": 7.89,
        "clouds": 75,
        "visibility": 10000,
        "wind_speed": 5.66,
        "wind_deg": 70,
        "weather": [
            {
                "id": 501,
                "main": "Rain",
                "description": "moderate rain",
                "icon": "10d"
            }
        ],
        "rain": {
            "1h": 1.78
        }
    }
}
```

Using System.Text.Json

In order to consume and deserialize the contents of the JSON returned to you, you need to use one of the following two options:

- Newtonsoft.Json (requires a NuGet package)
- System.Text.Json

Newtonsoft has been around for many years and is a go-to option for many developers. System.Text.Json has become its successor and is my recommendation for this scenario, especially as it is backed by Microsoft and James Newton-King, the author of Newtonsoft, works for Microsoft.

Let's go ahead and use *System.Text.Json* as it is the recommended way to proceed and ships with .NET MAUI out of the box.

Now that you have seen what the data looks like, you can start to build the model classes that will allow you to deserialize the response coming back from the API.

Creating Your Models

I highlighted that you really don't need all of the information that is returned from the API. Thankfully you only need to build your model to cover the detail that you require and allow the rest to be ignored during the deserialization process.

Let's create the model classes you require. You do this in the reverse order that they appear in the JSON due to the fact that the outer elements need to refer to the inner elements.

First, add a new folder to keep everything organized and call it Communications.

Now, add a new class file and call it Weather.cs.

```
namespace WidgetBoard.Communications;

public class Weather
```

```
{
    public string Main { get; set; }

    public string Icon { get; set; }

    public string IconUrl => $"https://openweathermap.org/img/
    wn/{Icon}@2x.png";
}
```

Your `Weather` class maps to the `weather` element in the JSON returned from the API. You can see that you are mapping to the `main` and `icon` elements and you have added a calculated property that returns a URL pointing to the icon provided by the Open Weather API. The last property you are mapping, `IconUrl`, is yet another great example of remote data. The API provides you with an icon that can be rendered inside your application representing the current weather of the location. Based on the example in your original JSON, you see the `icon` value of 10d. This represents rain.

You will notice that the casing of your property names does not match the element names in the JSON. This will actually result in the deserialization process to mapping as you require. When you get to the deserialization part, you will see how to handle this scenario.

Your next model class to add should be called `Current` and, similarly to the `Weather` class, it will map to the element that matches its name: current. Your `Current` class file should have the following contents:

```
using System.Text.Json.Serialization;

namespace WidgetBoard.Communications;

public class Current
```

```
{
    [JsonPropertyName("temp")]
    public double Temperature { get; set; }

    public int Sunrise { get; set; }

    public int Sunset { get; set; }

    public Weather[] Weather { get; set; }
}
```

This class will contain an array of Weather, the Sunset and Sunrise times, and the current Temperature. With the Temperature property mapping, you can see how it is possible to map from a property in your model to an element in JSON that has a different name. This functionality is extremely valuable when building your own models because it allows you to name the properties to provide better context. I personally prefer to avoid abbreviations and stick with explicit names to make the intentions of the code clear.

Your final model class to add should be called Forecast.cs and will have the following contents:

```
namespace WidgetBoard.Communications;

public class Forecast
{
    public string Timezone { get; set; }

    public Current Current { get; set; }
}
```

This class maps to the top-level element in the returned JSON. You are mapping to the Timezone element and also the Current, which will contain your previously mapped values.

Now that you have created the model classes that can be mapped to the JSON returned from the Open Weather API, you can proceed to calling the API in order to retrieve that JSON.

Connecting to the Open Weather API

Before you start to build the implementation for accessing the API, you are going to create an interface to define what it should do. This has the added benefit that when you wish to unit test any class that depends on the IWeatherForecastService, you can supply a mock implementation rather than requiring that the unit tests will access the real API. I will cover why that is a bad idea in Chapter 14, but the simple answer here is that you have a limited number of calls you are allowed to make for free and you don't want unit tests eating that allowance up.

```
namespace WidgetBoard.Communications;

public interface IWeatherForecastService
{
    Task<Forecast> GetForecast(double latitude, double
    longitude);
}
```

A common naming approach to classes that interact with APIs is to add the suffix *Service* to show that it provides a service to the user. Therefore let's create your service by adding a new class file and calling it WeatherForecastService.cs. Add the following contents:

```
using System.Text.Json;

namespace WidgetBoard.Communications;

public class WeatherForecastService : IWeatherForecastService
{
    private readonly HttpClient httpClient;
```

308

```csharp
private const string ApiKey = "ENTER YOUR KEY";
private const string ServerUrl = "https://api.open
weathermap.org/data/2.5/onecall?";

public WeatherForecastService(HttpClient httpClient)
{
    this.httpClient = httpClient;
}

public async Task<Forecast> GetForecast(double latitude,
double longitude)
{
    var response = await httpClient
        .GetAsync($"{ServerUrl}lat={latitude}&lon={longitude}
        &units=metric&exclude=minutely,hourly,daily,alerts&
        appid={ApiKey}")
        .ConfigureAwait(false);

    response.EnsureSuccessStatusCode();

    var stringContent = await response.Content
        .ReadAsStringAsync()
        .ConfigureAwait(false);

    var options = new JsonSerializerOptions
    {
        PropertyNameCaseInsensitive = true
    };

    return JsonSerializer.Deserialize<Forecast>(string
    Content, options);
}
}
```

You added a fair amount into this class file so let's walk through it step by step and cover what it does.

First is the HttpClient backing field, which is set within the constructor and supplied by the dependency injection layer. You also have constants representing the URL of the API and also your API key that you generated in the earlier sections.

Next is the main piece of functionality in the GetForecast method. The first line in this method handles connecting to the Open Weather API and passing your latitude, longitude, and API key values. You also make sure to set ConfigureAwait(false) because you do not need to be called back on the initial calling thread. This helps to boost performance a little as it avoids having to wait until the calling thread becomes free.

```
var response = await httpClient
    .GetAsync($"{ServerUrl}lat={latitude}&lon={longitude}
    &units=metric&exclude=minutely,hourly,daily,alerts&appid=
    {ApiKey}")
    .ConfigureAwait(false);
```

Then you make sure that the request was handled successfully by calling

```
response.EnsureSuccessStatusCode();
```

Note that the above will throw an exception if the status code received was not a 200 (success ok).

Then you extract the string content from the response.

```
var stringContent = await response.Content
    .ReadAsStringAsync()
    .ConfigureAwait(false);
```

Finally, you make use of the *System.Text.Json* NuGet package you installed earlier in order to deserialize the string content into the model classes that you created.

```
var options = new JsonSerializerOptions
{
    PropertyNameCaseInsensitive = true
};

return JsonSerializer.Deserialize<Forecast>(stringContent,
options);
```

I mentioned earlier that you had to explicitly opt-in to matching your property names to the JSON elements case-insensitively. You can see from the above code that you can do this through the use of the `JsonSerializerOptions` class and specifically the `PropertyNameCaseInsensitive` property.

Now that you have created the service, you should add your weather widget and make use of the service.

Creating the WeatherWidgetView

In order to create your widget, you need to add a new view. Add a new .NET MAUI ContentView (XAML) into your Views folder and call it WeatherWidgetView. This results in two files being created: WeatherWidgetView.xaml and WeatherWidgetView.xaml.cs. You need to update both files.

WeatherWidgetView.xaml

```
<?xml version="1.0" encoding="utf-8" ?>
<ContentView
    xmlns="http://schemas.microsoft.com/dotnet/2021/maui"
    xmlns:x="http://schemas.microsoft.com/winfx/2009/xaml"
    xmlns:viewmodels="clr-namespace:WidgetBoard.ViewModels"
```

```
x:Class="WidgetBoard.Views.WeatherWidgetView"
x:DataType="viewmodels:WeatherWidgetViewModel">

<VerticalStackLayout>
    <Label
        Text="Today"
        FontSize="20"
        VerticalOptions="Center"
        HorizontalOptions="Start"
        TextTransform="Uppercase" />

    <Label
        VerticalOptions="Center"
        HorizontalOptions="Center">

        <Label.FormattedText>
            <FormattedString>
                <Span
                    Text="{Binding Temperature,
                    StringFormat='{0:F1}'}"
                    FontSize="60"/>

                <Span
                    Text="°C" />
            </FormattedString>

        </Label.FormattedText>

    </Label>

    <Label
        Text="{Binding Weather}"
        FontSize="20"
        VerticalOptions="Center"
```

```
            HorizontalOptions="Center" />
        <Image
            Source="{Binding IconUrl}"
            WidthRequest="100"
            HeightRequest="100"/>
    </VerticalStackLayout>
</ContentView>
```

Some of the above XAML should feel familiar based on the previous code you have written. Some bits are new, so let's cover them.

`Label.FormattedText` enables you to define text of varying formats inside a single `Label` control. This can be helpful especially when parts of the text changes dynamically in length and therefore result in the contents moving around. In your example, you are adding a `Span` with a text binding to your `Temperature` property in the view model and a second `Span` with the degrees Celsius symbol.

The second new concept is the use of the `Image` control. The binding on the `Source` property looks relatively straightforward; however, it is worth noting that .NET MAUI works some magic for you here. You are binding a string to the property. Under the hood, .NET MAUI converts the string into something that can resemble an image source. In fact, the underlying type is called `ImageSource`. Further to this, it will inspect your string and if it contains a valid URL (e.g., starts with https://), then it will aim to load it as a remote image rather than looking in the applications set of compiled resources. .NET MAUI will also potentially handle caching of images for you to help reduce the amount of requests sent in order to load images from a remote source. In order to make use of this functionality, you need to provide a `UriImageSource` property on your view model rather than the `string` property.

The process of converting from one type to another is referred to as TypeConverters and can be fairly common in .NET MAUI. I won't go into detail on how they work, so please go to the Microsoft documentation site at https://learn.microsoft.com/dotnet/api/system.componentmodel. typeconverter.

WeatherWidgetView.xaml.cs

You also need to make the following adjustments to the WeatherWidgetView.xaml.cs file. This part is required because you haven't created a common base class for the widget views. At times there can be good reason to create them; however, because you want to keep the visual tree as simple as possible, there isn't a common visual base class to use.

```
using WidgetBoard.ViewModels;

namespace WidgetBoard.Views;

public partial class WeatherWidgetView : ContentView,
IWidgetView
{
    public WeatherWidgetView()
    {
        InitializeComponent();
    }

    public IWidgetViewModel WidgetViewModel
    {
        get => BindingContext as IWidgetViewModel;
        set => BindingContext = value;
    }
}
```

Now that you have created your widget view, you should create the view model that will be paired with it.

Creating the WeatherWidgetViewModel

The view model that you need to create in order to represent the weather-related data that can be bound to the UI requires some work that you are familiar with and some that you are not as familiar with. Let's proceed to adding the familiar bits and then walk through the newer concepts. First, add a new class file in the ViewModels folder and call it WeatherWidgetViewModel.cs. The initial contents should be modified to look as follows:

```
using WidgetBoard.Communications;

namespace WidgetBoard.ViewModels;

public class WeatherWidgetViewModel : BaseViewModel,
IWidgetViewModel
{
    public const string DisplayName = "Weather";

    public int Position { get; set; }

    public string Type => DisplayName;
}
```

The above should look familiar as it is very similar to the ClockWidgetViewModel you created earlier on in the book. Now you need to add in the weather-specific bits.

First, add a dependency on the IWeatherForecastService you created a short while ago.

```
private readonly IWeatherForecastService
weatherForecastService;

public WeatherWidgetViewModel(IWeatherForecastService
weatherForecastService)
```

```
{
    this.weatherForecastService = weatherForecastService;

    Task.Run(async () => await LoadWeatherForecast());
}

private async Task LoadWeatherForecast()
{
    var forecast = await weatherForecastService.
    GetForecast(20.798363, -156.331924);

    Temperature = forecast.Current.Temperature;
    Weather = forecast.Current.Weather.First().Main;
    IconUrl = forecast.Current.Weather.First().IconUrl;
}
```

Inside of your constructor you keep a copy of the service and you also start a background task to fetch the forecast information. Quite often you wouldn't start something like this from within a constructor; however, given that you know your view model will only be created when it is being added to the UI, this is perfectly acceptable.

Finally, you need to add the properties that your view wants to bind to.

```
private string iconUrl;
private double temperature;
private string weather;

    public string IconUrl

{
    get => iconUrl;
    set => SetProperty(ref iconUrl, value);
}

public double Temperature
```

```
{
    get => temperature;
    set => SetProperty(ref temperature, value);
}

public string Weather
{
    get => weather;
    set => SetProperty(ref weather, value);
}
```

That's all you need in the view model for now. You can now register the widget and get it ready for your first test run.

Registering Your Widget

You first need to make use of a NuGet package in order to follow some recommended practices for the registration and usage of the HttpClient class. Go ahead and add the *Microsoft.Extensions.Http* NuGet package and then take a look at how to use it.

- Right-click the *WidgetBoard* solution.

- Select **Manage NuGet Packages**.

- Search for *Microsoft.Extensions.Http*.

- Select the correct package.

- Click **Add Package**.

Inside your MauiProgram.cs file you need to add the following lines into the CreateMauiApp method:

```
builder.Services.AddHttpClient<WeatherForecastService>();
```

```
builder.Services.AddSingleton<IWeatherForecastService,
WeatherForecastService>();
```

```
WidgetFactory.RegisterWidget<WeatherWidgetView, WeatherWidgetVi
ewModel>(WeatherWidgetViewModel.DisplayName);
builder.Services.AddTransient<WeatherWidgetView>();
builder.Services.AddTransient<WeatherWidgetViewModel>();
```

The above code registers your widget's view and view models with the dependency injection layer and also registers it with your `WidgetFactory`, meaning it can be created from your add widget overlay.

Testing Your Widget

If you run your application and add a weather widget, you can see the result in Figure 10-1.

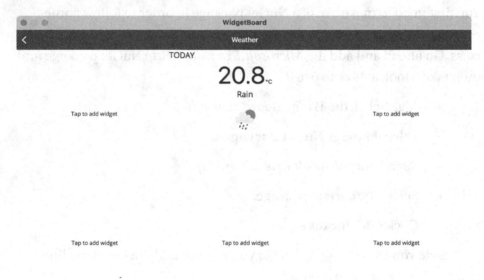

Figure 10-1. *Application running and showing your weather widget rendering correctly*

This works fine provided you have a good network connection. The moment you have a slow connection or even no connection, you will notice that things don't load quite as expected. In fact, you will likely observe a crash. You knew this could happen based on your earlier investigation into the things you need to consider when handling remote data. Let's now apply some techniques to handle these scenarios.

Adding Some State

The first thing you want to do is to consider the different possible states that your process can be in. There are three key scenarios that you need to handle and provide visual feedback to your users on:

1.   The widget is loading the data.

2.   The widget has the data.

3.   The widget has encountered an issue loading the data.

Let's handle these three scenarios.

First, create an enum that will represent the above scenarios.

```
public enum State
{
    None = 0,
    Loading = 1,
    Loaded = 2,
    Error = 3
}
```

You also want to modify your loading code in the view model to make use of this new State.

```
private async Task LoadWeatherForecast()
{
```

```
try
{
    State = State.Loading;

    var forecast = await weatherForecastService.GetForecast
    (20.798363, -156.331924);

    Temperature = forecast.Current.Temperature;
    Weather = forecast.Current.Weather.First().Main;
    IconUrl = forecast.Current.Weather.First().IconUrl;

    State = State.Loaded;
}
catch (Exception ex)
{
    State = State.Error;
}
}
```

And you also need to add the State property and backing field.

```
private State state;

public State State
{
    get => state;
    set => SetProperty(ref state, value);
}
```

Converting the State to UI

This section may well deserve a more prominent setting; however, to allow the content to flow through this book, I opted to only expose parts based on the context of the topics you are learning as you build your application.

Quite often in .NET MAUI there are scenarios where you wish to bind a piece of data to the UI but that data type does not match the desired type in the UI. To avoid having to add additional properties and potentially adding view-related information into your view models, you can make use of a concept called *converters*. A converter enables you to define how a specific data type can be converted from its type to another type. I always find the best way to cover something like this is to see it in action so let's create a converter to convert from your new State enum above into a bool value ready for binding to the IsVisible property in your view.

Add a new folder and call it Converters and then add a new class file and call it IsEqualToStateConverter.cs and then you can add the following contents:

```
using System.Globalization;
using WidgetBoard.ViewModels;

namespace WidgetBoard.Converters;

public class IsEqualToStateConverter : IValueConverter
{
    public State State { get; set; }

    public object Convert(object value, Type targetType, object
    parameter, CultureInfo culture)
    {
        if (value is State state)
        {
            return state == State;
        }

        return value;
    }

    public object ConvertBack(object value, Type targetType,
    object parameter, CultureInfo culture)
```

```
    {
        throw new NotImplementedException();
    }
}
```

The IValueConverter interface allows you to define how a value passed in can be converted. Implementations of this interface are for use within a binding using the Converter property.

Displaying the Loading State

It is worth noting that at times data can be loaded very quickly and the act of showing a spinner can provide a negative experience if it flashes very quickly. Of course, it is impossible to know which calls will take longer than others as there are so many factors which can affect the network. At times like this, I like to make sure that there is always a minimum amount of time that you display the spinner so that there isn't this weird flash to the user.

```xml
<?xml version="1.0" encoding="utf-8" ?>
<ContentView
    xmlns="http://schemas.microsoft.com/dotnet/2021/maui"
    xmlns:x="http://schemas.microsoft.com/winfx/2009/xaml"
    xmlns:viewmodels="clr-namespace:WidgetBoard.ViewModels"
    xmlns:converters="clr-namespace:WidgetBoard.Converters"
    x:Class="WidgetBoard.Views.WeatherWidgetView"
    x:DataType="viewmodels:WeatherWidgetViewModel">

    <ContentView.Resources>
        <converters:IsEqualToStateConverter
            x:Key="IsLoadingConverter"
            State="Loading" />
    </ContentView.Resources>
```

```
<VerticalStackLayout>
    <Label
        Text="Today"
        FontSize="20"
        VerticalOptions="Center"
        HorizontalOptions="Start"
        TextTransform="Uppercase" />

    <!-- Loading -->
    <VerticalStackLayout
        IsVisible="{Binding State, Converter={StaticResource
        IsLoadingConverter}}">

        <ActivityIndicator
            IsRunning="{Binding State, Converter={Static
            Resource IsLoadingConverter}}" />

        <Label
            Text="Loading weather data" />
    </VerticalStackLayout>
</VerticalStackLayout>
</ContentView>
```

Displaying the Loaded State

In order to handle the error state, you need to add another instance of your IsEqualToStateConverter, this time with the State property set to Loaded.

```
<converters:IsEqualToStateConverter
    x:Key="HasLoadedConverter"
    State="Loaded" />
```

You can then use this converter in a binding to show/hide the following UI:

```xml
<!-- Loaded -->
<VerticalStackLayout
    IsVisible="{Binding State, Converter={StaticResource
    HasLoadedConverter}}">
    <Label
        VerticalOptions="Center"
        HorizontalOptions="Center">
        <Label.FormattedText>
            <FormattedString>
                <Span
                    Text="{Binding Temperature, String
                    Format='{0:F1}'}"
                    FontSize="60"/>
                <Span
                    Text="°C" />
            </FormattedString>
        </Label.FormattedText>
    </Label>

    <Label
        Text="{Binding Weather}"
        FontSize="20"
        VerticalOptions="Center"
        HorizontalOptions="Center" />

    <Image
        Source="{Binding IconUrl}"
        WidthRequest="100"
        HeightRequest="100"/>
</VerticalStackLayout>
```

Displaying the Error State

In order to handle the error state, you need to add another instance of your IsEqualToStateConverter, this time with the State property set to Error.

```
<converters:IsEqualToStateConverter
    x:Key="HasErrorConverter"
    State="Error" />
```

You can then use this converter in a binding to show/hide the following UI:

```
<!-- Error -->
<VerticalStackLayout
    IsVisible="{Binding State, Converter={StaticResource
    HasErrorConverter}}">
    <Label
        Text="Unable to load weather data" />

    <Button
        Text="Retry"
        Command="{Binding LoadWeatherCommand}" />

</VerticalStackLayout>
```

You may have noticed that you have added a Button and bound its command to the view model. You need to add this to your view model if you wish to compile and run the application. The aim of the Button is to allow the user to request a retry of loading the weather information if the Error state is being shown.

Inside your WeatherWidgetViewModel.cs file you need to make the following change:

```
public ICommand LoadWeatherCommand { get; }
```

Then you need to update the constructor with the changes in bold:

```
public WeatherWidgetViewModel(WeatherForecastService
weatherForecastService)
{
    this.weatherForecastService = weatherForecastService;

    LoadWeatherCommand = new Command(async () => await
    LoadWeatherForecast());

    Task.Run(async () => await LoadWeatherForecast());
}
```

This means that when a load fails for whatever reason, the user will have the option to press the retry button and the widget will attempt to load the weather details again. It will walk through the states you added, so the UI will show the different UI options to the user as this happens.

This type of failure handling is considered manual. There are ways to automatically handle retries through a package called Polly.

Simplifying Webservice Access

The previous sections covered how you can interact directly with a web service at the most basic level. It requires a bit of setup but thankfully in your scenario this wasn't too complicated. Some web services can require a lot more setup or even return a lot more data.

When building your applications, the aim is to write as little code as possible as it reduces the amount of code you need to maintain. This statement isn't advocating for writing shortened code that can be difficult for a human to understand but instead stating that you want to focus on the details that are core to the application that you are building and not things like consuming a web service. Sure, you want to know that you are but having to write the underlying bits through the use of HttpClient can become cumbersome. Thankfully there are packages out there that can help you!

Prebuilt Libraries

I first recommend that you investigate whether the web service provider also provides a client library to make the consumption easier. Quite often providers supply a library, especially when there is a layer of authentication required. There are no official client libraries for the Open Weather API; however, there are a number of NuGet packages that provide some support for using the API.

Code Generation Libraries

If no client library is available, you can look to using an auto generation package to reduce the amount of code you need to write. Refit is a fantastic package for this purpose. It allows you to define an interface representing the web service call and then Refit will do the rest.

So why didn't I just start here? In a new project, you probably would do so, but I always strongly feel that you need to gain an understanding of what packages like Refit are doing before you really start to use them. This can be invaluable when things go wrong and you have to debug exactly what and why things are going wrong!

Adding the Refit NuGet Package

Let's go ahead and add the *Refit.HttpClientFactory* NuGet package and then take a look at how to use it.

- Right-click the *WidgetBoard* solution.
- Select **Manage NuGet Packages.**
- Search for *Refit.HttpClientFactory.*
- Select the correct package.
- Click **Add Package.**

Now that you have the NuGet package installed, you can use it.
Open your IWeatherForecastService.cs file and make the following
modifications shown in **bold**:

using Refit;

```
namespace WidgetBoard.Communications;

public interface IWeatherForecastService
{
```
**[Get("/onecall?lat={latitude}&lon={longitude}&units=metric&
    exclude=minutely,hourly,daily,alerts&appid=APIKEY")]**
```
    Task<Forecast> GetForecast(double latitude, double
    longitude);
}
```

The fantastic part of the above code is that you do not need to write
the implementation. Refit uses source code generators to do it for you! In
fact, it means you can delete your WeatherForecastService class as it is no
longer required.

The final change you are required to make is to change how you
register the IWeatherForecastService with your MauiAppBuilder in the
MauiProgram.cs file. Open it up and make the following changes.

First, add the using statement.

```
using Refit;
```

Then replace

```
builder.Services.AddSingleton<IWeatherForecastService,
WeatherForecastService>();
```

with

```
builder.Services
    .AddRefitClient<IWeatherForecastService>()
    .ConfigureHttpClient(c => c.BaseAddress = new Uri("https://
    api.openweathermap.org/data/2.5"));
```

This new line of code makes use of the Refit extension methods that enable you to consume an implementation of IWeatherForecastService whenever you register a dependency on that interface. It is worth reiterating that the implementation for the IWeatherForecastService is automatically generated for you through the Refit package. For further reading on this package, I thoroughly recommend their website at https://reactiveui.github.io/refit/.

Further Reading

You have added some complexities into your application in order to handle the scenario when webservice access doesn't load as expected. There are two really great libraries that can really help to reduce the amount of code you need to write around these parts.

Polly

To quote the about section on the GitHub repository,

> *Polly is a .NET resilience and transient-fault-handling library that allows developers to express policies such as Retry, Circuit Breaker, Timeout, Bulkhead Isolation, and Fallback in a fluent and thread-safe manner.*

Polly can really help to reduce writing complex code around the failure scenarios of webservice access. I thoroughly recommend checking out the GitHub repository at https://github.com/App-vNext/Polly.

StateContainer from CommunityToolkit.Maui

You had to build in converters and apply `IsVisible` bindings to control which view is being displayed when your widget is in a specific state. The `StateContainer` reduces that overhead so you "just" need to define the states and the views for those states.

If you love to write less code, I recommend checking out the Microsoft documentation at `https://learn.microsoft.com/dotnet/communitytoolkit/maui/layouts/statecontainer`.

Summary

In this chapter, you

- Learned about remote data

- Learned how you can interact with it

- Covered the common considerations

- Looked a concrete example with the Open Weather API

- Built your own implementation to consume the Open Weather API

- Covered how to consume the data returned

- Talked through scenarios where things can go wrong

- Provided implementations to handle those scenarios

- Looked at how you can reduce the complexity of your implementation with Refit

- Added in your Weather Widget

In the next chapter, you will

- Learn about permissions on the various platforms and how to request them.

- Learn how to use the Geolocation API.

- Cover how to write your own platform-specific interaction when necessary.

- Discover how to tweak the UI based on the platform on which your application is running.

- Learn to tweak the UI through the use of the handler architecture.

Source Code

The resulting source code for this chapter can be found on the GitHub repository at https://github.com/Apress/Introducing-MAUI/tree/main/ch10.

Extra Assignment

There are so many possibilities for accessing remote data in your application! Here are some extra widgets I would like you to consider creating.

TODO Widget

The go-to example application to build in tutorials is a TODO application. I would like you to expand upon this idea and add a TodoWidget into your application. There are several TODO APIs that you could utilize to do this. Do you have a favorite TODO service that you use? I personally like the

Microsoft TODO option. There is some good documentation over on the Microsoft pages to help get you started at `https://learn.microsoft.com/graph/todo-concept-overview`

Quote of the Day Widget

I know I certainly like to be inspired with a feel-good quote. Why don't you consider building a widget to refresh daily and show you a quote of the day?

The *They Said So Quotes API* offers a good API for doing this exact job with the documentation hosted at `https://quotes.rest/`.

The other concept that you will need to consider is how to trigger your `Scheduler` class to trigger the refresh at midnight.

NASA Space Image of the Day Widget

I love some of the images that come from NASA. It is so cool to be able to see into the reaches of space! Quite handily, they have a decent set of APIs that can enable you to build a widget and show off these images! The documentation on the NASA website really is great and should be able to guide you through the process of accessing the data you need. The NASA API documentation can be found at `https://api.nasa.gov/`.

I really can't wait to see these widgets in action!

PART IV

Utilizing the platforms

CHAPTER 11

Getting Specific

In this chapter, you will be learning about .NET MAUI Essentials and how it enables you to access platform-specific APIs without having to worry about any of the platform-specific complexities. Two concrete examples of are requesting permissions on each platform and accessing the device's geolocation information. You will explore what is required if you really do need to interact with platform-specific APIs that have not been abstracted for you. Finally, you will cover multiple techniques, concepts, and architectures that enable you to tweak the UI and behavior of your applications based on the platforms they are running on.

.NET MAUI Essentials

In the previous chapter, you created a Weather widget. You did not finish the job, though, as it currently only loads the weather for Maui, Hawaii. I don't know about you, but I am not lucky enough to live there! In this section, you will discover what the current device's location is in terms of longitude and latitude, and you will then send that information up to the Open Weather API for a much more accurate weather summary of the user's current location.

In order to achieve this, you need an understanding of two key concepts: the permissions system of each operating system, and how to access the APIs specific to GPS coordinates. Thankfully .NET MAUI has

© Shaun Lawrence 2023
S. Lawrence, *Introducing .NET MAUI*, https://doi.org/10.1007/978-1-4842-9234-1_11

you covered for both scenarios, but you do need to be aware of how they work and any platform-specific differences. Let's take a look at each to get a better understanding.

Permissions

A common theme I have been discussing in this book is how .NET MAUI does a lot of the heavy lifting when it comes to dealing with each supported platform. This continues with permissions because .NET MAUI abstracts a large number of permissions.

It is worth noting that every operating system is different. Not all require permissions for certain features. Refer to the Microsoft documentation on what .NET MAUI supports and what is required for each platform at `https://learn.microsoft.com/dotnet/ maui/platform-integration/appmodel/permissions- available-permissions`.

There are two key methods that enable you to interact with the permission system in .NET MAUI.

Checking the Status of a Permission

In order to check whether the user has already granted permission to your application, you can use the `CheckStatusAsync` method on the class. For your Weather widget, you need access to the devices geolocation information. You have two options in terms of the permission to use:

- `LocationWhenInUse`: This only allows the application to access the geolocation information while the app is open in the foreground.

- LocationAlways: This allows the application to also access the geolocation information even when the app is backgrounded. This can be particularly useful for exercise tracking applications that need to monitor the user's movement.

You only need the LocationWhenInUse option for your application.

```
PermissionStatus status = await Permissions.
CheckStatusAsync<Permissions.LocationWhenInUse>();
```

It is recommended that you check the status of the permission before requesting it to gain an understanding of whether the user has been asked before. On iOS, you are only allowed to ask once and then you are required to prompt the user to go to the Settings app and enable permission if they wish to change their mind. Sadly, Android provides a different approach and will return a status of Denied even if the user has not been prompted before. In this scenario you are then recommended to call ShouldShowRationale to check whether the user really has been prompted.

The possible values for PermissionStatus are as follows:

- Unknown: The permission is in an unknown state, or on iOS, the user has never been prompted.

- Denied: The user denied the permission request.

- Disabled: The feature is disabled on the device.

- Granted: The user granted permission or it is automatically granted.

- Restricted: In a restricted state

Requesting Permission

Once you have confirmed that the user has not been prompted with a permission request, you can proceed to prompting them by using the `Permissions.RequestAsync` method along with the specific permission to request. In your example, this will be the `LocationWhenInUse` permission.

```
PermissionStatus status = await Permissions.
RequestAsync<Permissions.LocationWhenInUse>();
```

It is worth noting that the `RequestAsync` method needs to be run on the main or UI thread. This is needed because it can result in presenting the built-in system UI in order to ask the user if they wish to give permission. Therefore, whenever you call `Permissions.RequestAsync` you must make sure your code is already running on the main thread with the `MainThread.IsMainThread` property, or you can dispatch out to the main thread with the `MainThread.InvokeOnMainThreadAsync` method.

It is considered best practice to only prompt the user for permission to use a specific feature when they first try to use that feature. This helps to provide context to the user around why the permission is being requested. You may also find that the different platform providers (e.g., Apple, Google, and Microsoft) have different rules they apply when reviewing and approving the applications you submit to their stores. For this, I recommend working with the most restrictive rules to save yourself pain and effort.

Handling Permissions in Your Application

The following section of code comes recommended from the Microsoft documentation site at https://learn.microsoft.com/dotnet/maui/ platform-integration/appmodel/permissions?#example. It has been included and left unchanged as it helps to really highlight the differences between platforms.

First, create the new folder and class for this new piece of functionality. Call the folder Services. Add a new interface file and call it ILocationService.cs under the Services folder. The contents of this new interface should be updated to the following

```
namespace WidgetBoard.Services;

public interface ILocationService
{
    Task<Location> GetLocationAsync();
}
```

This provides a definition of what a location service implementation will provide: an asynchronous method that will ultimately return a Location object.

Next, create an implementation. Add a new class file under the Services folder and call it LocationService.cs. Modify the initial contents to the following:

```
namespace WidgetBoard.Services;

public class LocationService : ILocationService
{

}
```

Now that you have a blank class, you can add the method for handling permission requests ready for use.

```
private async Task<PermissionStatus>
CheckAndRequestLocationPermission()
{
    PermissionStatus status = await Permissions.
    CheckStatusAsync<Permissions.LocationWhenInUse>();

    if (status == PermissionStatus.Granted)
    {
        return status;
    }

    if (status == PermissionStatus.Denied && DeviceInfo.
    Platform == DevicePlatform.iOS)
    {
        // Prompt the user to turn on in settings
        // On iOS once a permission has been denied it may not
        be requested again from the application
        return status;
    }

    if (Permissions.ShouldShowRationale<Permissions.
    LocationWhenInUse>())
    {
        // Prompt the user with additional information as to
        why the permission is needed
    }

    status = await Permissions.RequestAsync<Permissions.
    LocationWhenInUse>();

    return status;
}
```

Now that you have added the ability to request the user's permission to use the geolocation APIs on the device, you can proceed to using it.

Using the Geolocation API

.NET MAUI provides the ability to access each platform's geolocation APIs in order to retrieve a longitude and latitude representing where in the world the device running the application is currently located. Full details of what the API provides can be found at https://learn.microsoft.com/dotnet/maui/platform-integration/device/geolocation.

Registering the Geolocation Service

Open the MauiProgram.cs file and register the geolocation implementation so that you can use it via the dependency injection layer. You need to add the following line into the CreateMauiApp method:

```
builder.Services.AddSingleton(Geolocation.Default);
```

Using the Geolocation Service

This now means that you can add a dependency on the IGeolocation interface and wherever .NET MAUI provides you with an instance. Let's use the IGeolocation implementation in your LocationService.cs file. There are a few modifications you need to make, so I will walk through each one.

Add a field for the IGeolocation implementation in the root of the class.

```
private readonly IGeolocation geolocation;
```

Assign the IGeolocation implementation in the constructor.

```
public LocationService(IGeolocation geolocation)
{
```

```
    this.geolocation = geolocation;
}
```

Provide the method to return a Location object.

```
public async Task<Location> GetLocationAsync()
{
    return await MainThread.InvokeOnMainThreadAsync(async () =>
    {
        var status = await CheckAndRequestLocationPermission();

        if (status != PermissionStatus.Granted)
        {
            return null;
        }

        return await this.geolocation.GetLocationAsync();
    });
}
```

This implementation first makes sure that you are running on the main thread, which is required for location-based access. Then it calls your permission handling method and, if the app has permission, it calls the IGeolocation implementation and returns the resulting Location object. Now you are ready to make use of the LocationService.

Registering the LocationService

Open the MauiProgram.cs file and register the LocationService implementation so that you can use it via the dependency injection layer. You need to add the following line into the CreateMauiApp method:

```
builder.Services.AddSingleton<ILocationService,
LocationService>();
```

Using the ILocationService

Let's use the ILocationService implementation in your
WeatherWidgetViewModel.cs file. There are a few modifications you need
to make, so I will walk through each one

Add a field for the ILocationService implementation in the root of
the class.

```
private readonly ILocationService locationService;
```

Assign the ILocationService implementation in the constructor;
changes are in **bold.**

```
public WeatherWidgetViewModel(
    IWeatherForecastService weatherForecastService,
    ILocationService locationService)
{
    this.weatherForecastService = weatherForecastService;
    this.locationService = locationService;
    LoadWeatherCommand = new Command(async () => await
LoadWeatherForecast());
}
```

Modify your State enum to include a new value so that you can
handle when something goes wrong with permission access. Add a
PermissionError value, as can be seen below in **bold.**

```
public enum State
{
    None = 0,
    Loading = 1,
    Loaded = 2,
    Error = 3,
    PermissionError = 4
}
```

Modify your LoadWeatherForecast method to call your new
ILocationService implementation in order to find out the device's
location and then use that to call the Open Weather API to find out the
weather at the device's location.

```
private async Task LoadWeatherForecast()
{
    State = State.Loading;

    try
    {
        var location = await this.locationService.
        GetLocationAsync();

        if (location is null)
        {
            State = State.PermissionError;
            return;
        }

        var forecast = await weatherForecastService.
        GetForecast(location.Latitude, location.Longitude);

        Temperature = forecast.Current.Temperature;
        Weather = forecast.Current.Weather.First().Main;
        IconUrl = forecast.Current.Weather.First().IconUrl;

        State = State.Loaded;
    }
    catch (Exception ex)
    {
        State = State.Error;
    }
}
```

You have introduced a few changes here so let's break them down.

First, you are calling the `locationService` to get the device's location. If it returns null, it means the application does not have permission and you set the `State` to `PermissionError`.

If you have permission, you pass the device's current location into the `weatherForecastService.GetForecast` method.

Displaying Permission Errors to Your User

You have added the new state value and also assigned it in your view model when you either fail to retrieve the permission setting or the user has denied permission to the `LocationWhenInUse` feature. Now you can add in support into your UI to respond to this value and show something appropriate to the user. Open the `WeatherWidgetView.xaml` file and make the following modifications.

Add in the converter instance inside the `<ContentView.Resources>` tag.

```
<converters:IsEqualToStateConverter
    x:Key="HasPermissionErrorConverter"
    State="PermissionError" />
```

Then you can add a section that will render when the `State` property is equal to `PermissionError`. You should add this into the `WeatherWidgetView.xaml` file after the following section:

```
<!-- Error -->
<VerticalStackLayout
        IsVisible="{Binding State,
Converter={StaticResource HasErrorConverter}}">
    ...
</VerticalStackLayout>
```

The section you want to add is as follows:

```
<!-- PermissionError -->
<VerticalStackLayout
    IsVisible="{Binding State, Converter={StaticResource
    HasPermissionErrorConverter}}">

    <Label
        Text="Unable to retrieve location data" />

    <Button
        Text="Retry"
        Command="{Binding LoadWeatherCommand}" />

</VerticalStackLayout>
```

Now that you have added all of the required bits of code to call into the Permissions and Geolocation APIs, you need to configure each of your supported platforms to enable the location permission.

Configuring Platform-Specific Components

This is where .NET MAUI stops holding your hand and requires you to do some work in the platform-specific folders. Many of the APIs that are provided by .NET MAUI, as detailed in this section of the documentation site at https://learn.microsoft.com/dotnet/maui/platform-integration/, have the potential to require some level of platform-specific setup. This will vary per platform. For example, for haptic support, only Android requires some setup, whereas for the Geolocation API, all platforms require some setup.

Thankfully .NET MAUI provides helpful exceptions and error messages if you miss any of the platform-specific setup and they usually indicate the action required to fix the issue. Topics like this do make it imperative that you really test your application on each of the platforms you wish to support to verify that it behaves as expected.

Let's set up each platform so that your app can fully support accessing the devices' current location.

Android

Android requires several permissions and features to be configured in order for your application to use the LocationWhenInUse permission. You can configure them inside the Platforms/Android/MainApplication.cs file so open it and make the following additions in **bold**:

```
using Android.App;
using Android.Runtime;

[assembly: UsesPermission(Android.Manifest.Permission.
AccessCoarseLocation)]
[assembly: UsesPermission(Android.Manifest.Permission.
AccessFineLocation)]
[assembly: UsesFeature("android.hardware.location",
Required = false)]
[assembly: UsesFeature("android.hardware.location.gps",
Required = false)]
[assembly: UsesFeature("android.hardware.location.network",
Required = false)]

namespace WidgetBoard;
```

Note that the use of the assembly keyword requires that the attributes are applied at the assembly level and not on the class like the current [Application] attribute usage. For further reference on how to get started with geolocation, refer to the Microsoft documentation at https://learn.microsoft.com/dotnet/maui/platform-integration/device/geolocation?tabs=android-get-started.

If you run the application on Android now, you will see that the first time you add a Weather widget onto a board, the system will present the following popup to the user asking them to allow permission for your application to use the location feature. Figure 11-1 shows the result of running your application on Android.

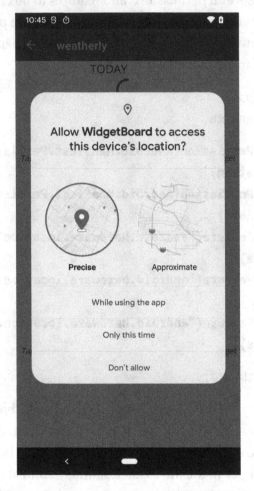

Figure 11-1. The application running on Android showing the permission prompt when a weather widget is first added to a board

iOS/Mac

Apple requires that you specify the reason your application wants to use the Geolocation feature in the process of defining that your application uses the feature. You can configure this by modifying the `Platforms/iOS/Info.plist` and `Platforms/MacCatalyst/Info.plist` files for iOS and Mac Catalyst, respectively. Both files require the same change, so let's open them and add the following lines in. Note that I am opting to edit the files inside Visual Studio Code as I find it provides a better editing experience. There is a built-in editor inside Visual Studio but I personally prefer to edit the XML directly. Add the following lines inside the `<dict>` element:

```
<key>NSLocationWhenInUseUsageDescription</key>
<string>In order to provide accurate weather
information.</string>
```

For further reference on how to get started with Geolocation refer to the Microsoft documentation at `https://learn.microsoft.com/dotnet/maui/platform-integration/device/geolocation?tabs=ios - get-started`

If you run the application on iOS and macOS now, you will see that the first time you add a Weather widget onto a board, the system will present the following popup to the user asking them to allow permission for your application to use the location feature. Figure 11-2 shows the result of running the application on iOS.

Figure 11-2. *The application running on iOS (left) and macOS (right) showing the permission prompt when a weather widget is first added to a board*

Windows

Windows applications have the concept of capabilities and it is up to developers to declare which capabilities are required in their applications. In order to do so for your application, you need to modify the

Platforms/Windows/Package.appxmanifest file. Note that I am opting to edit the files inside Visual Studio Code as I find it provides a better editing experience. Add the following line inside the <Capabilities> element:

```
<DeviceCapability Name="location"/>
```

For further reference on how to get started with Geolocation refer to the Microsoft documentation at https://learn.microsoft.com/dotnet/ maui/platform-integration/device/geolocation?tabs=windows- get-started.

If you run the application on Windows now, you don't see a permission request popup. Figure 11-3 shows the result of running the application on Windows.

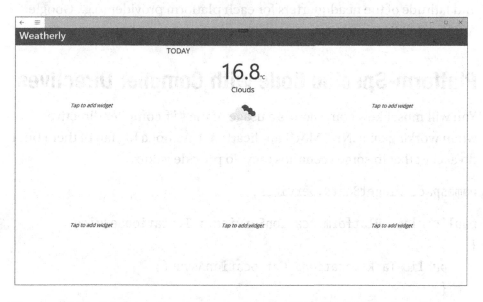

Figure 11-3. *The application running on Windows showing the permission prompt when a weather widget is first added to a board*

Platform-Specific API Access

While .NET MAUI does provide you with a lot of functionality out of the box, there can be times when you need to write your own interaction with the platform-specific layer to achieve your goals. Whatever functionality can be achieved on a specific platform can also be achieved within a .NET MAUI application. You just might have to do the heavy lifting yourself. If your implementation is considered useful enough to other developers, you should propose the changes back to the .NET MAUI team.

There are two main concepts you can utilize when building platform-specific code in .NET MAUI. Let's take a look at each one through the simple example of building a LocationService that returns the longitude and latitude of the headquarters for each platform provider (e.g., Google, Apple, and Microsoft).

Platform-Specific Code with Compiler Directives

You will most likely come across a usage of the #if compiler directive when working on a .NET MAUI application. I am not a big fan of them but I do accept that in some scenarios they do provide value.

```
namespace WidgetBoard.Services;

public class PlatformLocationService : ILocationService
{
    public Task<Location> GetLocationAsync()
    {
        Location location;

#if ANDROID
        location = new Location(37.419857, -122.078827);
#elif WINDOWS
        location = new Location(47.639722, -122.128333);
```

```
#else
        location = new Location(37.334722, -122.008889);
#endif

        return Task.FromResult(location);
    }
}
```

The above code will be compiled in different ways based on the target platform. The resulting compiled code for the Android platform looks as follows:

```
namespace WidgetBoard.Services;

public class PlatformLocationService : ILocationService
{
    public Task<Location> GetLocationAsync()
    {
        Location location;

        location = new Location(37.419857, -122.078827);

        return Task.FromResult(location);
    }
}
```

This means that only the code specific to the platform will be compiled and shipped to that platform.

This approach can work well in this scenario, but as soon as you need to use multiple classes or other platform-specific libraries, the code will become complex very quickly. In more complex scenarios, you can use the platform-specific folders created in your project for you.

Platform-Specific Code in Platform Folders

I briefly covered these folders in Chapter 2. Each platform has a folder and the files inside each folder (e.g., /Platforms/Android/) will only be compiled for that platform when you are targeting it. In order to create the same PlatformLocationService from the previous section, you first need to create a partial class under the Services folder with the following contents:

```
namespace WidgetBoard.Services;

public partial class MultiPlatformLocationService :
ILocationService
{
}
```

The above code will not compile now because you haven't implemented ILocationService. This is expected until you add in your platform-specific implementations, so don't worry. You add the partial keyword because this is only a partial implementation. The platform-specific files and classes you will add shortly will complete this partial implementation.

Next, you need to create your Android platform-specific implementation. To do this, you add a new class file under the /Platforms/Android/ folder and call it PlatformLocationService.cs, just like the one above. You want to modify its contents to the following:

```
namespace WidgetBoard.Services;

public partial class MultiPlatformLocationService
{
    public Task<Location> GetLocationAsync()
    {
        return Task.FromResult(new Location(37.419857,
        -122.078827));
    }
}
```

This class will only be compiled when the Android platform is being targeted and therefore you get a very similar compiled output to the one in the "Platform-Specific Code with Compiler Directives" section. The key difference is that you don't need to add any of those unpleasant #if directives.

When building platform-specific implementations this way, the namespace of your partial classes must match! Otherwise, the compiler won't be able to build a single class.

Overriding the Platform-Specific UI

One fundamental part of .NET MAUI is in the fact that it utilizes the underlying platform controls to handle the rendering of our applications. This will result in our applications looking different on each of the platforms. In the majority of scenarios, this is considered a good thing because the application is in keeping with the platform's look and feel. At times, though, you will need to override some of the platform-specific rendering or even just to tweak how controls render in your application on a specific platform.

OnPlatform

A common example of needing to change control properties are around the sizing of text or spacing around controls (Margin or Padding). I always find that the final finishing touches to get an application feeling really slick and polished can result in needing to tweak details like this per platform. There are two main ways to achieve this, and they depend on whether you are a XAML or C# oriented UI builder. Let's look over both with an example.

OnPlatform Markup Extension

XAML, as mentioned, is not as feature-rich in terms of what can be written and achieved. Therefore, additional functionality is provided by .NET MAUI to overcome these limitations. One such example is the OnPlatform markup extension. XAML markup extensions help enhance the power and flexibility of XAML by allowing element attributes to be set from a variety of sources.

You might decide that in your ClockWidgetView.xaml file the FontSize property is too large for iOS and Android and opt to change it only for those platforms. Let's take a look at the code and see how you can modify the property based on the platform the application is running on.

```xml
<?xml version="1.0" encoding="utf-8" ?>
<Label
    xmlns="http://schemas.microsoft.com/dotnet/2021/maui"
    xmlns:x="http://schemas.microsoft.com/winfx/2009/xaml"
    xmlns:viewmodels="clr-namespace:WidgetBoard.ViewModels"
    x:Class="WidgetBoard.Views.ClockWidgetView"
    FontSize="60"
    VerticalOptions="Center"
    HorizontalOptions="Center"
    x:DataType="viewmodels:ClockWidgetViewModel"
    Text="{Binding Time}">

    <Label.BindingContext>
        <viewmodels:ClockWidgetViewModel />
    </Label.BindingContext>

</Label>
```

The code above shows that the FontSize property is currently fixed to a value of 60. With the OnPlatform markup extension, you can change this value based on the platform the application is running on. The following code example shows how you can retain the default value of 60 and then override for the platforms that you wish:

```
FontSize="{OnPlatform Default=60, Android=25, iOS=30}"
```

The code example above states that all platforms will default to using a FontSize of 60 unless the application is running on Android and a value of 25 will be used or if the application is running on iOS and a value of 30 will be used.

Conditional Statements

If you had built your UI in C# or wanted to at least modify the FontSize property of a Label control in a similar way you could write the following conditional C# statement:

```
public ClockWidgetView()
{
    if (DeviceInfo.Platform == DevicePlatform.Android)
    {
        FontSize = 25;
    }
    else if (DeviceInfo.Platform == DevicePlatform.iOS)
    {
        FontSize = 30;
    }
    else
    {
        FontSize = 60;
    }
}
```

For further information on using the OnPlatform markup extension and other possible markup extensions that enable the customization of your application, please refer to the Microsoft documentation at https://learn.microsoft.com/dotnet/maui/xaml/markup-extensions/ consume#onplatform-markup-extension.

There will be times when just overriding values like this is not enough. For the more complex scenarios, you need to consider an architecture that is completely new to .NET MAUI and that is the handler architecture.

Handlers

Handlers are an area where .NET MAUI really shines! If you have come from a Xamarin.Forms background, you will appreciate the pain that custom renderers brought. If you don't have any Xamarin.Forms experience, you are very lucky! I won't dig down too deep into the details of the old approach as this is a book on .NET MAUI and not the past; however, I feel there is value in talking about the old issues and how they have been overcome by the new handler architecture.

In both Xamarin.Forms and .NET MAUI, we predominantly build our user interfaces with abstract controls: controls defined in the Microsoft namespace and not specifically any platform controls. These controls eventually need to be mapped down to the platform-specific layer. In the Xamarin.Forms days, you would have a custom renderer. The renderer would be responsible for knowing about the abstract control and also the platform-specific control and mapping property values and event handlers and such between the two. This is considered a tightly coupled design, meaning that it becomes really quite difficult to enhance the controls and their rendering. If you wanted to override a small amount of behavior, you would have to implement a full renderer responsible for mapping all properties/events. This was very painful!

In .NET MAUI, this concept of renderers has been entirely replaced with handlers. This new architecture provides some extra layers between the abstract controls in the .NET MAUI namespace and the underlying platform-specific controls being rendered in our applications. This is considered much more loosely coupled, mainly due to the fact that each control will implement a number of interfaces and it is the handler's responsibility to interact with the interface rather than the specific control. This has many benefits including the fact that multiple controls can all implement the same interface and ultimately rely on the same single handler. It also provides the ability to define smaller chunks of common functionality and, as you all know, smaller classes and files are much easier to read, follow, and ultimately maintain. Figure 11-4 shows how the abstract Button class in .NET MAUI is mapped to the specific controls on each platform.

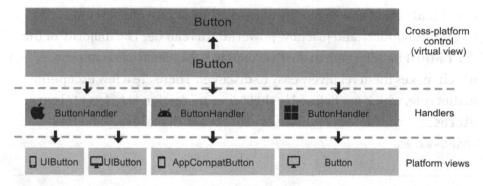

Figure 11-4. *The handler architecture in .NET MAUI*

If you wish to create a new control that needs to map to platform-specific implementations, you should follow the pattern shown in Figure 11-4. For example, if you made your FixedWidgetBoard a control in this manner, you would also create an IFixedWidgetBoard interface and then a FixedWidgetBoardHandler and then map from the virtual view across to a platform view. You didn't take this approach in your scenario because there was no benefit. In fact, it would result in more code because you would need to map to each platform individually. This concept may sound like it will always cause more effort; however, in the situation of a Button, it makes sense because each platform already has a definition of what a button is and how it behaves.

Quite often as application developers you will be using existing controls rather than building your own controls, so rather than needing to build everything you see in Figure 11-4, you can customize controls through the use of handlers.

Customizing Controls with Mappers

Mappers are key to the handler architecture. They define the actions that will be performed when either a property is changed or a command is sent between cross-platform controls and platform-specific views. This piece of information in itself might not be that helpful, but once you gain an understanding of how to modify these actions or provide new ones, you can start to understand just how powerful this can be. The majority of the .NET MAUI handlers are in the Microsoft.Maui.Handlers namespace, which makes them relatively easy to discover. There are a few exceptions to that rule, which are defined in their documentation at https://learn.microsoft.com/dotnet/maui/user-interface/handlers/#handler-based-views.

It is important to note that by modifying the mappers for handlers, you will be overriding the behavior for all implementations of the control it handles. You can overcome this by creating a class (e.g. MyButton) that inherits from the control you wish to enhance (e.g. Button) and then having your handler target the new class (MyButton).

Scoping of Mapper Customization

All controls in .NET MAUI that utilize the handler architecture also provide
HandlerChanging and HandlerChanged events, or OnHandlerChanging
and OnHandlerChanged methods, meaning you can subscribe to them and
customize the look and feel of a specific control instance.

Further Reading

One great example of overriding controls in such a way is a talk by Peter
Marchev, a Telerik developer, showing how you can customize individual
components in their charting control with very limited amounts of code.
The talk can be viewed at www.youtube.com/watch?v=s7WfTT-MVSg.

Summary

In this chapter, you

- Learned about permissions on the various platforms
  and how to request them

- Learned how to use the Geolocation API

- Wrote your own platform-specific interaction when
  necessary

- Discovered how to tweak the UI based on the platform
  upon which your application is running

- Further tweaked the UI through the use of the handler
  architecture

In the next chapter, you will

- Learn what testing is and why it is important.

- Cover what unit testing is and how you can apply it to a .NET MAUI application.

- Learn what snapshot testing is and how you can implement it.

- Gain an understanding of device tests and how you can apply them to your applications.

- Look to the future for yet more testing goodness.

Source Code

The resulting source code for this chapter can be found on the GitHub repository at `https://github.com/Apress/Introducing-MAUI/tree/main/ch11`.

Extra Assignment

You have only scratched the surface on the platform integration APIs that .NET MAUI offers you. I would love for you to look over the other possible APIs and build your own widgets that would benefit from them. The documentation for the platform integration APIs can be found at `https://learn.microsoft.com/dotnet/maui/platform-integration/`.

Barometer Widget

You can make use of the Barometer API in order to report the ambient air pressure back to the user. In fact, this might be a good addition to the Weather widget rather than a whole new widget. The documentation for this API can be found at `https://learn.microsoft.com/dotnet/maui/platform-integration/device/sensors?#barometer`.

Geocoding Lookup

I am reluctant to enable permissions like location access to apps I don't believe really need them. Perhaps you can enhance your Weather widget to allow the user to supply their nearest city, town, or postal code and then use the Geocoding API to reverse lookup the longitude and latitude information required for the Open Weather API. The documentation for the Geocoding API can be found at `https://learn.microsoft.com/dotnet/maui/platform-integration/device/geocoding`.

CHAPTER 12

Testing

Testing is such an important part of the software development process; it enables you to verify that what you have delivered is what was required and also validate that the software behaves correctly. It also provides the safety net of catching regressions in the products that you build.

There are many different approaches for designing and writing tests and where they fit into the software development process. This chapter is not intended to provide full insight into those approaches, but it will expose you to various methods of testing a .NET MAUI application, why they can be beneficial, and pique your interest in learning to use them in more depth.

Unit Testing

Unit testing is the process of ensuring that small units, typically a method or class, of an application meet their design and behave as intended. One big benefit of testing such a small unit of the code is that it makes it easier for you to identify where issues may lie or creep in as part of regression. I have worked on many legacy systems throughout my career where the teams neglected to apply unit testing and the experience when trying to identify the cause of a bug in a large system really can be costly in terms of time and money.

Despite unit testing featuring near the end of this book, it is a concept that should be adopted early in the development process. Unit testing can aid in the design and building of code that is easier to read and maintain

© Shaun Lawrence 2023
S. Lawrence, *Introducing .NET MAUI*, https://doi.org/10.1007/978-1-4842-9234-1_12

because it forces you to expose these small units of functionality and ultimately follow SOLID principles.

Unit testing itself will not catch all bugs in the system and should not be relied upon as a sole means of testing your applications. When used in combination with other forms of testing such as integration, functional, or end-to-end testing, you can build up confidence that your application is stable and delivers what is required.

Let's see how to implement unit testing with .NET MAUI.

Unit Testing in .NET MAUI

.NET MAUI applications are, as the name suggests, .NET-based projects, meaning that any of the existing .NET-based unit testing frameworks can be used.

As it currently stands, the default .NET MAUI project is not compatible with a unit test project. I will cover how to solve this in the "Adding a Unit Test Project to Your Solution" section.

There are three well-known frameworks that come with template support in Visual Studio, meaning you can create them with File ➤ Add New Project option. The three frameworks are listed below.

xUnit

xUnit appears to be the choice of the .NET MAUI team. One main reason for this is likely the support around being able to run xUnit-based unit tests on actual devices, meaning you can test device-specific implementations.

```
https://xunit.net
```

NUnit

NUnit is an old favorite of mine. I have used it on so many projects in the past! It has some great features like being able to run the same test case with multiple sets of data to reduce the amount of testing code you need to write and ultimately maintain.

https://nunit.org

MSTest

MSTest is a testing framework that is built and supplied by Microsoft. It doesn't appear as feature rich as NUnit or xUnit but it still does a great job.

https://learn.microsoft.com/dotnet/core/testing/unit-testing-with-mstest

Your Chosen Testing Framework

We will be using xUnit for this book mainly due to the benefits it brings with being able to also run the unit tests on devices.

Tests in xUnit are decorated with the [Fact] attribute with the expectation that as the author of the test methods you will name them in a way that defines a fact which the test will prove to be true.

Most of the test frameworks are quite similar and tend to differ in terms of keywords when identifying tests. Go with whatever testing framework you are most comfortable with. If you do not have much experience with any, perhaps experiment with each to see which gives you the best experience. At the end of the day, you will be building and maintaining these tests so it needs to benefit you and your team.

Adding Your Own Unit Tests

There are some steps that you need to follow in order to make sure that you can unit test your .NET MAUI application. Let's add a test project to the solution and then make the necessary changes.

Adding a Unit Test Project to Your Solution

1. Click the **File** menu.

2. Click **Add.**

3. Click **New Project.**

4. Enter *Test* in the ***Search for templates*** box.
   Figure 12-1 shows the Add a new project dialog in Visual Studio.

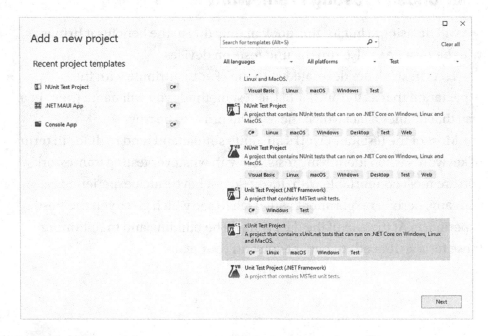

Figure 12-1. *Add a new project dialog in Visual Studio*

5. Select **xUnit Test Project.**

6. Click **Next.**

7. Enter a name for the project. I opted for
    WidgetBoard.Tests and find that appending .Tests or
    .UnitTests provides a common way to distinguish
    between application and test projects. This is also
    a common naming convention that simplifies
    searching for all unit test projects when running
    in a CI pipeline. I will cover this in more detail in
    Chapter 14.

8. Click **Next.**

9. Select the framework. The default should be fine;
    just make sure it matches the target version of the
    .NET MAUI application project.

10. Click **Create.**

Modify Your Application Project to Target net7.0

Sadly, the current .NET MAUI project template does not include the
net7.0 target framework, meaning that it is not initially compatible with
a standard unit test project. In order to correct this, you can manually
add the net7.0 target framework. Open the WidgetBoard/WidgetBoard.
csproj file in Visual Studio Code or your favorite text editor and make the
following changes.

Modify the first TargetFrameworks element to include net7.0; changes
are in **bold:**

```
<TargetFrameworks>net7.0;net7.0-android;net7.0-ios;net7.0-
maccatalyst</TargetFrameworks>
```

Add a Condition attribute to the OutputType element; changes are in **bold:**

```
<OutputType Condition="'$(TargetFramework)' != 'net7.0'">Exe
</OutputType>
```

Without this second change you will see a compilation error reporting that *error CS5001: Program does not contain a static 'Main' method suitable for an entry point.* This is due to the fact that you are building an application and .NET applications expect to have a static Main method as the entry point to the application. The OutputType for .NET MAUI applications **must** be Exe, which might feel slightly confusing as you rarely end up with an exe file that will be delivered.

If you are building against a newer version of .NET MAUI, you can replace net7.0 with the version you are using, such as net8.0.

Adding a Reference to the Project to Test

Now you need to add a reference from your test project onto the main application project.

1. Right-click **WidgetBoard.Tests.**

2. Click **Add.**

3. Click **Project Reference.**

4. Select **WidgetBoard** from the list. Figure 12-2 shows the Reference Manager dialog in Visual Studio.

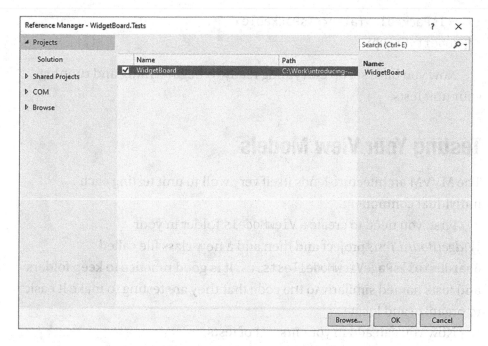

Figure 12-2. *Reference Manager in Visual Studio*

5.   Click **OK.**

Modify Your Test Project to Use MAUI Dependencies

The final step is to make your test project bring in the .NET MAUI
dependencies just like the main application project. Open up the
WidgetBoard.Tests/WidgetBoard.Tests.csproj file in Visual Studio
Code or your favorite text editor and make the following changes

Add <UseMaui>true</UseMaui> into the top-level PropertyGroup
element, which should now look like this; the changes are in **bold:**

```
<PropertyGroup>
    <TargetFramework>net7.0</TargetFramework>
    <ImplicitUsings>enable</ImplicitUsings>
    <Nullable>enable</Nullable>
    <UseMaui>true</UseMaui>
```

```
    <IsPackable>false</IsPackable>
</PropertyGroup>
```

Now you have set up everything ready to begin writing and running your unit tests.

Testing Your View Models

The MVVM architecture lends itself very well to unit testing each individual component.

First, you need to create a ViewModels folder in your *WidgetBoard.Tests* project and then add a new class file called BoardDetailsPageViewModelTests.cs. It is good practice to keep folders and tests named similarly to the code that they are testing to make it easier to organize and locate.

Now you can add in your first set of tests.

Testing BoardDetailsPageViewModel

Inside the class file that you just created, add the following:

```
[Fact]
public void SaveCommandCannotExecuteWithoutBoardName()
{
    var viewModel = new BoardDetailsPageViewModel(null, null);

    Assert.Null(viewModel.BoardName);
    Assert.False(viewModel.SaveCommand.CanExecute(null));
}

[Fact]
public void SaveCommandCanExecuteWithBoardName()
```

```
{
    var viewModel = new BoardDetailsPageViewModel(null, null);

    viewModel.BoardName = "Work";

    Assert.True(viewModel.SaveCommand.CanExecute(null));
}
```

Testing INotifyPropertyChanged

I covered in Chapter 4 that INotifyPropertyChanged serves as the mechanism to keep your views and view models in sync; therefore, it can be really useful to verify that your view models are correctly implementing INotifyPropertyChanged by ensuring that it raises the PropertyChanged event when it should.

The following test shows how to create an instance of the BoardDetailsPageViewModel, subscribe to the PropertyChanged event, modify a property that you expect to fire the PropertyChanged event, and then Assert that the event was invoked:

```
[Fact]
public void SettingBoardNameShouldRaisePropertyChanged()
{
    var invoked = false;
    var viewModel = new BoardDetailsPageViewModel(null, null);

    viewModel.PropertyChanged += (sender, e) =>
    {
        if (e.PropertyName.Equals(nameof(BoardDetailsPageView
        Model.BoardName)))
        {
            invoked = true;
        }
```

```
    };

    viewModel.BoardName = "Work";

    Assert.True(invoked);
}
```

This provides you with the confidence to know that if the BoardName is not showing in your user interface, it will probably not be an issue inside the view model.

Testing Asynchronous Operations

Many modern applications involve some level of asynchronous operation and a perfect example is your use of the Open Weather API in order to load the current location's weather. The WeatherWidgetViewModel relies on an implementation of the IWeatherForecastService interface you created in Chapter 10. Unit tests against specific implementations like this can be considered flaky. A flaky test is one that provides inconsistent results. Web service access can exhibit this type of behavior when unit testing given access limits on the API or other potential issues that could impact a reliable test run.

In order to remove test flakiness, you can create a mock implementation that will provide a set of consistent behavior.

Creating Your ILocationService Mock

Create a new folder in your *WidgetBoard.Tests* project and call it Mocks. I covered this before but organizing your code in such a way really can make it much easier to maintain. With this new folder, you can create a new class file inside and call it MockLocationService.cs. Modify the contents to the following:

```
using WidgetBoard.Services;

namespace WidgetBoard.Tests.Mocks;

internal class MockLocationService : ILocationService
{
    private readonly Location? location;
    private readonly TimeSpan delay;

    private MockLocationService(Location? mockLocation,
    TimeSpan delay)
    {
        location = mockLocation;
        this.delay = delay;
    }

    internal static ILocationService ThatReturns(Location?
    location, TimeSpan after) =>
        new MockLocationService(location, after);

    internal static ILocationService
    ThatReturnsNoLocation(TimeSpan after) =>
        new MockLocationService(null, after);

    public async Task<Location?> GetLocationAsync()
    {
        await Task.Delay(this.delay);

        return this.location;
    }
}
```

The implementation you provided for the GetLocationAsync
method forces a delay based on the supplied TimeSpan parameter in
the constructor to mimic a network delay and then return the location
supplied in the constructor.

One key detail I really like to use when building mocks is to make the usage of them in my tests as easy to read as possible. You can see that the MockLocationService cannot be instantiated because it has a private constructor. This means that to use it you must use the ThatReturns or ThatReturnsNoLocation methods. Look at this and see how much more readable it is:

```
MockLocationService.ThatReturns(new Location(0.0, 0.0), after:
TimeSpan.FromSeconds(2));
```

The above is much more readable than the following because it includes the intent:

```
new MockLocationService(new Location(0.0, 0.0), TimeSpan.
FromSeconds(2));
```

Creating Your WeatherForecastService Mock

You can add a second file into the Mocks folder and call this class file MockWeatherForecastService.cs. Modify the contents to the following:

```
using WidgetBoard.Communications;

namespace WidgetBoard.Tests.Mocks;

internal class MockWeatherForecastService :
IWeatherForecastService
{
    private readonly Forecast? forecast;
    private readonly TimeSpan delay;

    private MockWeatherForecastService(Forecast? forecast,
    TimeSpan delay)
    {
        this.forecast = forecast;
        this.delay = delay;
```

```
}

internal static IWeatherForecastService
ThatReturns(Forecast? forecast, TimeSpan after) =>
    new MockWeatherForecastService(forecast, after);

internal static IWeatherForecastService
ThatReturnsNoForecast(TimeSpan after) =>
    new MockWeatherForecastService(null, after);

public async Task<Forecast?> GetForecast(double latitude,
double longitude)
{
    await Task.Delay(this.delay);

    return forecast;
}
}
```

The implementation you provided for the GetForecast method forces a delay based on the supplied TimeSpan parameter in the constructor to mimic a network delay and then return the forecast supplied in the constructor.

Creating Your Asynchronous Tests

With your mocks in place, you can write tests that will verify the behavior of your application when calling asynchronous and potentially long running operations. You need to add a new class file to your ViewModels folder in the WidgetBoard.Tests project and call is WeatherWidgetViewModelTests.cs and then modify the contents to the following:

```
using WidgetBoard.Tests.Mocks;
using WidgetBoard.ViewModels;
```

```
namespace WidgetBoard.Tests.ViewModels;

public class WeatherWidgetViewModelTests
{
}
```

Now you can proceed to adding three tests to cover a variety of different scenarios.

```
[Fact]
public async Task NullLocationResultsInPermissionErrorState()
{
    var viewModel = new WeatherWidgetViewModel(
        MockWeatherForecastService.ThatReturnsNoForecast(after:
        TimeSpan.FromSeconds(5)),
        MockLocationService.ThatReturnsNoLocation(after:
        TimeSpan.FromSeconds(2)));

    await viewModel.InitializeAsync();

    Assert.Equal(State.PermissionError, viewModel.State);
    Assert.Null(viewModel.Weather);
}
```

This first test, as the name implies, verifies that if a null location is returned from the ILocationService implementation, the view model State will be set to PermissionError and no Weather will be set.

```
[Fact]
public async Task NullForecastResultsInErrorState()
{
    var viewModel = new WeatherWidgetViewModel(
        MockWeatherForecastService.ThatReturnsNoForecast(after:
        TimeSpan.FromSeconds(5)),
```

```
        MockLocationService.ThatReturns(new Location(0.0, 0.0),
        after: TimeSpan.FromSeconds(2)));

    await viewModel.InitializeAsync();

    Assert.Equal(State.Error, viewModel.State);
    Assert.Null(viewModel.Weather);
}
```

This second test, as the name implies, verifies that if a null forecast is
returned from the IWeatherForecastService implementation, the view
model State will be set to Error and no Weather will be set.

```
[Fact]
public async Task ValidForecastResultsInSuccessfulLoad()
{
    var weatherForecastService =
        MockWeatherForecastService.ThatReturns(
            new Communications.Forecast
            {
                Current = new Communications.Current
                {
                    Temperature = 18.0,
                    Weather = new Communications.Weather[]
                    {
                        new Communications.Weather
                        {
                            Icon = "abc.png",
                            Main = "Sunshine"
                        }
                    }
                }
            },
```

```
            after: TimeSpan.FromSeconds(5));
    var locationService = MockLocationService.ThatReturns(
            new Location(0.0, 0.0),
            after: TimeSpan.FromSeconds(2));

    var viewModel = new WeatherWidgetViewModel(
        weatherForecastService,
        locationService);

    await viewModel.InitializeAsync();

    Assert.Equal(State.Loaded, viewModel.State);
    Assert.Equal("Sunshine", viewModel.Weather);
}
```

This final test, as the name implies, verifies that if a valid forecast is returned from the IWeatherForecastService implementation, the view model State will be set to Loaded and the Weather will be correctly set.

Testing Your Views

It is possible to write unit tests that will verify the behavior of your views.

Creating Your ClockWidgetViewModel Mock

In order to verify your ClockWidgetView, you need to provide it with a view model. Your ClockWidgetViewModel currently has some complexities in it that will make it difficult to use in the test. It displays the current date/time. Let's create a mock to remove this potential difficulty. Inside your Mocks folder, add a new class file called MockClockWidgetViewModel.cs and modify the contents to match the following:

```
using WidgetBoard.ViewModels;
```

```
namespace WidgetBoard.Tests.Mocks;

public class MockClockWidgetViewModel : IWidgetViewModel
{
    public int Position { get; set; }

    public string Type => "Mock";

    public MockClockWidgetViewModel(DateTime time)
    {
        Time = time;
    }

    public DateTime Time { get; }

    public Task InitializeAsync() => Task.CompletedTask;
}
```

Now you can use this in your unit tests to verify that your ClockWidgetView binds correctly to its view model.

Creating Your View Tests

First, create a Views folder in your *WidgetBoard.Tests* project and then add a new class file called ClockWidgetView.cs.

```
using WidgetBoard.Tests.Mocks;
using WidgetBoard.Views;

namespace WidgetBoard.Tests.Views;

public class ClockWidgetViewTests
{
    [Fact]
    public void TextIsUpdatedByTimeProperty()
    {
```

```
        var time = new DateTime(2022, 01, 01);

        var clockWidget = new ClockWidgetView();

        Assert.Null(clockWidget.Text);

        clockWidget.WidgetViewModel = new MockClockWidgetView
        Model(time);

        Assert.Equal(time.ToString(), clockWidget.Text);
    }
}
```

The test `TextIsUpdatedByTimeProperty` creates a new
`ClockWidgetView`, assigns a your new `MockClockWidgetViewModel`, and
then verifies that that the Text property of the widget is correctly updated
to reflect the value from the Time property on your view model through its
binding.

Device Testing

Device testing is really a form of unit testing; however, it provides some
unique abilities so it deserves its own top-level section. It essentially
enables you to write unit tests that can be run on a device and therefore
truly test any platform-specific pieces of functionality. A perfect example
of this is to test the `PlatformLocationService` you implemented in the
previous chapter to return the longitude and latitude coordinates of each
platform provider's headquarters.

Creating a Device Test Project

You need to create another project in order to handle the running of the device tests. The documentation on the GitHub repository covers all that is needed, so go to https://github.com/shinyorg/xunit-maui. Check in the code repository called *WidgetBoard.DeviceTests* if you get stuck; there is an already created project to use as a template.

Adding a Device-Specific Test

```
using WidgetBoard.Services;
using Xunit;

namespace WidgetBoard.DeviceTests.Services;

public class PlatformLocationServiceTests
{
    [Fact]
    public async Task GetLocationAsyncWillReturnPlatform
    SpecificLocation()
    {
        var locationService = new PlatformLocationService();

        var location = await locationService.
        GetLocationAsync();

#if ANDROID
        Assert.Equal(37.419857, location.Latitude);
        Assert.Equal(-122.078827, location.Longitude);
#elif WINDOWS
        Assert.Equal(47.639722, location.Latitude);
        Assert.Equal(-122.128333, location.Longitude);
#else
        Assert.Equal(37.334722, location.Latitude);
```

```
        Assert.Equal(-122.008889, location.Longitude);
#endif
    }
}
```

Now that you have written your tests, you can run them on your devices.

Running Device-Specific Tests

In order to run your tests on a device, you first need to set your *WidgetBoard.DeviceTests* project as the startup project. You can do this as follows:

- Right-click the *WidgetBoard.DeviceTests* project in Solution Explorer.

- Select **Set as Startup Project.**

Now start the application from Visual Studio., Figure 12-3 shows the device test runner screen running on Windows.

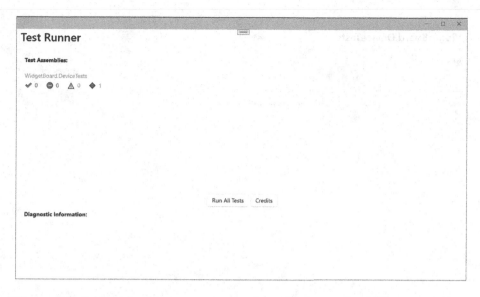

Figure 12-3. *Device test runner on the Windows platform*

You can click on a specific test and choose to run it, or you can simply **Run All Tests**. This part is entirely manual so it will require a human to perform these tasks but it can be left to run for as long as the tests need.

Finally you will see the results of the test runs and you can click them to see more information. Figure 12-4 shows the device test runner and a set of test results.

385

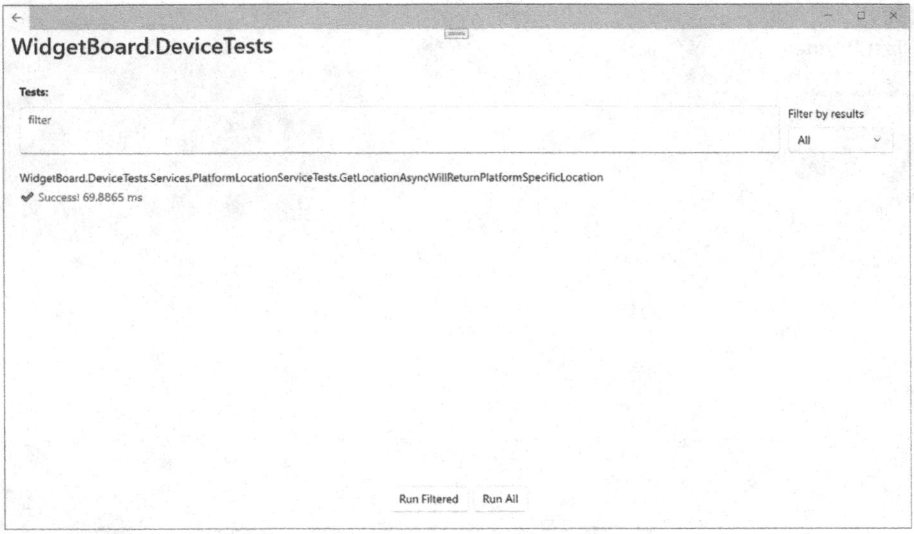

Figure 12-4. *Test run result for the GetLocationAsyncWillReturn PlatformSpecificLocation device test*

You can run these tests on all the platforms that you support to make sure that the code does what is expected.

Snapshot Testing

Snapshot testing is similar to unit testing, but it avoids the need to write Assert statements to manually define each expectation in the test. Instead the result of a test is compared to a *golden master*. A golden master is a snapshot of a previous test run that you as the test author accept as the expected result for subsequent test runs. A snapshot can be anything ranging from a screenshot of the application to a serialization of an object in memory. If you take a look at the `WeatherWidgetViewModel` you unit tested in the earlier section, you can see that a serialization of the state of the `ValidForecastResultsInSuccessfulLoad` test will result in the following golden master being created:

```
{
  LoadWeatherCommand: {},
  IconUrl: https://openweathermap.org/img/wn/abc.png@2x.png,
  State: Loaded,
  Temperature: 18.0,
  Weather: Sunshine,
  Type: Weather
}
```

When this test is run, each time the serialized output of the WeatherWidgetViewModel will be compared to the above golden master. If any of the values are different from those in the golden master, the test will fail.

Snapshot Testing Your Application

In order to snapshot test your application, you will make use of the excellent library called *VerifyTests*. VerifyTests has some really great documentation and examples to get you started over at https://github. com/VerifyTests/Verify.

You will additionally need to consume the Verify.Xunit NuGet package. I have opted to create a separate project just to keep things clearly separated for the purpose of this example. You can repeat the steps in sections "Adding a Unit Test Project to Your Solution" and "Adding a Reference to the Project to Test," except that you will name the project *WidgetBoard.SnapshotTests*.

Using VerifyTests, you can take a copy of your WeatherWidgetViewModelTests class in the *WidgetBoard.Tests* project and modify it to the following. The limited changes are shown in **bold** to highlight the differences from the original.

```
[UsesVerify]
public class WeatherWidgetViewModelTests
{
    [Fact]
    public async Task
NullLocationResultsInPermissionErrorState()
    {
        var viewModel = new WeatherWidgetViewModel(
            new MockWeatherForecastService(null),
            new MockLocationService(null));

        await viewModel.InitializeAsync();

        await Verify(viewModel);
    }

    [Fact]
    public async Task NullForecastResultsInErrorState()
    {
        var viewModel = new WeatherWidgetViewModel(
            new MockWeatherForecastService(null),
            new MockLocationService(new Location(0.0, 0.0)));

        await viewModel.InitializeAsync();

        await Verify(viewModel);
    }

    [Fact]
    public async Task ValidForecastResultsInSuccessfulLoad()
    {
        var viewModel = new WeatherWidgetViewModel(
            new MockWeatherForecastService(new Communications.
            Forecast
```

```
        {
            Current = new Communications.Current
            {
                Temperature = 18.0,
                Weather = new Communications.Weather[]
                {
                    new Communications.Weather
                    {
                        Icon = "abc.png",
                        Main = "Sunshine"
                    }
                }
            }
        }),
        new MockLocationService(new Location(0.0, 0.0)));

        await viewModel.InitializeAsync();

        await Verify(viewModel);
    }
}
```

You remove the Assert statements and replace them by calling the
Verify method. In your original scenario, you were only asserting a small
number of things, but you can imagine that if the number of Assert
statements were to grow, then this single method call to Verify really does
reduce the complexity of your tests.

Brand new tests will always fail until you accept the golden master.
There is tooling that can make this task easier, which is again provided by
the *VerifyTests* developers.

Passing Thoughts

I end this snapshot testing section with the statement that it is not for everyone. Some people really like the reduction in test case size, while it verifies more than most typical unit tests by the sheer fact that it verifies the whole object under test. As a counter argument, some people dislike that the expected state or golden master is in a file separate to the tests. I personally believe they provide great value, and I hope that this introduction to snapshot testing will give you enough context to decide whether it is going to be a good fit for you and your team, or at least give you the desire to experiment with the concept.

Looking to the Future

I really wished this chapter could cover how to write and build tests that can test your UI via automation tests. Sadly, this is not quite ready yet. It is certainly something that is being looked at, but there is nothing concrete or ready.

If you are coming in with a background in Xamarin.Forms, you may well be aware of Xamarin.UITesting. This proved to be a little difficult to work with and it was inconsistent at times, but it did provide the groundwork for writing automation tests for a Xamarin.Forms application. Currently the .NET MAUI team is evaluating a number of options to enable you to test your applications.

There is currently the ability to test through the use of Appium (`https://appium.io`); however, it can be clunky and unreliable at times.

I am most excited by the work that Jonathan Dick (the .NET MAUI lead) is doing with Maui.UITesting. This is very much in its infancy at the time of writing but I am expecting good things to come from it. You should check out the details over on the GitHub repository at `https://github.com/Redth/Maui.UITesting`.

Summary

Now you have an overview of different testing techniques and the benefits they bring. You may prefer snapshot over writing your own asserts. I don't mind either way so long as you do test your code.

In this chapter, you

- Learned what testing is and why it is important

- Explored unit testing and how you can apply it to a .NET MAUI application

- Learned about snapshot testing and how you can implement it

- Explored what device tests are and how you can apply them to your applications

- Looked to the future for yet more testing goodness

In the next chapter, you will

- Learn what .NET MAUI Graphics is

- Gain an insight into some of the power provided by .NET MAUI Graphics

- Build your own sketch widget with the .NET MAUI `GraphicsView` control

Source Code

The resulting source code for this chapter can be found on the GitHub repository at `https://github.com/Apress/Introducing-MAUI/tree/main/ch12`.

CHAPTER 13

Lets Get Graphical

In this chapter, you will learn what .NET MAUI Graphics is, how it can be used, and some practical examples of why you would want to use it. You will also gain insight into some of the power provided by .NET MAUI Graphics and how you can use it to build your own sketch widget with the .NET MAUI `GraphicsView` control.

.NET MAUI Graphics

.NET MAUI Graphics is another one of my favorite topics! I am currently exploring the idea of building a game engine on top of it given the amount of power it already offers. If you are interested in the game engine, please feel free to check out the repository on GitHub at `https://github.com/bijington/orbit`.

It has the potential to offer the ability for so much to be achieved, things like rendering chart controls or other fancy concepts all through a cross-platform API, meaning you only really need to focus on the problems you are trying to solve and not worry about each individual platform.

Essentially .NET MAUI Graphics offers a surface that can render pixel-perfect graphics on any platform supported by .NET MAUI. Consider .NET MAUI Graphics as an abstraction layer, like .NET MAUI itself, on top of the platform-specific drawing libraries. So we get all the power of each platform but with a simple unified .NET API that we as developers can work with.

S. Lawrence, *Introducing .NET MAUI*, https://doi.org/10.1007/978-1-4842-9234-1_13

Drawing on the Screen

.NET MAUI provides GraphicsView, which you can use to draw shapes on the screen. You need to assign the Drawable property on GraphicsView with an implementation that knows how to draw. This implementation must implement the IDrawable interface that defines a Draw method.

Updating the Surface

In order to trigger the application or GraphicsView to update what is rendered on screen, you must call the Invalidate method on GraphicsView. This will then cause the IDrawable.Draw method to be invoked and your code will be given the chance to update the canvas.

The way to interact with the ICanvas implementation is to first set the values you need such as fill color (FillColor) or stroke color (StrokeColor) and then call the draw method you are interested in (FillSquare() or DrawSquare(), respectively).

Let's look at some basic examples to get a better understanding of how to use the graphics layer.

Drawing a Line

Inside the Draw method you can interact with the ICanvas to draw a line using the DrawLine method. The following code shows how this can be achieved:

```
public void Draw(ICanvas canvas, RectF dirtyRect)
{
    canvas.StrokeColor = Colors.Red;
    canvas.StrokeSize = 6;
    canvas.DrawLine(0, 20, 100, 50);
}
```

You set StrokeColor and StrokeSize before calling the DrawLine method. Order is important and you must set these properties before you draw. Figure 13-1 shows the result of the Draw method from above.

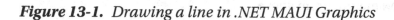

Figure 13-1. *Drawing a line in .NET MAUI Graphics*

In addition to drawing lines, you can draw many different shapes such as ellipse, rectangle, rounded rectangle, and arc. You can draw even more complex shapes through paths.

Drawing a Path

Paths are not to be confused with the Shapes API provided with .NET MAUI. Paths in .NET MAUI Graphics enable you to build up a set of coordinates in order to draw a more complex shape.

```
public void Draw(ICanvas canvas, RectF dirtyRect)
{
    PathF path = new PathF();
    path.MoveTo(40, 10);
    path.LineTo(70, 80);
    path.LineTo(10, 50);
    path.Close();
    canvas.StrokeColor = Colors.Red;
    canvas.StrokeSize = 6;
    canvas.DrawPath(path);
}
```

You first build up a PathF through the MoveTo, LineTo, and Close methods. The MoveTo method moves the current location of the path to the specified coordinates, and then the LineTo method draws a line from the current location that you just set in MoveTo to the coordinates specified in the LineTo method call. Finally, the Close method allows you to close the path. This means that the final location will have a line added back to the starting location. Notice that you didn't explicitly add a LineTo(40, 10) method call in; Close does this for you. Then you set the StrokeColor and StrokeSize before calling the DrawPath method. Figure 13-2 shows the result of the Draw method from above.

Figure 13-2. *Drawing a path in .NET MAUI Graphics*

It is this DrawPath method that you will be utilizing in the new widget you will be building as part of this chapter.

Maintaining the State of the Canvas

There can be times when you want to preserve some of the settings that you apply to the canvas, such as properties like StrokeColor and FillColor. All properties related to Stroke and Fill, plus others like transformation properties, can be preserved. This can be done through the SaveState method, which will save the current state. This saved state can then be restored through the RestoreState method. It is also possible to reset the current graphics state back to the default values with the ResetState method. These three methods can provide a large amount of functionality in specific scenarios. Say you have implemented a chart rendering control where the chart is rendered and then each individual series is rendered separately. You want to preserve the state of the charts graphics settings but wish to reset each time you render a series (e.g., each column in a bar chart).

Further Reading

You have only scratched the surface of what is possible with the .NET MAUI Graphics layer. I strongly recommend that you refer to the Microsoft documentation at `https://learn.microsoft.com/dotnet/maui/user-interface/graphics/` where it shows much more complex scenarios such as painting patterns, gradients, images, rendering text, and much more.

Building a Sketch Widget

My daughters love to doodle and leave me little notes when I am away from my desk, so I thought why not give them the ability to draw digital sketches and help save some trees. Let's create a new widget and then piece together this new drawing mechanic

Creating the SketchWidgetViewModel

As with all of the widgets, you want to create a view model to accompany the view. Let's add a new class file into the `ViewModels` folder and call it `SketchWidgetViewModel.cs`. Modify it with the following contents:

```
namespace WidgetBoard.ViewModels;

public class SketchWidgetViewModel : IWidgetViewModel
{
    public const string DisplayName = "Sketch";

    public int Position { get; set; }

    public string Type => DisplayName;

    public Task InitializeAsync() => Task.CompletedTask;
}
```

The view model is relatively simple as it only really needs to implement the basics of the IWidgetViewModel interface. If you decided to add more functionality into your widget, you have the infrastructure in place to do so.

Let's now deal with the view and user interaction.

Representing a User Interaction

When a user interacts with the new widget, they will be drawing on the screen. You will need to record this interaction so that it can be rendered inside the Draw method that the SketchWidgetView implements through the IDrawable interface. Add a new a new class file, call it DrawingPath.cs in the root of the project, and modify it to have the following contents:

```
public class DrawingPath
{
    public DrawingPath(Color color, float thickness)
    {
        Color = color;
        Thickness = thickness;
        Path = new PathF();
    }

    public Color Color { get; }
    public PathF Path { get; }
    public float Thickness { get; }

    public void Add(PointF point) => Path.LineTo(point);
}
```

The class has three main properties:

- Color represents the color of the line being drawn.

- Thickness represents how thick the line is.

- Path contains the points that make up the line.

You also have a single method that adds a new point into the Path property. This ties in well with the .NET MAUI Graphics layer as you receive the point when the user interacts with the surface and then you can also use the same type to render the line on the screen.

Let's create the widget view that will make use of this class.

Creating the SketchWidgetView

As with each of the widget views, you will be creating a XAML-based view. It will be inside the view where most of the logic resides because this widget is largely view-related.

Add a new .NET MAUI ContentView (XAML) to your Views folder and call it *SketchWidgetView*.

Modifying the SketchWidgetView.xaml

The contents of the SketchWidgetView.xaml file should be modified to the following. Remember that you want to keep your visual tree as simple as possible. You only need to declare the GraphicsView itself and no other container controls.

```xml
<?xml version="1.0" encoding="utf-8" ?>
<GraphicsView
    xmlns="http://schemas.microsoft.com/dotnet/2021/maui"
    xmlns:x="http://schemas.microsoft.com/winfx/2009/xaml"
    x:Class="WidgetBoard.Views.SketchWidgetView"
    StartInteraction="GraphicsView_StartInteraction"
    DragInteraction="GraphicsView_DragInteraction"
    EndInteraction="GraphicsView_EndInteraction" />
```

The GraphicsView provides several events that you can subscribe to in order to handle the user's interaction with the surface. You are only interested in the following:

- StartInteraction: This is when the user first interacts, so basically when the first touch/mouse click happens.

- DragInteraction: This follows from the start and involves the touch/mouse moving around on the surface.

- EndInteraction: This is when the user lifts their finger from the screen or mouse button.

When you add these events in the XAML file, it will automatically create some C# code in the SketchWidgetView.xaml.cs file that you will expand on shortly.

Modifying the SketchWidgetView.xaml.cs

Visual Studio will have created this file for you already so you need to open it and modify it to the following:

Note that the types in the event handlers have been shortened (e.g., from System.Object to object). This is mainly to make it clearer to read.

```
Using Microsoft.Maui.Controls;
using WidgetBoard.ViewModels;

namespace WidgetBoard.Views;

public partial class SketchWidgetView : GraphicsView,
IWidgetView, IDrawable
{
    public SketchWidgetView()
    {
        InitializeComponent();
```

```
        this.Drawable = this;
    }

    public IWidgetViewModel WidgetViewModel
    {
        get => BindingContext as IWidgetViewModel;
        set => BindingContext = value;
    }

    private void GraphicsView_StartInteraction(object sender,
    TouchEventArgs e)
    {
    }

    private void GraphicsView_DragInteraction(object sender,
    TouchEventArgs e)
    {
    }

    private void GraphicsView_EndInteraction(Object sender,
    TouchEventArgs e)
    {
    }

    public void Draw(Icanvas canvas, RectF dirtyRect)
    {
        throw new NotImplementedException();
    }
}
```

Each of the event handles and the Draw method have the blank or default implementation. Let's build this file up slowly and discuss the key parts as you do so.

First, you need to add the backing fields to store the interactions from the user.

```
private DrawingPath currentPath;
private readonly IList<DrawingPath> paths = new
List<DrawingPath>();
```

The first event handler to modify is for the StartInteraction event.

```
private void GraphicsView_StartInteraction(object sender,
TouchEventArgs e)
{
    currentPath = new DrawingPath(Colors.Black, 2);
    currentPath.Add(e.Touches.First());
    paths.Add(currentPath);

    Invalidate();
}
```

In this method, you first create a new instance of the DrawingPath class, assigning a color and thickness. They can, of course, be expanded to allow selections from the user so they can have custom colors. Next, you add the first touch into the current path so you have your first point of interaction. Then you add the current path to the list of all paths so that they can eventually be rendered on screen. Finally, you call Invalidate, which will trigger the Draw method to be called and the paths can be drawn.

The next event handler to modify is for the DragInteraction event.

```
private void GraphicsView_DragInteraction(object sender,
TouchEventArgs e)
{
    currentPath.Add(e.Touches.First());

    Invalidate();
}
```

In this method, you add the current touch to the current path and again call `Invalidate` to cause the `Draw` method to be called.

The final event handler to modify is for the `EndInteraction` event.

```
private void GraphicsView_EndInteraction(object sender,
TouchEventArgs e)
{
    currentPath.Add(e.Touches.First());

    Invalidate();
}
```

This has the exact same implementation as the `DragInteraction` event handler.

The final set of changes to make is inside the `Draw` method so you can actually see something on the screen.

```
public void Draw(ICanvas canvas, RectF dirtyRect)
{
    foreach (var path in paths)
    {
        canvas.StrokeColor = path.Color;
        canvas.StrokeSize = path.Thickness;
        canvas.StrokeLineCap = LineCap.Round;
        canvas.DrawPath(path.Path);
    }
}
```

This method loops through all of the paths that you have created from the user interactions, setting the stroke color, size, and then drawing the path that was built up by the three event handlers that you just implemented.

Registering Your Widget

The last part in your implementation of the sketch widget is to register your view and view model with the `MauiAppBuilder`. Let's open up the `MauiProgram.cs` file and add the following lines into the `CreateMauiApp` method:

```
WidgetFactory.RegisterWidget<SketchWidgetView, SketchWidgetView
Model>(SketchWidgetViewModel.DisplayName);
builder.Services.AddTransient<SketchWidgetView>();
builder.Services.AddTransient<SketchWidgetViewModel>();
```

Taking Your Widget for a Test Draw

You should be able to run your application on all platforms, add a widget of type *Sketch* to a board, and then interact with the widget to leave a fancy doodle. Figure 13-3 shows the new sketch widget rendered on a board.

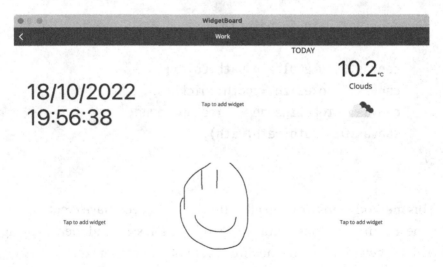

Figure 13-3. *The sketch widget showing my terrible doodling skills running on macOS*

Summary

In this chapter, you have

- Learned what .NET MAUI Graphics is

- Gained an insight into some of the power provided by .NET MAUI Graphics

- Built your own sketch widget with the .NET MAUI GraphicsView control

In the next chapter, you will

- Explore the concepts of distributing your application

- Learn about concepts like continuous integration and continuous delivery to improve your development processes

- Learn about linking, what it is, and how it can benefit/ hinder you

- Learn why it is important to collect analytical and crash information

- Explore why you might want to consider obfuscating your code

Source Code

The resulting source code for this chapter can be found on the GitHub repository at https://github.com/Apress/Introducing-MAUI/tree/main/ch13.

Extra Assignment

Think of another concept where you can use .NET MAUI graphics. Maybe the chart control idea I discussed or even just showing the battery level in a widget or other device information.

PART V

Finishing Our Application

CHAPTER 14

Releasing Our Application

Once you have built your application, you need to get it to your users. There are many ways to achieve this. You can publish a release build and ship it directly to your customers or you can make use of the stores that each platform provider offers.

Shipping directly to an end customer can sometimes be the best option, such as when you are building an internal application and you don't want it to be publicly accessible.

Most often the recommended way to ship applications to users is to go through the stores provided by each platform provider (e.g., App Store from Apple, Play Store from Google, and Microsoft Store from Microsoft). This does involve agreeing to terms and conditions, and these providers take a percentage of any income you make. There are many benefits that justify paying the fees. They provide trusted platforms for users to find and download your applications. The store will provide a much wider reach for your intended audience. The store also manages the ability to provide updates seamlessly.

Distributing Your Application

The aim of this section is not to give a step-by-step guide on distributing to each of the stores mentioned above. Initially, I wanted to provide this information, but the details around doing so have changed numerous

© Shaun Lawrence 2023
S. Lawrence, *Introducing .NET MAUI*, https://doi.org/10.1007/978-1-4842-9234-1_14

times during the time it has taken to write this book. For this reason alone, I will defer to the platform providers and Microsoft's documentation on how to achieve distribution. What this chapter will cover is details around distributing applications, why you need to do it, and some of the common issues that crop up during the process.

One very important thing to note is that apps built with .NET MAUI follow the same rules and common issues that native applications follow. Therefore, when encountering issues with each specific store, sometimes a search engine will return better results if you omit the .NET MAUI part.

Android

Android has the biggest mobile user base. However, given the model it follows of allowing manufacturers to customize the Android operating system as well as providing varying sets of hardware, it can be the most problematic.

An *Android Package*, or APK for short, is the resulting application file that runs on an Android device. If you wish to provide a mechanism to download this file (e.g., a website or file share), users can side load the application onto their Android device. This is not recommended in the public domain because it can be very difficult to trust the packages that are freely downloaded from the Internet.

When you wish to distribute using the Google Play Store, you are required to build an *Android App Bundle*, or AAB for short. It contains all of the relevant files needed to compile an APK ready for installation on a user's device.

Essentially you build an Android App Bundle, sign it with a specific signing key that you own, and upload the bundle to Google Play. Google uses this bundle when a user comes to download your application and compiles a specific APK for that device. This is the way to do things now. If you have worked with Android apps in the past, you may recall building the APK yourself. This runs into the issue that the APK is architecture-specific, and in the current market where there are multiple architectures supported by the various Android devices, you can end up with an application size that is the sum of the number of architectures multiplied by the actual size (for example, if there are four architectures and the application size is 25MB, the resulting APK is 100MB).

Additional Resources

Both Microsoft and Google provide documentation on how to distribute applications via the Google Play Store. See the following links.

- **Microsoft**: How to publish an application ready for the Play Store, `https://learn.microsoft.com/dotnet/ maui/android/deployment/overview`

- **Google**: How to upload your application to the Play Store, `https://developer.android.com/studio/ publish/upload-bundle`

- It is also worth noting that other stores/platforms provide the ability to distribute, install, and run Android applications. Amazon devices such as the Kindle Fire are built on top of Android and allow the running of Android applications. Amazon provides its own store, details of which can be found at `https:// developer.amazon.com`.

iOS

iOS and macOS are considered really painful when dealing with distributing and signing. Having spent several years going through this pain, I want to break down the key concepts to hopefully reduce the pain that you might experience. Thankfully the Apple tooling has come a long way since I started building mobile apps in 2007, so you don't have to relive all those painful memories.

The following sections cover the development and application settings you will need to create on the Apple developer website at `https://developer.apple.com`.

Certificate

You need to generate a certificate on the machine that will build your application. Most documentation takes you through the complex scenarios of creating a Certificate Signing Request and then uploading to Apple. There is actually a far simpler way by using Xcode. The following steps can help to achieve this:

- Click the **Xcode** main menu.

- Click on **Settings.**

- Click on the **Accounts** tab.

- Click the **Manage Certificates** button, shown in Figure 14-1.

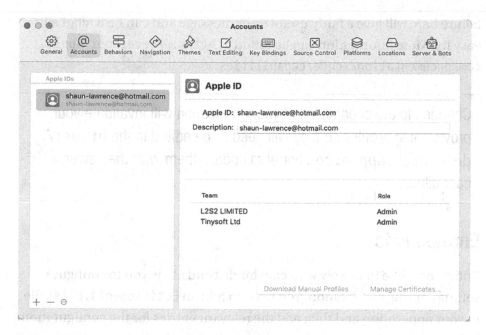

Figure 14-1. *Apple settings screen showing how to manage certificates*

Identifier

This represents your application. It requires you to define unique details to identify the application that will be exposed to the public store as well as defining what capabilities your application requires.

Capabilities

iOS applications run under a sandboxed environment. Apple provides a set of App Services that can be utilized by your applications and enhance its capabilities. Capabilities include services like in-app purchasing, push notifications, Apple Pay, and such. The use of these services needs to be defined at compile time and the usage of them will be reviewed when you upload your application to Apple for review. Therefore, it's important that you make sure you only have the ones you need. Don't worry, though; a failure here will give a fairly useful error message and can be a relatively easy fix. More information can be found at `https://developer.apple.com/documentation/xcode/capabilities`.

Changes to the capabilities of your application will invalidate your provisioning profiles so they will need to be edited in the `https://developer.apple.com` portal to update them with the newer capabilities.

Entitlements

Entitlements tie in closely with capabilities and allow you to configure settings during compilation. You need to add an `Entitlements.plist` file to your application and then add the relevant entries for the configuration. Information on how to configure this can be found at `https://learn.microsoft.com/dotnet/maui/ios/deployment/entitlements`

Provisioning Profiles

Provisioning profiles determine how your application will be provisioned for deployment. There are two main types:

- **Development**: This is what you need when running a debug build of your application on your own device.

- **Distribution**: This is required for the release builds when you ship to the App Store.

A common issue around provisioning profiles is when trying to run the application on your device and the tooling reports back *Unable to deploy app to this device, no provisioning profiles were found*. When observing this a good starting point is to double check that you have the provisioning profile installed and whether the profile has been invalidated by changing any Capabilities.

Additional Resources

Both Microsoft and Apple provide documentation on how to distribute applications via the Apple App Store.

- **Microsoft**: How to publish an application ready for the App Store, `https://learn.microsoft.com/dotnet/maui/ios/deployment/overview`

- **Apple**: How to upload your application to the App Store, `https://developer.apple.com/app-store/`

macOS

When distributing your .NET MAUI application for macOS, you can generate an `.app` or a `.pkg` file. An `.app` file is a self-contained app that can be run without installation, whereas a `.pkg` is an app packaged in an installer.

Additional Resources

Both Microsoft and Apple provide documentation on how to distribute applications via the Apple App Store.

- **Microsoft**: How to publish an application ready for the App Store, `https://learn.microsoft.com/dotnet/maui/macos/deployment/overview`

- **Apple**: How to upload your application to the App Store, `https://developer.apple.com/macos/distribution/`

Windows

When distributing your .NET MAUI app for Windows, you can publish the app and its dependencies to a folder for deployment to another system. Publishing a .NET MAUI app for Windows creates an MSIX app package, which has numerous benefits for the users installing your app.

MSIX is a Windows app package format that provides a modern packaging experience to all Windows apps.

Additional Resources

Microsoft provides documentation on how to distribute applications via the Microsoft Store.

- **Microsoft**: How to publish an application ready for the App Store, `https://learn.microsoft.com/dotnet/ maui/windows/deployment/overview`

- **Microsoft**: How to upload your application to the Microsoft Store, `https://developer.microsoft.com/ microsoft-store/`

Things to Consider

Many issues can crop up when you make the jump from a debug build running on a simulator, emulator, or physical device to building a release build ready to run on an end user's machine.

Following Good Practices

Each of the platform-specific sections prior to this one contained information or links to resources that show how to deploy your applications to each platform provider's public store. This is all great but one key detail that is lacking is the use of continuous integration and continuous delivery (CI/CD) in order to provide a clean environment that can reliably produce a build that can be deployed.

Continuous integration (CI) is the practice of merging all developers' working copies to a shared mainline.

Continuous delivery (CD) is a software engineering approach in which teams produce software in short cycles, ensuring that the software can be reliably released at any time and, when releasing the software, without doing so manually. It aims at building, testing, and releasing software with greater speed and frequency. The approach helps reduce the cost, time, and risk of delivering changes by allowing for more incremental updates to applications in production. A straightforward and repeatable deployment process is important for continuous delivery.

Both concepts are usually considered together as they help to make it a far smoother experience when working in a team. I was there in the early stages of learning and building apps and I neglected this part. If I could go back and tell a much younger Shaun some advice, it would be to get this part set up and early in the development process. Thanks to the dotnet CLI that is available to us, the setup to provide the necessary steps is straightforward. On top of that, tools like GitHub, Azure DevOps, TeamCity, and others will likely provide some level of out of the box support for this.

If you imagine that each of the applications can be built with the dotnet CLI, for example

```
dotnet publish -f:net7.0-android -c:Release
```

I am using `net7.0` here because my application is built against .NET 7.0. If you are working against a different version of .NET, replace `net7.0` with your chosen version. If you are unsure what version you are using, open your csproj file and look at the value inside the `<TargetFrameworks></TargetFrameworks>` tags.

There are more required arguments to pass to the build, which involve signing key passwords and more, but this shows how easily this can be added to a set of automated steps that run each time code is committed or a merge request is opened.

You should also consider the testing that you added in Chapter 12 and see how this can also be incorporated into a CI environment.

```
dotnet test
```

This is far simpler than the publishing step. Running the tests in a CI environment really should be considered a critical set of criteria when building any application. The safety net that this provides in making sure your changes do not unintentionally break other bits of functionality alone makes it worthwhile.

Performance

Android has always been one of the slower platforms when building mobile applications. Don't get me wrong; the applications can perform well on the higher-end devices, but Android devices come in a wide range of specifications, and typically in the business environment it is the cheaper devices that get bought in bulk and are expected to perform well. There are some concepts that you should consider when publishing your Android applications in order to boost the performance of your applications.

Startup Tracing

There are some extra steps that you can do in order to boost the startup times of your Android applications. Startup tracing essentially profiles an application when it starts to determine what libraries and other initializations are required so when you release the application it will benefit from a faster startup time. It is worth noting that boosting the startup time can result in an increase in application size so I recommend playing around with the settings to find the right balance for your application.

Microsoft has published two great blog posts on how startup tracing can be configured, the improvements it makes, and how the application can be affected:

- https://devblogs.microsoft.com/dotnet/dotnet-7-performance-improvements-in-dotnet-maui/

- https://devblogs.microsoft.com/xamarin/faster-startup-times-with-startup-tracing-on-android/

Image Sizes

One thing that can perform really poorly is the use of images that do not match the dimensions in which they need to be rendered on screen. For example, an image that displays at 100x100 pixels in the application really should be that size when supplied. If you were to render an image that was actually 300x300 pixels, it will not only look poor on the device due to scaling, but it will slow the application down. Plus, it involves storing an image that is bigger than really needed. Therefore, make sure that your images are correctly sized to gain the best experience when rendering them.

Use of ObservableCollection

A lot of common coding examples show how to bind an
ObservableCollection to the ItemsSource property of a control. This
can have its uses, but it can have a big performance overhead. The reason
is that each time an element is added to the collection, a UI update will
be triggered because the control is monitoring for changes against the
ObservableCollection. If you do not need live updating items in a
collection, it is typically much faster to use a List and simple raise the
PropertyChanged event from INotifyPropertyChanged instead.

Let's take a look at the code you added in Chapter 9 and see how it can
be improved:

```
public ObservableCollection<Board> Boards { get; } = new
ObservableCollection<Board>();

public void LoadBoards()
{
    var boards = this.boardRepository.ListBoards();

    foreach (var board in boards)
    {
        Boards.Add(board);
    }
}
```

You can improve the performance of the above code by implementing
it with a List as follows:

```
private IList<Board> boards;

public IList<Board> Boards
{
    get => this.boards;
```

```
    private set => SetProperty(ref this.boards, value);
}

public void LoadBoards()
{
    Boards = this.boardRepository.ListBoards();
}
```

This new code will result in the UI only being updated once rather than once per each board that is added to the Boards collection.

Linking

While devices these days do tend to offer generous amounts of storage space, it is still considered a very good practice to minimize the amount of memory your apps really consume, especially when considering mobile devices that have limited data networks in order to download the apps.

What Is Linking?

Linking is performed by the Linker to remove unused code from compiled assemblies. This helps to reduce the size of your applications by trimming out any unused parts of libraries that you use.

Linking is a highly complex topic and I am only really scratching the surface. For further reference, I recommend checking out the Microsoft documentation at https://learn.microsoft.com/xamarin/ios/deploy-test/linker.

The Linker provides the fantastic ability to reference the full .NET base class library so when you compile your application ready for distributing, it will only include the parts of that BCL that you actually reference and use within your application.

Issues That Crop Up

As you can imagine, if the Linker is unable to detect that something is really used in your application and it is removed, things can go very wrong at runtime. Your application will most likely crash when it tries to use a type that isn't included in your build.

This can quite often happen when only referring to types in XAML. As I covered in Chapter 5, the XAML compiler isn't as powerful as the C# compiler and it can miss scenarios.

Reflection is another option to really avoid. Not only can it trick the compiler into not realizing APIs are used but it can also not perform well.

It is worth considering that some third-party packages that you end up using in your applications may not be Linker safe. For this reason, the default setting of **Link SDK assemblies only** is set. This means that only the assemblies provided by Microsoft will be linked because they are built to be Linker safe. In an ideal world, the third-party libraries would also be Linker safe, but I can safely say that the people building these fantastic packages are already spread thin building them, so if it is something that you really require, I strongly urge you to investigate helping them provide it or sponsoring the people that build it to help them.

Crashes/Analytics

Given that I have covered how things can go wrong, I would like to cover a way in which you can gain insight to when that happens. Each of the platform providers do offer a way to collect crash information and report them it to you in order to make sure that you can prevent things like crashes from ruining the experience your applications provide.

There are frameworks/packages that aim to make this process easier by collecting and collating information from each platform into a centralized site. Further to this, you can enable the collection of analytic information to aid your understanding of how your users like to interact with your application and identify areas that you can improve upon.

In fact, a lot of the effort in my day job goes into finding ways to improve products. This only truly comes to light when you learn how your users interact with your applications. Capturing analytic information isn't the sole route I recommend taking. End user engagement can also be a fantastic thing to do if you have the opportunity. I would also like to highlight things like App Tracking Transparency by Apple and the Google equivalent as you want to make sure that when collecting analytic information you are not passing on information that can be used to track your users, or you at least make them aware of it. Further to this, it is considered good practice to allow users to opt in to enable the collection of analytical information rather than just capturing it or making them opt out.

There are some companies that provide solutions for this already. They are fee-based but do offer a free tier with fewer features.

Sentry

Sentry offers a .NET MAUI package that will make it easier to collect crash and analytical information. The website contains details on its usage and pricing: https://sentry.io/for/dot-net/.

Sentry also has the source code open sourced on GitHub and provides usage examples as well as assisting in understanding what the code does:

https://github.com/getsentry/sentry-dotnet/tree/main/src/ Sentry.Maui

App Center

App Center offers a wide range of features but the main one to focus on for here is the concept of collecting crash and analytical information. The website contains details on its usage and pricing: https://appcenter.ms.

Andreas Nesheim has written a great article on how you can get started with using App Center diagnostics in .NET MAUI: www.andreasnesheim. no/using-app-center-diagnostics-analytics-with-net-maui/.

Obfuscation

It is a very safe assumption that if you are providing a compiled application to user's devices that any of the code in the application can be compromised, intellectual property (IP) can be stolen, or an attacker can learn about vulnerabilities in your application. If you really wish to retain your IP, then you likely want to keep it on a server-side component and have your application call it via a web API. That being said, there is still serious value in making use of tools that obfuscate the compiled codebase to make it more difficult for an attacker to decipher what the application is doing.

Let's take a look at a simple class and how it will look when decompiled after obfuscation.

```
public class SomethingSecure
{
    private string PrivateSecret { get; } = "abc";
    internal string InternalSecret { get; } = "def";
    public string PublicSecret { get; } = "ghi";
}
```

The code decompiled using ILSpy without being obfuscated first looks as follows:

```
using System;

public class SomethingSecure
{
    private string PrivateSecret { get; } = "abc";

    internal string InternalSecret { get; } = "def";

    public string PublicSecret { get; } = "ghi";
}
```

If you run the original code through an obfuscation tool and then decompile the source, you will end up with something like the following:

```
// \u0008\u0002
using System;

[\u000f\u0002(1)]
[\u000e\u0002(0)]
public sealed class \u0008\u0002
{
    private readonly string m_\u0002 = \u0002\u0003.\
    u0002(-815072442);

    private readonly string m_\u0003 = \u0002\u0003.\
    u0002(-815072424);

    private readonly string m_\u0005 = \u0002\u0003.\
    u0002(-815072430);

    private string \u0002()
    {
        return this.m_\u0002;
```

```
    }

    internal string \u0003()
    {
        return this.m_\u0003;
    }

    public string \u0005()
    {
        return this.m_\u0005;
    }
}
```

It is clear from the above that it is much more difficult now to follow what this code is doing.

Obfuscation doesn't make it impossible for attackers to gain an understanding of what the code does. It does, however, make that task much more difficult.

Distributing Test Versions

There are a lot of different tools and websites that help you ship test builds out to people who can test your application. I have become most fond of using the deployment options provided by Apple and Google. The main reason I prefer to do it this way is that you do not need to change any of your deployment processes. You can continue to publish applications ready for releasing to the public via each store. In fact, these processes even upload the builds to the store portals. They simply allow you to release the application to a subset of users.

As is in keeping with this chapter, I won't walk you through each of these portals because the details can change from time to time. I refer you to the documentation provided by each platform provider and strongly urge you to investigate.

- Apple TestFlight, `https://testflight.apple.com`

- Google Play Internal Testing, `https://play.google.com/console/about/internal-testing/`

Summary

In this chapter, you have

- Explored the concepts of distributing your application

- Learned about continuous integration and continuous delivery to improve your development processes

- Learned about linking, what it is, and how it can benefit/hinder you

- Covered why it is important to collect analytical and crash information

- Explored why you may want to consider obfuscating your code

- Reached the end of our application-building journey together

CHAPTER 15

Conclusion

Wow! If you made it this far, I want to thank you so much! I really hope that you have enjoyed reading this book as much as I enjoyed writing it. This book was designed to give you an insight into what .NET MAUI offers and how you can use it to build real world applications. The sample we built together covers a lot of the key concepts. Of course I could have filled the book with hundreds more pages, adding in so many more widgets and features to the application. This application is a concept that is near and dear to my heart so I can tell you that it will continue to evolve over time. I would love to hear where you decide to take it next, and I would love to see what you create next.

Looking at the Final Product

The application we just finished building together has been a pet project of mine for years, so thank you for helping me to finally reach this dream! Let's take a trip down memory lane to review what exactly we have built. Figure 15-1 shows my prototype sketch.

© Shaun Lawrence 2023
S. Lawrence, *Introducing .NET MAUI*, https://doi.org/10.1007/978-1-4842-9234-1_15

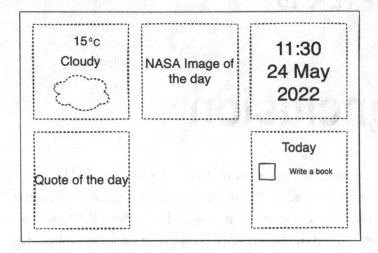

Figure 15-1. Sketch prototype of the application

The process of building this application has taken you through many different concepts including

- Creating a .NET MAUI application project

- Reviewing the possible architecture patterns you can use to build .NET MAUI applications

- Learning about the building blocks that make up your application's UI

- How you can further expand on the UI through styling

- How to make your application accessible

- How to create your own layout and utilize some cool features like BindableLayout to do a lot of the heavy lifting

- How to store data and the scenarios around where best to store each type of data

- How to access different types of remote data and the scenarios around when things go wrong

- How to customize your application on a per-platform basis

- How to test your application

- The concept of distributing your application

All of the items above made for a really fun journey! And the end result is almost identical to my original plan. Figure 15-2 shows the final application with the widgets.

Figure 15-2. *The final application showing the widgets that we have added plus the results of some of the extra assignment sections*

Taking the Project Further

One main reason I really love this project is that I believe the possibilities of future widgets is wide open! I could provide a list as long as my arm on ideas that we could continue to achieve together. If I could, I would have fit them all in this book, but I would probably never have finished.

Here is a short list of the things that I think we could achieve based on the knowledge that you have gathered during the book:

- Family planning calendar
- Image widget
  - Slide show from device
  - Slide show from external webservice
- Shopping list
- Home assistant integration
- OctoPrint status widget
- Smart meter widget
- Social media follower count widget

I am repeating myself here, but I would really love to hear from you about your experience reading this book and where you have decided to take our application next.

Useful Resources

There are so many great places to find information on either building .NET MAUI applications or solving issues that may arise during that experience. The following list is a collection of websites that provide some really great content along with a few specific examples of content creators on those platforms.

StackOverflow

StackOverflow is a question-and-answer site where you can seek assistance for issues that you encounter. Often someone else has already asked the question so you can find the answer you need. If you can't find a .NET MAUI-specific question/answer, it is worth also looking for Xamarin. Forms question/answers given that it is the predecessor to .NET MAUI.

    https://stackoverflow.com

GitHub

GitHub is where the .NET MAUI repository is hosted and the framework is developed in the open. I strongly recommend keeping up to date with the discussions and issues on this repository.

    https://github.com/dotnet/maui

YouTube

There are some really great content creators providing video tutorials on how to build .NET MAUI applications. Two great creators are in fact Microsoft employees; however, they build this content in their own free time, which I believe goes to show just how passionate they are about the framework.

Gerald Versluis

www.youtube.com/c/GeraldVersluis

James Montemagno

www.youtube.com/c/JamesMontemagno

Social Media

There is a whole host of social media options such as LinkedIn, Discord, Twitter, and Facebook. I urge you to find the platform that works best for you and start finding and following people that work on or with the technology.

Yet More Goodness

It is impossible to provide a curated list of all the great content creators or resources in printed form. It will instantly become outdated. In fact, by the time you have finished this book you have may well have become another name to add to this list! For that reason, here is a great resource that provides a curated list: `https://github.com/jfversluis/learn-dotnet-maui`.

Looking Forward

While .NET MAUI offers us a lot, there is still so much more that will evolve. I fully expect there to be some extensive work applied to improving the ability to test the user interfaces of .NET MAUI applications along with further enhancements in the usage of .NET MAUI graphics, which has the potential to not only render applications identically across each platform (which is very similar to how Flutter works) but also to boost performance by moving away from the native controls that come with Android. Some key areas to keep an eye on are as follows.

Upgrading from Xamarin.Forms

I would like to see where the dotnet upgrade assistant goes. This will likely prove vital to any existing applications built against Xamarin.Forms. There has been work on it so far, but at the time of writing it is in preview. There are documented steps on how to manually migrate applications with the following two links covering how this can be achieved:

```
https://learn.microsoft.com/dotnet/maui/get-started/migrate
https://learn.microsoft.com/dotnet/maui/migration/
```

I can confirm that I have followed through the above steps in order to migrate a relatively simple application from Xamarin.Forms to .NET MAUI. Of course, if your application is more involved and uses concepts that are now obsolete (Renderers, Effects, etc.), then the migration process could be much more involved. While I do expect the dotnet upgrade assistant to make this task easier, I highly doubt it will get to a point where it will do everything for us. In fact, I suggest you take this as a good exercise to review what your Xamarin.Forms application currently does and whether there are better ways to achieve things moving forwards.

Comet

I have been surprised by what Comet has to offer despite it also being in preview/proof of concept at the time of writing. David Ortinau, a Program Manager on the .NET MAUI team, has praised the work that has come out of the Comet investigation, stating that a lot of the evolutionary steps from Xamarin.Forms to .NET MAUI were largely influenced by this work.

```
https://github.com/dotnet/Comet
```

Testing

The topic of testing really does excite me! I have spent recent months working with development and test teams to help build processes and infrastructure focused heavily on testing. Having the ability to automate testing of applications will be a huge leap forwards. As I covered in Chapter 12, there is the Xamarin.UITest framework for testing Xamarin. Forms applications. Like the technology it was testing, it had its failings/challenges. Therefore, the idea of rewriting and exploring new testing approaches is very much a good thing in my book. I won't lie; I would have loved it sooner–certainly before this book was published–but nonetheless having it being worked on is positive.

I know that I will be keeping an eye on this repository, and if testing is important to you (and it should be), you should do so also. One further great advantage is that with the framework being developed in the open, we as the potential consumers have the power to get involved and influence the final result.

```
https://github.com/Redth/Maui.UITesting
```

Index

A

AbsoluteLayout.LayoutFlags
attached property, 125

Accessibility
applications, 200
AutomationProperties, 207
AutomationProperties.
ExcludeWithChildren, 207
AutomationProperties.
IsInAccessibleTree, 207
checklist, 216–218
definition, 199
features, 211
guidelines, 201
principles, 200, 201
scenarios, 199
screen readers, 202
SemanticProperties class, 202
SemanticProperties.
Description, 202, 204
SemanticProperties.
HeadingLevel, 204
SemanticProperties.Hint, 204
SemanticScreenReader,
205–207
suitable contrast, 208–210
testing

Android, 215
iOS, 215, 216
macOS, 216
Windows, 216
text size, 210
fixed sizes, 211–214
font auto scaling, 214, 215
minimum sizes, 214
ActivityIndicator, 300
Adaptive icon, 118
AddWidgetCommand, 228
AddWidgetFrame control, 241, 242,
247, 248
AddWidget method, 269
Ahead-of-time (AOT), 11
Android, 48, 53, 67–69, 293, 347,
348, 410
Android App Bundle (AAB),
410, 411
Android applications
image sizes, 419
ObservableCollection, 420
startup tracing, 419
Android devices, 53, 411, 418
AndroidManifest.xml file,
48–50, 293
Android Package (APK), 410, 411